Drawing the Line

The Origin of the
American Containment Policy in East Asia

DRAWING

The Origin of the

THE LINE

American Containment Policy in East Asia

ROBERT M. BLUM

W · W · NORTON & COMPANY New York · London

Copyright © 1982 by Robert M. Blum
All rights reserved.
Published simultaneously in Canada by George J. McLeod Limited, Toronto.
Printed in the United States of America.

The text of this book is composed in Baskerville, with
display type set in Weiss Bold.
Manufacturing by The Haddon Craftsmen, Inc.
Book design by A. Christopher Simon.

LIBRARY OF CONGRESS CATALOGING IN PUBLICATION DATA

Blum, Robert M.
  Drawing the line.

  Includes bibliographical references and index.
  1. East Asia—Foreign relations—United States.
  2. United States—Foreign relations—East Asia.
  I. Title.
DS518.8.B58   327.7305   82-2187
                             AACR2

ISBN 0-393-01565-3

W. W. Norton & Company, Inc. 500 Fifth Avenue, New York, N. Y. 10110
W. W. Norton & Company Ltd. 37 Great Russell Street, London WC1B 3NU

1 2 3 4 5 6 7 8 9 0

This study is dedicated to my parents,

MARGARET MORTON

and

LEON SCHNEIDER BLUM

Contents

CONTENTS

Preface

Ten years ago I had the privilege of serving on the staff of the Senate Committee on Foreign Relations as a historian charged with studying American relations with Vietnam in the late 1940s. In the course of my research I discovered an interesting cache of documents in a group of safes in a dusty room in the Capitol Building. The documents, the executive session transcripts of the committee's closed hearings dating back to 1947, contained revealing, unedited comments of the committee members and the secret testimony of their executive branch witnesses. From those transcripts, I learned that the committee, which at the time was raking the Nixon administration over the coals for its continued involvement in Vietnam, had in fact been one of the key actors in the original American commitment to save Vietnam from communism, albeit a committee of a much earlier Congress. Spurred by the China debate that dominated the 81st Congress of 1949, the transcripts revealed that the committee had, without much thought to its ultimate consequence, attached an amendment to a major arms aid bill that authorized the president to spend 75 million unvouchered dollars in assistance to the "general area of China." The money was ultimately spent on the first direct-aid commitment to the French in Indochina who were then fighting Ho Chi Minh's Communist-dominated Viet Minh. By the time I had pieced the story together, however, the committee had lost interest in its historical inquiry, but was willing to publish its old transcripts in a "Historical Series."

After leaving the committee staff in 1974 and returning to graduate school at the University of Texas in Austin, I explored how the amendment related to American foreign policy throughout East Asia. This book is the result of that effort.

Like all historians, I owe a large debt to the many archivists who preserved the raw material from which this book is shaped. From the National Archives to the various private collections I visited, archivists maintained the records and provided them for researcher use, cheerfully and often under personally difficult working conditions.

Several institutions provided crucial financial support for research, including the Dora Bonham Fund at the University of Texas and the research fund at the Truman Library.

Many civil servants and private citizens who participated in the making of American policy toward Asia in the period discussed in this book consented to share their memories of the hectic months before the Korean War. I am grateful for their kindness in taking the time to talk and, on numerous occasions, extending their hospitality. Their names are listed on page 230.

I am most grateful to scholars who read various parts or all of one or more drafts of this book: Professor Robert A. Divine, who supervised it as a dissertation and long served as a model of what a judicious diplomatic historian should be; Professor W. W. Rostow, who would not allow me to take on anything less than a significant topic and see it through to the end; and Professor Louis Gould, who ruthlessly hunted down the passive voice and other awkward constructions. Drs. William Olsen and Michael Schaller provided valuable substantive and stylistic assistance. Remaining errors in style and content are, however, a responsibility reserved for the author.

ROBERT M. BLUM
September 1981
Washington, D.C.

Drawing the Line

The Origin of the
American Containment Policy in East Asia

1

China Roots

Introduction

At the end of the Pacific War in August 1945, the United States' fondest wish for East Asia was that its countries be at peace and independent, that its governments be stable, that its land mass not be dominated by a single power hostile to Western interests, and that the region participate in an economic system beneficial to both itself and the West. Yet, the region was far from enjoying this benign state. In rapid transition from one state of war to another, many parts of East Asia were doomed to suffer internal strife for many years to come. Where the battle lines in World War II had usually been drawn and the enemy singular, the Asian wars of the late 1940s were either civil wars or insurgencies without front lines and with almost bewildering political complexity. To make matters worse, most countries had an active Communist movement presumed to be Soviet controlled.

Despite the gap between its wish and reality, the United States took few direct measures of significance to arrest the chaos or curb communism in East Asia in the first five years after it defeated Japan. Only in conquered territory—Japan and Korea—were American troops stationed. In China, the United States maintained a half-hearted commitment to the survival of a Nationalist regime that was corrupt, unpopular with the

Chinese, and losing a civil war to the Communists. In Southeast Asia, a declining bastion of European colonialism, American influence was minimal.

In sharp contrast to the apparent American indifference toward East Asia, the United States pursued a forceful policy in Western Europe designed to thwart Soviet expansion and obtain an enduring peace. Although their numbers were reduced, American troops never left Europe after the close of the war. Within four years Washington had backed its policy in the region with massive economic assistance, a strong political commitment, and the promise of a strong defense treaty and massive military aid.

The reason for the disparity in commitment was not indifference or inattention to Asia. The American press and private reporting channels of the Truman administration adequately described Asia's troubles. The administration's senior officials devoted much of their attention throughout the second half of the 1940s to the region, especially China. Their relative inaction stemmed from several other reasons.

One was the perceived limitations of American power. The military believed that it could not make a significant commitment of American armed forces to both Europe and Asia at the same time for fear that the cold war might become hot in both regions. The budget makers in the Administration, who enjoyed firm backing in the White House and Congress, believed that there were severe limits to the amount of money the United States could apply overseas through economic and military assistance. As a result of the need to set priorities, American policy makers felt compelled to continue the tradition of emphasizing the security of Europe over Asia.

Beyond the constraint of limited resources, American inaction in the Orient in the early postwar years was encouraged by the inability of anybody in or out of government to devise a sensible plan to retrieve the declining situation in Asia. Short of a massive commitment of American ground forces in China, the Nationalists seemed doomed to lose to the Communists. The problems of Southeast Asia were still the responsibility of European colonial powers who resented American interference. Washington was also divided over how hard to push them to divest themselves of their colonies: on the one hand, American officials worried about alienating countries that played a vital role in European recovery and defense; on the other, they did not want the problems of the region

4

dumped in their own laps.

Finally, American politicians and diplomats, who were of European ancestry, who had occasionally traveled to Europe, and who were familiar with its languages and culture, felt much more comfortable dealing with the problems of Western Europe. Their images and understanding of Asia were much more vague. While some had traveled in China and thought they understood it, few had experience elsewhere in Asia. As a result, they turned their attention to Europe first and acted with vigor and imagination. They watched Asia, and especially China, worriedly, but held back from taking an activist role.

In 1949, as Europe appeared to be on its way to recovery and China was rapidly falling to the Communists, Washington's attention began to turn East with an eye toward positive action. By the end of the year, the administration decided to commit American power and prestige to containing the spread of communism throughout the Far East by drawing a line of containment around much of China. By the spring of 1950, months before the outbreak of the Korean War, Washington had begun to implement this policy.

The focus of the new policy was Southeast Asia. The policy arose, however, only in part as the result of the Truman administration's concern for events in the subcontinent. It also owed its creation to the intense debate in American politics in 1949 over the failure to thwart the Communists within China. The debate created both a perceived political need on the part of the administration to act forcefully somewhere in Asia and a $75 million contingency fund that provided money to embark on an activist policy in the region.

The result, which was clear at the time but thrown out of focus for subsequent students of the period by the dramatic American response to the Korean War, was that the United States became committed to playing a significant role in the defense of Southeast Asia against Communist domination months before 27 June 1950. The first crates of American military hardware, received in Saigon in July 1950, had been on their way for many months and owed their presence there to a complicated mixture of bureaucratic infighting within the Truman administration and to the support of a distracted and highly politicized Congress. This book attempts to tell the story of how the aid got there—how the initial decisions were made in 1949 that involved the United States in a containment policy in Southeast Asia.

5

America and the Chinese Civil War

The story has much to do with China. During the Pacific War, the Roosevelt and Truman administrations supported Generalissimo Chiang Kai-shek's Nationalist Chinese regime against Japan with a combination of encouraging rhetoric and limited supplies flown into China over the Himalayan "hump." The results of this assistance were discouraging. The Nationalists' will to resist aggression had never been strong and the American entry into the war did not significantly spark the regime's effort. Discouraged by the Nationalist malaise, American diplomats and soldiers in China studied with interest the Communist movement that controlled a large area of North China and, from an inferior position, competed with the Japanese and the Nationalists for authority over China. The two Chinese groups, which had been fighting a civil war since the late 1920s, agreed in 1936 to form a united front against the Japanese; they ceased most direct fighting but remained hostile.[1]

American wartime policy toward the Communists was always tentative. The United States supported the Nationalist government exclusively, but, for limited military and diplomatic purposes, sought working relations with Communist leader Mao Tse-tung's regime. The Nationalists did not want the United States to deal with the Communists but under pressure they acquiesced in the American desire to establish an observer group, known as the "Dixie Mission," in Communist-held Yenan in the summer of 1944. The mission's primary purpose was to obtain weather reports and order of battle information about Japanese troops, but a secondary purpose was to gather political intelligence about the Communists. The results of the second purpose were interesting. Communist leaders, who had once been hostile toward the United States, now appeared friendly and made known their interest in obtaining political and military support; Mao Tse-tung and Chou En-lai, both senior party leaders, even sought permission to travel to Washington to discuss postwar Sino-American relations with President Roosevelt. The trip never occurred and when the Americans continued their exclusive diplomatic and material support for the Nationalists, Communist ardor for their enemy's ally cooled.[2]

The United States continued its interest in Chinese politics after the Japanese surrender in 1945 with its major effort directed toward the creation of a stable and friendly China. During the Yalta Conference held in the last months of the war, President Roosevelt attempted to achieve

6

this goal by accommodating China to the expansionist interests of the Soviet Union. Without the foreknowledge of either the Chinese National-ists or Communists, the president agreed to allow Stalin port and railroad concessions in Manchuria and to preserve the status quo in Sino-Soviet border areas that had, in the period of Nationalist feebleness, pulled away from Chinese control. In return for these unauthorized concessions, Stalin agreed to join the Pacific War after Germany's defeat and, in effect, to support the Nationalists in their conflict with the Communists. It was not a happy bargain from the Chinese point of view, but Chiang Kai-shek eventually bought it when he assented to the terms of the Yalta Agree-ment in a Sino-Soviet Treaty of Friendship in December 1945.

While Roosevelt was compromising China's interests in Yalta, his rep-resentative in the wartime capital of Chungking, Ambassador Patrick J. Hurley, attempted to negotiate a settlement between the Communists and Nationalists. Hurley's strategy was to isolate the Communists, in-crease support for the Nationalists, and attempt to compel the former to join the latter. Because the Chinese Communists were still weaker than the Nationalists, and, perhaps, because of Stalin's apparent abandonment of his Chinese comrades, Mao Tse-tung considered it necessary to partic-ipate in the American-sponsored negotiations. The negotiations, how-ever, were tedious and their ultimate outcome not bright; overcome by frustration, the restless Hurley resigned his post in December 1945 after a long dispute with the State Department officers in his embassy. Immedi-ately after his resignation, President Truman appointed General George C. Marshall to continue the mediation effort.

Marshall took up where Hurley left off and succeeded in staving off civil war through the first ten months of 1946 while the United States supplied arms to the Nationalist regime. By midsummer, the Chinese Communists began to attack the United States openly in their propaganda. By mid-October, Marshall had given up his mission and the civil war began in earnest with most informed observers predicting an eventual Communist victory.

Despite the pessimism about the civil war's outcome, the increasingly anti-Communist American government, which was confronting Soviet pressure in Europe, continued to furnish the Nationalists with diplo-matic, economic, and military assistance. The support kept flowing as a result of a combination of forces within the United States. Compelled by America's sentimental attachment to a "Free" China and by a powerful domestic lobby for the Nationalists, Congress persisted in enacting aid legislation for the moribund regime. The Truman administration, ambivalent over the proper course of action and not wanting to risk support for its higher priority European policy by blocking further aid, followed the line of least resistance and sent assistance to Chiang Kai-shek.

By the beginning of 1948, most objective American observers in China saw that the aid was doing little good and that the Nationalists were losing the war with increasing momentum. The Communist "People's Liberation Army" held sway over most of Manchuria except for a corridor between the key cities of Mukden and Changchun. In North China, they controlled a large area south of Peiping and east of Yenan stretching to the Shantung peninsula in the east and as far south as Suchow. By May 1948 the Communists were approaching the Yangtze River and menaced the major cities of Manchuria and North China. On 1 November 1948, Mukden fell, followed by Suchow on 1 December, Tientsin on 15 January, and Peiping on 22 January. These reverses occurred notwithstanding an initial two-to-one Nationalist superiority in troops, a large reservoir of American arms, and assistance from American military advisors. By the end of 1948, Washington assumed that the Nationalists could not retrieve their declining fortunes.[3]

Formosa and the Nationalists

While the military trend was obvious, the shape of China's future was not clear in the winter of 1948–49. Most American observers foresaw eventual Communist domination of China, but after a period of regionalism or coalition government. Uncertainty about the future increased when Generalissimo Chiang Kai-shek "retired" from the presidency of the Republic of China on 21 January 1949, relinquishing his office to Vice President Li Tsung-jen. Acting President Li, a political rival to Chiang's reactionary wing of the Nationalist Party, immediately opened negotiations with the Communists after assuming office. Although he rejected a stringent eight-point ultimatum from Mao Tse-tung, Li sent a peace mission to Peiping in mid-February, which quickly collapsed. An even more fruitless one followed in early April in which several Nationalist delegates refused to return to Nanking.

After the failure of the second mission, the Communists launched an offensive, crossing the Yangtze River on 20 April. Both during the peace initiatives and after their failure, the Nationalist Party's contending factions refused to work together in any effective way. From retirement, Chiang Kai-shek continued to exercise his influence in the dwindling non-Communist areas of China through his control of the country's gold reserves and his influence with the army and the Nationalist Party.[4]

As Communist victories continued on the mainland, wealthy Chinese and large Nationalist military units retreated to Formosa. Conditions on the island in late 1948 were relatively tranquil but deteriorating under the impact of the mainland exodus. The island had only recently returned to Chinese control. In 1895 Japan had seized Formosa, exploiting it as a colony until 1945 when, in accordance with an Allied decision reached at Cairo in 1943 and reiterated at Potsdam two years later, China regained its lost real estate. The island's population at first welcomed its Chinese liberators but quickly developed misgivings. A new ruling class, composed of some of the worst elements in the Nationalist Party, replaced the Japanese overlords, who, at least, had made the economy work. Formosa's new rulers promptly displayed what one State Department official called a "genius for misgovernment."[5] In 1947 the Taiwanese revolted but were crushed with great cruelty; thereafter, the island's native population seethed but was impotent in the face of the Nationalist's military power.

The State Department viewed the indigenous population with sympathy but considered its leaders to be weak, disorganized, and not a political alternative to either the Nationalists or the Communists. It hoped, however, that "progressive" elements in the Nationalist Party might join with the Taiwanese to form a political movement strong enough to replace the existing corrupt regime. This new political force would give the island political stability and make it a democratic model for the mainland. By January 1949, the hope was not bright. The department's Far Eastern Bureau believed Formosa to be filled with men "whose gross incompetence [had] played into the hands of the Communists in China." The department thought that Formosa, although relatively secure from Communist attack, might eventually fall either by "the classic Communist technique of infiltration, agitation and mass revolt" or "the classic Chinese technique of a deal at the top." In response to this declining situation, American diplomats saw the need for vigorous but discreet measures to keep it out of Communist hands. The discretion was imperative because of the need not to alienate the Chinese Communists any more than necessary or furnish them with an irredentist issue to be turned against the United States.[6]

9

The Communist Puzzle

The United States knew much more about Formosa and the non-Communist Chinese than about the Communists. In their rapidly expanding region of the mainland, the crucial question was the orientation of the new regime once it took power. While the Communists' relations with the United States had dissolved into hostility during the Marshall mission, developments in Eastern Europe in 1948 held some encouragement. In the summer, Marshall Josip Broz Tito, the leader of Communist Yugoslavia, broke openly with Stalin, left the Cominform, and began to chart an independent foreign policy while keeping his country Communist in internal policies. Since the Chinese Communists were coming to power by the force of their own arms in a manner similar to the Yugoslav Communists' takeover, some American observers speculated that the Soviet-Yugoslav split might be repeated in China.

Studying this new phenomenon from his vantage point in Nanking, American Ambassador J. Leighton Stuart, a missionary-educator who had lived in China for half a century, wrote the State Department on 4 August 1948 that "the Yugoslavia affair" was pertinent to China "because the Chinese Communists in recent months have been guilty of precisely those sins for which Tito is being attacked."[7] Stuart's was one of the earliest suggestions from China hinting at the prospect of "Chinese Titoism," but his optimism, which would fluctuate between extremes in the next year, soon began to fade.

In the late fall of 1948 the tone of Communist propaganda took a sharp, unfriendly turn in its attacks on the United States. In a 30 October radio broadcast, a commentator alleged that the United States had established an espionage organization in China, an allegation soon followed by publication and broadcast of hostile statements by the Party's top leaders. In a long telegram in late November, Stuart informed Washington that "until 2 or 3 months ago [the Communists] had been pursuing a distinctly conciliatory and moderate line in the vein of the new democracy." However, he continued, signs of conciliation vanished with the broadcast of a recent article by Liu Shao-chi, a high ranking party leader. Echoing a theme Soviet ideologue Andrei Zhdanov expressed a year earlier, Liu described a world divided into two mutually antagonistic camps with American imperialists in one and China and the Soviet Union in the other.* "The emphasis now," Stuart noted, "is entirely in accord

*For discussion of the Zhdanov speech, see Chapter 7, p. 109.

with [the] Soviet line," which included a requisite denunciation of Marshal Tito and Yugoslavia.[8]

The ambassador found further evidence of Chinese Communist orthodoxy in an 8 November article by Mao Tse-tung celebrating the Soviet October Revolution of 1917. It revealed "parallelism of CCP foreign policy" to Russia's "so overwhelming that we can hardly see how Kremlin planners could wish for any improvement in professed CCP foreign policy." The "coincidence of CCP foreign policy with that of the USSR" was such, he concluded, "as to permit no further doubt on this score."[9]

The Chinese Communists soon matched their propaganda with deeds. The first important point of contact between the People's Liberation Army and an official United States diplomatic establishment was in Mukden, the site of the main American consulate general serving Manchuria. Two weeks after the Communist takeover on 1 November 1948, local officials confiscated the consulate general's short wave radio and cut the staff off from all but sporadic communication with the outside world. Consul General Angus Ward, an elderly Sinologist with long experience in China, continued to function with his small staff as an unrecognized diplomatic agent, but under close scrutiny and with no business to transact.[10] In Dairen, a northern Manchurian city under joint Sino-Soviet jurisdiction, life for the American consular staff was especially difficult. Local authorities in North China were more tolerant of American consulates and allowed consular officials use of their shortwave radios (Tientsin was disallowed use of its radio for several weeks) but ignored their official status. The State Department attributed the different pattern of behavior evidenced in Manchuria and North China to a greater Russian influence in Manchuria and found much to object to in treatment of its personnel in both areas.[11]

In the face of the Communist's hostility toward the United States and a corresponding increase in praise for the Soviet Union, the State Department fell back on the hope that things were not what they seemed, or, at least, were not always doomed to be so. The assessment of past Sino-Soviet tension by the Bureau of Far Eastern Affairs (FE) nourished this hope. Russia had a history of pursuing its interest in both Central and East Asia at China's expense, both before and after the 1917 revolution. Sino-Soviet Communist Party relations had been troubled since the birth of the Chinese party in 1920 and, at the Yalta Conference in 1945, Stalin clearly pursued Russian interests at the expense of his Chinese comrades. When the tide of the Chinese civil war turned in favor of the Communists,

Stalin continued relations with the dying regime and negotiated a treaty of commerce to secure Russia's special interests in the far western Chinese province of Sinkiang.[12]

In addition to historic strains in Sino-Soviet relations, another factor encouraged American analysts: China's economy, especially along the coast, had been Western-oriented since the days of the first Opium War. Given the new regime's need to rebuild China after the civil war, the State Department thought it likely that the Communists would turn toward the West for trade and aid, regardless of ideology. This hypothesis further held that the Soviets could not afford to give the new government the large amount of aid or commercial intercourse it needed. In short, State Department analysts thought it possible that a combination of economic necessity and Soviet aggression would abet the natural "Titoist" forces within the Chinese Communist Party.

Evidence supporting the Chinese Tito hypothesis was vague and fleeting in the winter of 1948–49, but could be found if one looked carefully. One indication was the Soviet failure to praise Communist battlefield successes. American officials adduced evidence of this frosty attitude from Soviet censorship of a *Herald Tribune* correspondent's article from Moscow; the Russians deleted a sentence in the dispatch noting that "from the Soviet point of view [the] Chinese revolution constitutes continuation and extension [of the] Bolshevik Revolution [in] Russia."[13] By February, however, Soviet press silence began to yield to praise for Russia's comrades in China and the American embassy in Moscow reversed its interpretation; the change indicated "clear evidence" of "solid alignment" with the Chinese Communists.[14]

Other evidence, however, suggested that the Sino-Soviet relationship remained less than harmonious. The Soviets conducted negotiations with the retreating Nationalist government over Russian interests in Sinkiang province and they appeared to be controlling Manchuria in their own interest through Chinese more loyal to Moscow than to Mao. Reacting to these reports in late January, John Paton Davies, a diplomat veteran of the "Dixie Mission" and China expert on the State Department's Policy Planning Staff, warned his chief, George Kennan, that "a strong odor of bad fish is emanating from Sino-Soviet relations." Davies observed that the continuing Soviet negotiations with the Nationalists over Sinkiang appeared "somewhat uncalled for" if the Communists should either form a coalition government with the Nationalists or simply conquer them. He warned that if the United States should "find the USSR continues to recognize a [non-Communist] government in South China after the formation of a Communist government in the North, we should not wear an ah-ha look on our faces" or "permit our Ambassador to be sucked south in anxious bafflement."[15]

As Davies predicted, the Soviet-bloc embassies migrated to Canton with the Nationalist government in mid-February. The embassies of all non-Communist countries remained in Nanking to await contact with China's new rulers. In analyzing recent developments in Sino-Soviet relations, FE reported that "the actions of the Soviets in negotiating at this time a long-term agreement with the Nationalist Government involving special rights to the USSR would seem to indicate something less than comradely trust between the Chinese Communists and Moscow."[16]

Truman and the State Department

The man charged with ultimate responsibility in shaping American policy toward China was President Harry S. Truman. By late 1948, Truman had revealed himself to be a president of two distinct parts. One was a narrow partisan who surrounded himself with cronies and second-rate men. He was quick to reward them, to defend them in the face of just criticism, and to smite their enemies. The second part, which was largely insulated from the first, was that of a statesman who hired men larger than himself to advise him on international affairs. These men tended to be from elite American society and the president, without deep examination, usually accepted their advice on foreign policy. His principal internal guiding light, which could lead him in many directions, was that world war was best avoided, that the Soviet Union was trying to take over the world by using the tool of international communism, and that the United States should not be dishonored.[17]

After 20 January 1949, Truman's chief foreign policy advisor was Secretary of State Dean G. Acheson. Well-bred and well-schooled, Acheson, a Yale-educated lawyer, had been a figure of note in Washington since the New Deal. After brief service in the Treasury Department and several years as a private attorney in Washington, he was summoned by President Franklin D. Roosevelt to the State Department in 1940. Shortly after Truman assumed office, Acheson became under secretary of state to Secretary James Byrnes and, later, George Marshall. During this period he gained exposure to the problems of China but made his chief contribution in European policy. In 1949, Truman asked him to replace Marshall.

13

As secretary of state, Dean Acheson brought to his job a sharp intelligence, a keen wit, which he could not always keep in reign, a mild arro-
gance, which was less pronounced than it would appear in later years, and
a belief in orderly administration and delegation of responsibility to
subordinates, especially in areas of secondary importance or about which
he was uncertain.[18]

Because Acheson was new at his job, unfamiliar with the details of
Asian policy, and initially more concerned with Europe, he rarely disputed the China policy recommendations that filtered up to him during
his first months in office. The most important initial decision he made on
the subject was to retain the men who shaped Asian policy in the Marshall
years. With respect to China, this involved two key figures: W. Walton
Butterworth, director of the Office of Far Eastern Affairs (FE), and Philip
D. Sprouse, chief of FE's subordinate Division of Chinese Affairs (CA).
Butterworth was a career foreign service officer from New Orleans. Edu-
cated at Princeton and Oxford (a Rhodes Scholar), he had served with
distinction in numerous diplomatic posts for over twenty years. During
the war he developed a reputation as a right-winger because of his support of the Roosevelt administration's policy of working with Franco's
Spain. After the war, the department sent him to China to run the American embassy in Nanking while General Marshall attempted to mediate the
civil war. While in China, Butterworth earned the special enmity of
Chiang Kai-shek and his advisors and the gratitude of General Marshall.
Not long after Truman made Marshall secretary of state, the general
appointed Butterworth FE director. Butterworth was not especially popular within the department, where some found his manner supercilious,
but he was thought to be able and not reluctant to report events as he
saw them. During his tenure he opposed large-scale China aid, for awhile
favored severing Taiwan from the mainland, was skeptical of accommodation with Chinese Communists, and generally lacked enthusiasm for
heavy American involvement in Asia. Although the secretary sometimes
found FE to be sluggish and lacking in creative ideas, Acheson respected
Butterworth's opinion and maintained with him an easy social relationship.[19]

Philip Sprouse was one of Butterworth's chief assets. A soft-spoken
career foreign service officer from Tennessee, Sprouse had served many
years in China, both before and after the Pacific War, had accompanied
General Marshall on his China mission, and was appointed CA chief after
Marshall became secretary. In his advice to Butterworth and Acheson,

Sprouse was guided by a strong sense of propriety that inhibited him from advocating abrupt abandonment of Chiang, an unemotional view of American interest, and an accurate perception of the realities of China.[20]

When Butterworth reported on events in Asia and made policy recommendations, he frequently conveyed his views through Deputy Under Secretary of State for Political Affairs Dean Rusk. Like Butterworth and Sprouse, Rusk had also been close to Marshall and, before 1949, served as assistant secretary for United Nations Affairs. Coming from a poor farm background in Georgia, Rusk had been a Rhodes Scholar and served in General Stilwell's army in China during World War II. As a bureaucrat, he was a man who then, as later, left few paper traces of his thoughts; he preferred to give advice orally, in private, and off the record. Within the State Department he was respected for his vitality and accurate reporting of other's views. Much more than Butterworth, he wanted the United States to take active measures to combat communism in Asia. Because Rusk's immediate superior, Under Secretary James Webb, was disinclined to become involved in policy, Acheson charged the deputy under secretary with overseeing policy in East Asia. He did not shrink from this responsibility.[21]

At Dean Rusk's level, there were two other senior advisors to whom Acheson paid attention when considering Asian policy in 1949. They were Ambassador at Large Philip Jessup, a Columbia University-trained international lawyer, and George Kennan, a career foreign service officer and director of the Policy Planning Staff. Of the two men, Acheson valued Jessup's advice more highly. In early 1949, Jessup negotiated an end to the Berlin blockade and was rewarded for the effort by being asked to devise a new American policy for Asia. Like Butterworth, his position with the secretary was buttressed by a warm social relationship. Unlike Butterworth, however, he was less blunt in asserting his views and less inclined to grasp the nettle when dealing with controversial subjects.[22]

Like his colleagues, George Kennan had reached his prime in the State Department under Secretary Marshall. While a career foreign service officer in the American embassy in Moscow and later as chief foreign policy planner for the State Department, Kennan's keenest interest was European policy and he supported only an off-shore containment policy in Asia. His staff's key China expert was John Davies. Davies was a foreign service officer with long experience in China and with a sprawling mind that allowed him to recommend both fine-tuned policies of coaxing Chinese Communists toward the West and policies of blunt coercion. Kennan's advice on China policy tended to reflect Davies' views. Acheson apparently began to lose interest in Kennan's thoughts about Asian policy and other subjects toward the end of 1949.[23]

Acheson received a daily briefing from his senior advisors every morning at 9:30. The usual attendants in 1949 were Webb, Rusk, Kennan, Jessup, Counselor Charles Bohlen, and Congressional Liaison Chief Ernest Gross. The secretary usually prepared for these meetings by reading a five- or six-page top secret summary of the previous day's cable traffic. He reviewed current problems, listened to advice, and gave his guidance. Following this conference, James Webb held an under secretary's meeting that office directors (later assistant secretaries) attended. This meeting cleared policy papers destined for the secretary's office and beyond and was used to convey policy guidance to the department's offices and divisions. Direct contact between the secretary and the office directors, however, frequently circumvented this chain of command. Acheson also maintained routine communication with the president whom he briefed twice a week and to whom he had quick access at all other times. For each meeting the department's executive secretariat, which constituted the secretary's personal staff, prepared a numbered agenda for Acheson to use in briefing Truman. During the meetings the secretary reviewed each item and returned to the State Department where he dictated a brief memorandum stating the president's views. President Truman made most of his decisions quickly and in accordance with Acheson's advice.

"National Military Establishment"

The National Military Establishment, created by the 1947 National Security Act, was a bureaucratic way station between the military disunity of the pre-1947 years and a more unified Department of Defense organized in late 1949. The establishment's titular leader was the secretary of defense who received advice from three civilian service secretaries and the Joint Chiefs of Staff. It was far from a harmonious group. The service rivalry over budgets in 1949 was intense and led to well-publicized congressional hearings about the strategic roles of the Navy and the Air Force. When it came to China policy, however, there was little disunity between the services or among the top civilian leaders. The concensus was that the United States should exert itself more vigorously to stop communism in China by rendering military assistance, short of committing American ground forces, to non-Communist forces on the mainland

and Formosa. The military leaders held this view during James Forrestal's tenure as defense secretary and found an even more vigorous champion of an active China policy in Louis A. Johnson.

Louis Johnson replaced Forrestal in late March 1949. A tall, native West Virginian, a prosperous Washington lawyer, and a former War Department executive, he earned Harry Truman's gratitude in 1948 by serving in the thankless job of Democratic Party treasurer. It proved to be a job suited to his talents. "Few men could have prospected more profitably in the arid wastes of the Democratic financial desert than Louis Johnson," a contemporary wrote many years later. "He knew which arms to stroke and which to twist."[24] These abilities, which served him well in 1948, impressed others less favorably after he became defense secretary. Instead of dealing with Democratic Party politicos, his new office forced him to deal with the cream of the foreign policy establishment. The two did not mix well.

David Lilienthal, Atomic Energy Commission chairman and an experienced Washington bureaucrat, spotted the problem when he first met the new defense secretary. "The first impression all of us got," he recorded in his diary,

> came before we [Lilienthal and his fellow AEC commissioners] were ushered into his office. The "characters" . . . hovering around the outer office . . . [had] the overfed, cigar-chewing, red-faced glum look that you see hanging around the courthouse and the city hall all over the country. The vultures who gather where there is dead meat (in the way of public contracts) and who think they know how to get a hunk of same.
>
> This impression was not changed very much by what we first ran into when we assembled in his office. He greeted us affably, a tall, soft-spoken, relaxed man, big and as handsome as a bald man ever is.
>
> [I]t was a picture of an able man who certainly feels his oats and is riding high. The amount of power he will shortly have . . . is terrific. This will be a strain for democracy.[25]

National Security Council

One tool Johnson and his predecessor used to force their views on the State Department and the president was the National Security Council (NSC). The National Security Act of 1947 created the NSC and gave it a broad mandate. As interpreted by the NSC's executive director, retired Admiral Sidney Souers, the council was to be "the instrument through which the president obtains the collective advice of the appropriate officials in the executive branch concerning the integration of domestic, foreign, and military policy relating to the national security." It was a convenient definition since it allowed the military to remove policy formulation from the exclusive domain of the State Department and place it in an arena weighted toward the "military point of view." The council consisted of four bodies: the members, a secretariat, and two separate groups of consultants and staff, both drawn from member agencies. From its origin through October 1949, the statutory membership consisted of the president, the secretary of state, the secretary of defense, the secretaries of the Army, Navy, and Air Force, and the chairman of the new National Security Resources Board, who was there, in theory, to represent a "civilian point of view." The administrator of the Economic Cooperation Administration, the director of the Central Intelligence Agency, the chairman of the Joint Chiefs of Staff, the treasury secretary, and others also frequently attended the meetings.[26]

Discussion in the council meetings revolved around numbered policy papers that usually originated in member agencies; occasionally the staff produced an independent study. The standard format was a brief statement of the "problem," a more lengthy "analysis," and the "conclusions." The conclusions, which contained policy recommendations, could be adopted, modified, rejected, or sent back to the staff for further consideration. If they were to become "national policy," the members forwarded them to the president with the recommendation that they become national policy. The president was free to do what he wished with the NSC's advice.

The Friends of China

Four other separate, but closely coordinated, groups influenced the Truman administration's China policies: a congressional China bloc, a private citizens' China lobby, a variety of individuals working within the executive branch, and the Chinese diplomatic mission in Washington and New York. Although no one group controlled another, they often coordinated their efforts and shared a common cause—the interest of Nationalist China in general and, frequently, the interest of Chiang Kai-shek in particular.

The China bloc was not a tightly organized body in either the 80th or the 81st Congress; at most, it was a loose coalition of senators and representatives, mostly Republicans, interested in China. In the House, Walter Judd, a Minnesota Republican, was the most persistent and forceful advocate. A missionary doctor in China in the 1920s and 1930s, Judd came to Congress in 1943 and thereafter berated the Roosevelt administration for its weak support of Chiang Kai-shek. By 1949, both Judd and his colleagues realized that he was over-identified with China; consequently he stepped back—but never very far—to allow other Republicans like John Vorys of Ohio and John Davis Lodge of Connecticut to take the lead. Perhaps out of frustration over their party's defeat in the 1948 election, many other Republicans were persuaded from time to time to join this activist core in their attacks on the administration's Far Eastern policy and policy makers. In the Senate, the key Republican China bloc members were William Knowland, a forceful newcomer from California, Styles Bridges, a senior party member from New Hampshire, and a new recruit, the prayerful H. Alexander Smith of New Jersey. Unlike their House colleagues, the Senate China bloc was better able to recruit Democrats to their ranks; best known in the majority party was the powerful and venomous Pat McCarran of Nevada.

A group of loosely organized American citizens known as the "China lobby" supported the congressional China bloc's efforts. Its origins dated back to the early days of World War II when China was fighting Japan alone. During the war a group of men with a mixture of ideological, emotional, and frequently financial, interests in the survival of a "Free" China headed the lobby. It persisted after the war and, by 1949, the two best-known organized groups were the "Committee to Defend America by Aiding Anti-Communist China," and the "American China Policy Association." Ten of the fifty-one committee directors were also directors of the smaller association, although the two groups appear to have operated independently. Frederick C. McKee, a Pittsburgh industrialist, directed the committee, devoting much of his effort to lobbying administration officials he knew from the period when he lobbied Congress for passage of both Lend-Lease and the Marshall Plan. Compared to the American China Policy Association's lobbying effort, McKee's effort was low-keyed and genteel.[27]

The American China Policy Association leaders were Alfred Kohlberg and William Loeb. Kohlberg, a lace handkerchief importer who moved to New York after the Japanese forced him from China, formed the group in 1946. The association made its public debut by sending a letter signed by "65 leading Americans" to President Truman protesting then Under Secretary of State Dean Acheson's "offer" of American training and support for Chinese Communist forces that might join the Chinese Nationalist Army. In the same year Kohlberg also founded the monthly publication *Plain Talk*.[28] Setting a tone for future editions, the first issue contained an article describing a "pro-Soviet group" in the State Department's China division and implicating foreign service officers John Service, John Davies, and John Carter Vincent, and State Department advisor Owen Lattimore, among others, as part of a "highly organized campaign" dedicated to altering American policy in accordance with the "soviet line."[29] Along with Loeb, the editor of the *Manchester* (N.H.) *Morning Union*, Kohlberg continued to suggest that the State Department's Far Eastern Bureau was run by pro-Communists.[30] The special contribution of these two men to the China debate was their drive and vindictiveness.

In addition to these citizen lobbyists, there was also an unorganized core of prominent men and women who made China their special cause. Included were Henry and Clare Boothe Luce of Time, Incorporated; Roy Howard of the Scripts-Howard Press; syndicated columnists Joseph and Stewart Alsop; former ambassador to France and the Soviet Union William C. Bullitt; former senior state department official Stanley Hornbeck; Harvard Law School Dean Emeritus Roscoe Pound; and retired Major General Claire L. Chennault, leader of the "Flying Tigers" in China.

There was also an unorganized group of government officials, drawn largely from the military establishment, who strongly supported the Nationalist government and occasionally lent themselves to its cause. Some of the higher ranking members of this group were Assistant Secretary of Defense Paul H. Griffith; the supreme commander of the Allied Forces in the Pacific, General Douglas MacArthur; National Military Establishment War Council member, Lieutenant General Albert C. Wedemeyer; Western Pacific Fleet commander, Admiral Oscar C. Badger; and Secretary of the Senate and friend of the president, Leslie L. Biffle. These individuals made their views known by explicit arguments in high government councils and by giving their superiors documents written by the Chinese embassy and the China lobby.[31]

A dual Chinese Nationalist government mission to the United States supported both the private and public China lobbies. The accredited Chinese ambassador, Columbia University-educated Dr. V. K. Wellington Koo, had faithfully served the Chinese republic since World War I; it was not always clear, however, which Chinese faction he was serving in 1949. Acting President Li Tsung-jen, his government's titular leader, controlled few levers of power; most real power remained in the hands of Chiang Kai-shek and his wing of the Nationalist Party. Koo's authority was also complicated by the long sojourn in New York City of Madame Chiang Kai-shek, who stayed in America from December 1948 to January 1950. Madame Chiang, who maintained direct communication with her husband, presided over a powerful group of Chinese ex-patriots, including Nationalist ideologue Chen Li-fu, her brother-in-law H. H. Kung, the Washington embassy's minister-counselor Chen Chih-mai, China's United Nations ambassador Dr. T. F. Tsiang, and her influential brother, currently without a government job, T. V. Soong. The Washington embassy and the collection of personages in New York did not always work in harmony, but they did work vigorously. For whom and for what part of China, however, was sometimes unclear to the State Department. It was a many-faceted operation ranging from honorable forms of diplomacy to crass mudslinging.[32]

Madame Chiang and Ambassador Koo usually took the high road. After several frustrating weeks in Washington in which she vainly lobbied for more aid, Madame Chiang retired to New York in late 1948 to work on the American government more indirectly, leaving Washington to Koo and her agents.[33] The ambassador held aloof from the embassy's day-to-day lobbying, reserving himself for high-level contacts within the Congress, the administration, and the diplomatic community. The task of pursuing Nationalist interests through China bloc and lobby manipulation fell to Chen Chih-mai, First Secretary Joseph Ku, and others. Much of their responsibility was, in turn, delegated to their paid American lobbyist, William J. Goodwin.[34]

The Chinese hired Goodwin as a member of the National Resources Commission of China in March 1948 as a result of an introduction by Alfred Kohlberg.[35] Goodwin held a position as "advisor on public relations" until he changed to the "China News Service" payroll in the following year. In both positions Goodwin, a public relations man, pursued a variety of activities on behalf of his employer and proved to be squarely in the Kohlberg tradition. Among other activities, he arranged meetings, usually dinners at Washington and New York hotels and clubs, between congressmen, friends of China, and members of the Chinese embassy. Between November 1948 and March 1949 Koo attended six of these functions.[36] He also conducted a mail campaign designed to nourish the perception that the State Department was Communist-dominated.[37]

Although the various friends of China in the United States did not form a centrally organized conspiracy, they were more than a scattered collection of like-minded individuals. They maintained close ties, sharing documents, ideas, money, and a special historical litany. According to their interpretation, the United States sold the Nationalists out to Stalin at the Yalta Conference and in China. At Yalta, China's betrayers were Alger Hiss and soft-headed liberals; in China, they were foreign service officers who constantly criticized the Chinese war effort against Japan. Particularly suspect was John Service, whose unflattering reports of the generalissimo's regime the Federal Bureau of Investigation (FBI) found in the safe of Philip Jaffe, editor of the left-leaning Asian affairs magazine *Amerasia*. After confiscating these and other classified documents, the FBI arrested Service and several other State Department officers. A federal grand jury unanimously no-billed Service after the FBI sought an indictment and he was reinstated in the department, but China's friends never took their eyes off him or forgave the State Department for not firing him.[38]

For the years 1945–46, the litany held that General George Marshall's mediation mission to China compounded treason and tragedy by "forcing" the Nationalists to form a coalition government with the Communists and by temporarily cutting off aid to Chiang. In 1947 China's enemies succeeded in suppressing a report that General Albert Wedemeyer made after a survey trip to China that might, had its recommendations been implemented, have saved Free China. In the next year the State Department quibbled about the Nationalists' shortcomings and delayed American aid while a Red Chinese army was rolling south.[39] China's friends chanted this litany relatively quietly before the 1948 presidential election, expecting that relief would soon come with the Dewey administration. When Truman won, they attempted to turn the charge of China's "sell-out" into a national political issue.

The friends of China had little significant organized opposition outside the State Department. There was no equally enthusiastic counter-China bloc in Congress; the best the administration could do was to keep the Democratic leadership and moderate Republicans well briefed on developments in China and lobby against offensive China aid bills. Few friendly senators or congressmen matched the China bloc blow for blow;

the State Department's strongest defender was Senate Foreign Relations Committee Chairman Tom Connally, a Texas Democrat who was not popular with his colleagues. There was also no equally vocal counter-China lobby. A significant number of American businessmen and missionary interests favored writing off China and working with the Communists, but their voices were less shrill than those of their competitors; their arguments were more complex and their influence on the public and congressional minds was relatively slight.[40]

Like the government, the American public was in a quandary about China. Its mind had long been awash in contradictory views of the Chinese and the present civil war only exacerbated the confusion. In late November 1948, the Gallup Poll asked a sample population if it thought the Chinese Communists were taking orders from Moscow. Fifty-one percent thought they were; 10 percent thought they were not. Thirty-two percent favored sending "about $5 billion worth of goods and military supplies" to aid Chiang Kai-shek; 34 percent were opposed. In early May 1949, another sample was asked what "the United States should do about China?" Forty-three percent considered China to be a "lost cause"; 22 percent favored sending some form of aid, "food, arms, money." Gallup asked another sample a week later about their opinion on trade with a Communist China. Thirty-four percent were for such trade; 46 percent opposed; and 20 percent had no opinion. Other polls inquiring about Russia and domestic communism indicated a high degree of anxiety about Communists at home and abroad. Popular opinion, in short, leaned against further involvement with the Nationalists and showed a pronounced tilt against accommodation with Communists in China or elsewhere. It was in such a political climate that Truman administration officials planned China policy in the winter of 1948–49 and that the friends of China plotted their opposition.[41]

2

China Policy Smorgasbord, 3 March 1949

With the Nationalist Chinese position deteriorating in mid-1948, the State Department and the military establishment found themselves at serious odds over China policy. The debate between diplomats and soldiers would be manifested in many forums over the next two years, but found its highest bureaucratic expression in battles over language in National Security Council (NSC) papers. One especially important battle, which produced three China policies rather than one, ended with the the administration adopting a group of policy papers on 3 March 1949. While the final products of this battle were a charade that papered over profound differences about policy, the exercise threw the differing bureaucratic views into broad relief.

Policy Papers

In mid-1948, the official US China policy was to continue backing the Nationalist regime with limited military, economic, and diplomatic support. Responding to the obvious need to revise a policy that was backing a losing cause, the State Department, in early September, sent the NSC a vague statement of what a new China policy should be.[1] Since the department preferred to keep the day-to-day conduct of policy to itself

.vey only a general sense of its thoughts on the subject, the
:ss was intentional. As one senior official put it, "at this stage the
.ould concern itself only with an overall strategic statement of
policy, leaving tactical planning and implementation to the operational
elements in the Government—particularly our Office of Far Eastern
Affairs."[2]

Assessing the Nationalist's prospects as hopeless, the paper suggested
a new policy of "fear and favor" toward the future Communist regime.
With American military strength dismissed as useless in the China, the
department recommended a variety of vaguely defined political, cultural,
and economic "forms" as potentially useful in the battle for the mind of
the new China. Diplomatic recognition (a political form) was to remain
with the Nationalist government until it fell and was then to be assigned
elsewhere as the circumstances dictated. The most important form was
economic. With "favor in hand in the shape of economic aid authorizations," the United States would have flexibility "to give or withold fully
or in part" economic assistance. "Only thus will U.S. politico-economic
influence be felt."[3]

The State Department-draft policy statement was not well received
either in the military or by the NSC staff, both of which wanted a tougher
anti-Communist foreign policy in Asia and, more generally, sought a
wider role in policy formulation and implementation. The NSC staff
countered with an alternative draft that called for "aggressive political
warfare" against the new regime for the purpose of overthrowing it. The
State Department found this draft unacceptable and produced two more
of its own that the military and the NSC staff also rejected.[4] The impasse
continued into the new year, and before the administration was able to
adopt a formal China policy, it was confronted with two important operational decisions that would have major policy implications. These decisions would, in effect, be made in a policy vacuum.

Aid for the Communists?

The Communists' march south forced the Truman administration to
consider the specific question of whether or not to continue the China aid
program. The program operated under several legislative authorizations,
but the largest was the "China Aid Act" of 1948.[5] Passed as part of an
omnibus foreign aid bill that also authorized Marshall Plan aid to Europe,
the China "act" authorized $125 million for military aid and $338 million

for economic aid. It specified that the money could be used q   h 3 April 1949, and be granted to the "Government of Chi   'r authority of this authorization, Congress later passed a sep   )- priation act with no time cut off that granted the full $12   ɔr military aid and only $275 million for economic assistance.[6]

The task of implementing the economic aid program fell to the newly established Economic Cooperation Administration (ECA)—created primarily to implement the Marshall Plan—which opened aid missions throughout China. Three men held key responsibility for administering the program: Roger Lapham, a liberal Republican and former mayor of San Francisco, currently the aid mission chief stationed in Shanghai; Harlan Cleveland, a young economist who had worked in China in the aid field after the war and was now the chief of ECA's China Aid Division in Washington; and Paul Hoffman, a Republican and former president of Studebaker Motors, the ECA administrator. Together they oversaw a large program containing several elements: food relief for China's several major cities; a commodity support program (raw cotton, petroleum, fertilizer, and tobacco), a rurul reconstruction program, and an industrialization and replacement program.[7] By November 1948, the men in charge of ECA were forced to consider what to do with their program in light of the Communists' advance south and addressed the question to the State Department and the president.

Roger Lapham first raised the question in a long telegram to headquarters in late November. In "TOECA 499," as ECA officially designated the telegram, Lapham warned that most of the coastal cities of China would soon fall to the Communists and recommended that the commodity program be completed under the Communists. He proposed that it be "subject to minimum of conditions, including publicity as to source of supplies granted Chinese people, freedom of activity to ECA personnel, and cooperation in complete present distribution arrangements."[8] Another supporter of a tentative aid program to the Communists, Consul General John Cabot in Shanghai, also later endorsed the concept of continued aid. He conceded privately, however, that his "suggestions may be—in fact probably are in certain respects—poison ivy from the domestic political viewpoint."[9]

TOECA 499 reached Washington on the evening of 27 November and presented the administration with an operational question that could not be deferred. The telegram met a hospitable reception in ECA, both Cleveland and Hoffman favoring Lapham's recommendation. The director, however, did not think a policy of aiding the Communists was feasible over the long term; Hoffman assumed that the Communists would violate the principles ECA demanded in the distribution of American goods. Yet, if Americans were to leave China, he preferred that they be thrown out, and that the onus of the break be left on the Communists.[10]

On 2 December, Cleveland and Hoffman approached their State Department counterparts, Butterworth and Acting Secretary of State Robert Lovett, in an effort to obtain policy guidance and, specifically, to discuss the possibility of continuing aid to a Communist China. They quickly learned the department's negative reaction. "The difficulty in considering this question, of course," Cleveland wrote Lapham after the meeting, "is compounded by the fact that there has been no determination as to the general policy." Cleveland noted Lovett's concern with the possible congressional response to aiding the Communists; once, he recorded, the acting secretary expressed concern over "getting away with it" in light of the clear legislative intent of the China Aid Act to help the Nationalists. Lovett's comments "were in terms of what was feasible or desirable from the standpoint of congressional and public reaction in this country, rather than what was desirable purely from the standpoint of our relationship with China or the Chinese people."[11]

Hoffman did not abandon his position. He soon obtained a garbled expression of congressional support for his views in an appearance before the joint congressional "Watchdog" Committee (established to monitor ECA) and then departed for China to look at the aid program firsthand.[12] In Shanghai he gave a press conference on 13 December in which he supported granting the new regime aid if conditions existed "which would permit continuation of free institutions." Were such conditions to exist, he thought "our government would be willing to accept a recommendation for continued aid."[13] He was soon proved wrong. Five days after his statement, Butterworth urged Lovett to raise the question of aiding the Communists in the next Cabinet meeting. He recommended that the acting secretary oppose the program's continuance in Communist-occupied areas, except for the dispersal of commodities either landed or being unloaded. When these goods were distributed, Butterworth wanted the ECA to withdraw.[14]

On 30 December 1948, with Hoffman not yet back in Washington, Lovett discussed the question with the president and won endorsement for Butterworth's position.[15] While the ECA administrator strenuously attempted to reverse this decision after his return, he was unable to

27

impress either the president or his Cabinet, which unanimously voted to back Truman.[16] The State Department's position had been based, first, on the belief that the United States should not be in a position of helping the new regime and, second, on an awareness of the problems such assistance would raise with Congress. In the wake of recent signs of Communist hostility toward the United States, it was apparently not willing to run a congressional gauntlet in order to bestow favors upon the Communists in China. The pay-off for such a policy—a Communist China weaned away from Moscow—was seen as too unlikely and, in any event, too long in coming. The possibility that such aid might be used as a lure to pull China toward the West was apparently not given much serious thought in the State Department outside of the Policy Planning Staff, despite the fact that it was a policy line suggested in earlier department-draft policy papers. The department's senior officials may have also anticipated the probable negative reaction to such a policy in the White House. If there was any mystery about the president's views on the subject, they were tersely summarized in a Cabinet meeting on 19 January, when Truman stated that "we can't be in the position of making any deals with a Communist regime."[17]

Military Aid for the Nationalists?

While the administration quickly decided not to furnish economic aid to the Communists, decisions about continuing military assistance to the Nationalists took several months to reach. The military aid program had three components: a military advisory group that advised the Chinese government on strategy and troop training; a naval advisory group that trained the Chinese navy, backed by a large unit of the United States Western Pacific Fleet stationed at Tsingtao; and material aid furnished under the China Aid Act's $125 million fund. By late November 1948, only approximately $17 million of the aid was thought to remain uncommitted, although no one could be quite sure. A significant amount of the arms that had been purchased were then, or soon would be, at sea on American ship en route to China.[18]

In a 14 December memorandum to Admiral Souers of the NSC, Defense Secretary Forrestal asked for guidance about the arms aid program's future. Noting that the president had recently urged that China aid be expedited, the secretary pointed out that the situation in China had greatly deteriorated in recent weeks.[19] Several days later, the NSC met and adopted a State Department request to defer decisions about the military aid program until the council could obtain the views of General David Barr, head of the American military mission in Nanking, and Ambassador Stuart.[20]

The council also dealt with the question of continuing the military advisory program. In late October the State Department had been concerned that Admiral Oscar Badger, the Tsingtao naval unit's commander, might engage in the city's defense against the Communists.[21] By mid-December the Joint Chiefs of Staff had disabused Badger of this notion and Lovett strongly recommended to the NSC on 14 December that the admiral be ordered to liquidate his shore facilities and withdraw to his ships. He also urged that the Navy not restation its ships at either Formosa or Amoy when it finally abandoned the Chinese mainland, something both Badger and the Joint Chiefs of Staff had wanted to do.[22] On 23 December, the NSC met again and, with the president's support, backed Lovett's position.[23] A decision had already been reached to begin phasing out General Barr's land-based advisory group.[24]

On 26 January, General Barr, reversing an earlier position that both he and Ambassador Stuart had taken recommending continued arms aid, urged that no further US military assistance be shipped to China. The arms, he feared, would either fall into Communist hands or be sold abroad by unscrupulous Nationalists.[25] Defense Secretary Forrestal sent Barr's views to the NSC along with three alternative policies for the council to consider in its meeting the following day: (1) *continue* the present military aid policy; (2) *suspend* the program; or (3) *terminate* it and send the unspent balance of the $125 million back to the Treasury.[26]

It is not clear what position the State Department took on the military aid question in an NSC meeting on 3 February. Philip Sprouse, chief of the FE's Division of Chinese Affairs, drafted a memorandum for Butterworth to send to Secretary of State Dean Acheson—who had been on the job for thirteen days—recommending that the department favor continuation of the military aid then en route on the narrow legal grounds that the supplies belonged to the Nationalists. In effect, this was an endorsement for Forrestal's first option. The memorandum carrying this recommendation, however, was either altered by Butterworth or Acheson before the latter read or summarized its contents before the NSC meeting. The document was returned to the files modified to state that the department opposed the "termination" of the aid program and recommended the "continued procurement of military aid supplies to the Chinese government, but the *suspension* of further delivery of supplies, including those now *en route* pending further developments in China." The revised document had been altered to endorse Forrestal's second option.[27] The council finally adopted the position that Truman "advise key members of Congress that [he] considers it to be in the interest of national security to suspend further shipments under the Military Aid Program for China . . . pending clarification and review of the situation, meanwhile permitting only such selective shipments as can be properly and effectively used."[28]

The next day, Truman discussed with his Cabinet the advisability of taking up the military aid question with the House Foreign Affairs and the Senate Foreign Relations Committees. On the advice of Vice President Alben Barkley, the president invited only the ranking majority and minority members of the committees to meet with him, Barkley, and Acheson on the following day, Saturday, 5 February.[29] During this meeting, the participants recommended that the president continue the program but, where possible, delay it without formal action. Truman quickly adopted this position.[30]

It is again not clear what course (if any) Acheson recommended to the president before the congressional leaders, but the final decision was consistent with the policy FE wanted. The Far Eastern Office's reasons, however, had changed from the legalistic motive Sprouse and butterworth had given earlier in the week. Before the meeting with the congressional leadership and the president, Butterworth advised Acheson to keep the aid program in operation in order to obscure the Formosa policy FE was then developing; the office was planning to turn the China aid program into a program to support an independent Formosa.[31]

Paper Policies

On 3 March 1949, after two key decisions had been reached about how to deal with both the Communists and the Nationalists, the Truman administration finally agreed on three NSC policy papers on China. Between them, the papers gave clouded guidance on what US policy should be toward the Communist- and non-Communist-held areas of the mainland and toward Formosa. The net effect was the promulgation of three policies that could justify a variety of contradictory actions as consistent with "national policy."

THE BROAD OUTLINE: NSC–34/2.   In devising policies for both the Communist and non-Communist mainland, the State Department produced a new policy paper that ultimately became part of a series designated NSC–34. Dated 28 February 1949, and numbered NSC–34/2, the document moved only slightly closer toward a precise definition of "U.S. Policy Toward China" than predecessor drafts that had been fought over by the military and State Department in 1948. In its analysis, the paper noted the progress of events since the council had considered earlier drafts in November 1948. The Communists were proceeding with their conquest and "eventually most or all of China will come under Communist rule." It noted also the Kremlin's "extraterritorial activities" in China, the dispatch of the Soviet ambassador to Canton and "the fact that the full force of nationalism" had yet to be released in Communist China. Heavy emphasis was placed on the folly of further military aid to the Nationalists since the material would be "ineffective," fall into Communist hands, and "solidify the Chinese people in support of the Communists and perpetuate the delusion that China's interests lie with the USSR." The paper also questioned whether the United States should continue to give political support to weak non-Communist figures in China. This analysis concluded with an assertion of what a wise policy would be:

> We should be seeking to discover, nourish and bring to power a new revolution, a revolution which may eventually have to come to a test of arms with the Chinese Communists, *if* it cannot in the meantime so modify the composition and character of the Chinese Communists that they become a truly independent government, existing in amicable relations with the world community.
>
> This is obviously a long-term proposition. There is, however, no short cut. . . . The Kremlin waited twenty-five years for the fulfillment of its revolution in China. We may have to persevere as long or longer.

The analysis section of an NSC paper is, as an historical document, interesting in what it reveals about the reasoning of its authors, but it is also somewhat academic; the council members voted only on a paper's conclusions, which contain the actual policy statements. The relationship between the conclusions, which are carefully negotiated within the executive bureaucracy, and the analysis, which is usually the product of fewer pens, is not necessarily intimate. In the case of NSC–34/2, the seven brief recommendations frequently strayed from the logic of the analysis and were themselves sometimes contradictory.

The first held that the United States

> should avoid military and political support of any non-communist regimes in China unless the respective regimes are willing actively to resist communism with or without U.S. aid and, unless further, it is evident that such support would mean the overthrow of, or at least a successful resistance to, the Communists.

Shortly after this tortuously qualified statement another recommendation asserted that the United States should recognize the Nationalist government "until the situation is further clarified." Since recognition was a form of political support and since the existing Nationalist regime was thought to have little chance of surviving, much less overthrowing the Communists, the two recommendations were inconsistent.

Two other statements called for a continued American presence in China. One sentence called for a program of covert operations on the mainland. Another laboriously worded recommendation explicitly endorsed a policy of fostering Chinese Titoism:

> While scrupulously avoiding the appearance of intervention, we should be alert to exploit through political and economic means any rifts between the Chinese Communists and the USSR and between the Stalinist and other elements in China both within and outside of the communist structure.[32]

The recommendation section was a smorgasbord. While the paper's accent was on abandoning the Nationalists and encouraging Chinese Titoism, the jumble of policies it recommended allowed the administration sufficient flexibility to move in practically any direction it wished.

THE TRADE WEAPON: NSC–41.   Like its predecessors, NSC–34/2 was short on specifics about how to encourage a Sino-Soviet rift. The State Department offered suggestions for one tactical approach in a companion paper on trade policy sent the NSC on 28 February. Designated NSC–41, the trade paper held that it was "in the field of economic relations with China that the United States has available its most effective weapons vis-a-vis a Chinese Communist regime." This belief assumed that the new regime would "be dependent largely on a resumption" of trade with Japan and the West "if it is to rehabilitate and expand China's existing industrial and transportation facilities." The prospect that China might be able to do without this trade was judged possible but not likely. The paper also conceded that trade with China was indirectly important to the United States. Although the Sino-American trade was not significant, Sino-Japanese trade was important if the United States wished to be relieved of the burden of supporting its former enemy.

In order to exploit Communist China's future need for foreign trade, NSC–41 outlined two alternative policies: one would be to mobilize "the political and economic power of the western world to combat openly, through intimidation or direct pressure a Chinese Communist regime." The State Department rejected this policy because it would help consolidate Communist leadership and force China even more firmly in the Soviet camp; in a pinch, the new regime could forego Western trade. A hostile policy would also cut off future Sino-Japanese trade.

The department preferred a second alternative that gave substance to the "fear and favor" policy. The United States would allow controlled trade between China, the West, and Japan. It would make the Communists "aware of the potential power of the United States, in collaboration with other western powers and SCAP [General MacArthur's "Supreme Commander of the Allied Powers" headquarters in Tokyo], to impose severe restrictions on trade" if the new government acted hostilely toward the United States. The department called for the establishment of a system of trade controls, which initially embargoed only strategic goods, that would indicate the "United States ability and intention to deal drastically with China's foreign trade if necessary." The hope, however, was that renewed Chinese trade with Japan and the West "might foster serious conflicts between Kremlin and Chinese Communist policy and thereby tend to produce an independent Communist regime." NSC–41 concluded by recommending that a system of export controls, coordinated with friendly foreign powers, be placed on foreign trade with China. Goods of military utility for Communist China or for other Communist countries would be prohibited. All other trade would be permitted but controls would allow it to be monitored and could be used, if tightened, to compel the Chinese to act properly toward the West.[33]

FORMOSA POLICY: NSC–37/5. The Truman administration's Formosa policy developed rapidly in late 1948. In November the Joint Chiefs of Staff advised Forrestal that the island was strategically important and recommended that it be denied the Communists "by application of such diplomatic and economic steps as may be appropriate" to keep it in friendly hands. The State Department agreed that the island was important and suggested that it might even be worth seizing militarily. A week before he left office, Robert Lovett advised the president that one method of blocking a Communist takeover might be "to foster a Chinese non-Communist local government which will itself successfully deny Formosa to the Communists."[34]

On 19 January, the department produced a paper, which it sent to the NSC, urging this course of action. "When the situation in China has developed to the point where we know what governing group we will have to deal with in Formosa," it recommended that "the U.S. should seek to develop and support a local non-Communist Chinese regime which will provide at least a modicum of decent government for the island."[35] A month later the department offered a specific proposal to achieve this result: the State Department would send a high-ranking diplomat to Formosa who would discuss with the governor the steps he needed to take to secure the island from internal revolt and, when assured that such steps would be taken, offer American diplomatic and economic assistance. All of this, however, was to be done in great secrecy so as not to attract Communist or Nationalist attention.[36]

Before the NSC reacted to the State Department paper, the Joint Chiefs of Staff (JCS) made their views known about Formosa. An overt military effort to seize the island was, they held, unwise because of the "current disparity between our military strength and our global obligations." Thus they supported the State Department's plan to deny the island to the Communists by diplomatic and economic means. The JCS also suggested something else. To the chagrin of the State Department, they persisted with a plan to station "minor numbers of fleet units . . . at a suitable Formosan port or ports."[37]

On 1 March, the NSC staff submitted a draft report on Formosa policy based on earlier State Department drafts. Numbered NSC–37/5, the brief paper recapitulated the department's recommendations for diplomatic and economic support and argued against stationing ships at Formosa. Along with two other policy papers, this document went to the NSC members for their discussion in a meeting scheduled for 3 March.[38]

American China Policies

On 3 March, the National Security Council members voted to recommend the conclusions of all three papers to the president as national policy. On the same day, the president agreed and charged the secretary of state with their implementation.[39]

The administration finally had not one but three China policies: one for Communist China, one for the non-Communist mainland, and one for Formosa. The tone of all three accented a hard line toward the Communists. All were fashioned by a State Department cognizant of the views of other bureaucracies within the administration, of Congress, and of public opinion. Taken together, they confronted the Communists with more "fear" than "favor." They apparently gave little thought to a softer approach, one that might offer the new regime more positive inducements to lean toward the West. The closest thing to a lure—the ECA recommendation that aid be continued under the Communists—had been dismissed in the last days of the first Truman administration. The only incentive offered the Communists in the 3 March package was "controlled trade" with the West and Japan. The balance of the remaining policies was, to varying degrees, disagreeable from the Chinese Communist perspective: continued recognition of the Nationalists; a program of covert aid to pro-Western groups on the mainland; possible future overt support for some anti-Communist force that might rise up against the Communists; continued shipments of military and economic aid to the Nationalists; and the policy of severing Formosa from the mainland. Many of these negative policies were designed in opposition to the Titoist hypothesis and appeared to rest on the counter-hypothesis that all Communists were in the same camp and should be staunchly opposed by the use of all practical devices.

The appearances were deceiving. The Titoist hypothesis was at the core of the State Department's China policies. Although the department, the main drafter of these papers, couched the policies in tough language, endorsed continued support of the Nationalists, and sprinkled in carefully qualified contingent policies that allowed other bureaucracies to sign off on the whole package, it still saw the prospect of a Sino-Soviet split as offering the most realistic policy goal. It could not propose a pure Titoist policy. In China, an avowed policy of encouraging Chinese Titoism would serve only to consolidate the position of the Communist Party's Stalinists (Tito, after all, had broken with Stalin without encouragement from the West). Within the administration, the military establishment was skeptical of the Tito hypothesis, as was President Truman himself. In Congress, the Democrats gave it no support and the Republicans reacted with hostility. Thus the State Department, which itself had mixed feelings about the hypothesis, asserted it cautiously before the National Security Council and the president.

The State Department may also have been trying to be clever with its policy smorgasbord. Many of the contradictions arose from the department's assumption that the Nationalist regime was doomed. The policy of continued recognition, a form of political support, would end with the government's demise. The continuation of economic and military aid to the non-Communist mainland would also cease being an irritant when the Communists controlled all the mainland. NSC–34/2's provision for aiding other forces opposed to the Communists—should they arise—was possibly a State Department sop thrown in to mollify administration officials who wanted to do something more active against communism than trade and wait. The department could support it because of the qualification that such groups would not be aided unless they were at first willing to fight unsupported and unless the American support would lead to "the overthrow of, or at least successful resistance to, the Communists." This placed a heavy burden of proof on anyone urging a program of aid to a non-Communist force on the mainland. The analysis section of the same paper dismissed as remote the chances of any such group being successful. The policies of 3 March applying to the mainland that were hostile to the policy of pursuing Titoism could thus be viewed as short term irritants that would not linger long to damage the goal of stimulating a rift between the new China and the Soviet Union. The policy toward the non-Communist mainland would, quite simply, vanish with the government of Nationalist China.

More difficult to reconcile with the Titoist policy was the State Department's Formosa policy. Far from being a policy forced upon a reluctant department by its hawkish bureaucratic competitors, FE and the Policy Planning Staff enthusiastically endorsed NSC–37/5. Yet the policy appears in retrospect to contain the seeds of the destruction of the Titoist policy toward the mainland. How, one must ask, could the State Department expect actively to foster Formosan independence from the mainland and not incur the Chinese Communists' wrath? The answer was that it should be done secretly; if the Communists did not know about the United States' effort to sever the island from the mainland, they would not blame America for its loss. Butterworth alluded to the need for secrecy, as well as FE's enthusiasm for the policy, in a 15 January "Top Secret" letter to the American consul in Taipei.

All of us in the Department feel strongly that we should seek by political and economic means to prevent the Chinese Communists regime from control of the Island. . . . [D]o not be surprised if you get instructions requesting you to persuade the authorities in control of Formosa to disassociate themselves from any arrangement made on the mainland and maintain a separate regime. *We would wish, however, to avoid too obvious an association while giving them aid.* [40]

The FE director concluded by asking the consul to burn the letter.

Dean Acheson made the point even more forcefully in the 3 March NSC meeting. Rebutting the JCS recommendation to station minor fleet units on Formosa, the secretary stressed that he was "most anxious to avoid raising the spectre of an American-created irredentist issue just at the time we shall be seeking to exploit the genuinely Soviet-created irredentist issue in Manchuria and Sinkiang." It was "a cardinal point in our thinking that if our policy is to have any hope of success in Formosa, we must carefully conceal our wish to separate the island from mainland control." [41] Through discreet implementation of both the Formosa and mainland policies, the administration apparently thought it could have its Formosa cake and Chinese Titoism too.

After the president agreed to the recommendations of the China papers on 3 March, the administration, in essence, embraced three official policies overlapping the three NSC papers. Neither the papers nor the policies settled the dispute between the State Department and the military. The latter had doubts about the wisdom of NSC–41, was hostile to the whole concept of Chinese Titoism, and preferred a constant hard line approach to the Communists. So also did President Truman; yet, since he had entrusted foreign policy formulation and conduct to Dean Acheson and the State Department, he was not prepared to challenge the Tito hypothesis if, in fact, he understood it. The three China papers, in any case, were sufficiently hard line in their sound and substance that Truman probably agreed to them without much difficulty. As the year progressed, the State Department would find that he needed more convincing on the premise of its mainland policy. The military would also need to be dealt with again on the China question, especially after Louis Johnson became secretary of defense. After 3 March, however, the two groups with which the State Department found it most imperative to deal were the United States Congress and the Chinese Communist Party.

3

First China Bloc Offensive

Truman administration officials wrestled with the China question in late 1948 against an uncertain domestic political background. One reason the State Department did not forcefully pursue a "Tito" policy in China before the 1948 presidential election may have been the assumption that a Thomas E. Dewey administration would reverse that policy when it took office in January 1949. The presumed president-elect was a moderate on China by Republican standards but was willing to "renew and strengthen our ancient ties of friendship with this great wartime ally" once he took office.[1] Unfortunately for Governor Dewey and Chiang Kai-shek, Harry Truman won and the Democrats regained control of Congress. Conditions within the State Department, however, remained in flux even after the election. Secretary Marshall, ill and planning to retire, left control of the department to Under Secretary of State Robert Lovett. While Lovett was a strong leader, he was not inclined to press forward with new policies that a new secretary of state might soon replace. The China policy papers begun during the fall were thus left in draft form for the new secretary to deal with on 21 January 1949.

Round Robin, 7 February

Dean Acheson took office aware of the influence groups lobbying for China had on postwar American-Asian policy. As under secretary of state between 1945 and 1947, he had frequently felt their pressure, and, in the last year of his tenure, he bore the brunt of an early version of McCarthyism when he defended John Carter Vincent, then chief of the Far Eastern Bureau, from Senator Bridges's charge that Vincent was "soft on Communism."[2] Acheson may have also known that the China bloc had enough legislative clout in 1948 to compel the administration to recommend a China aid program to Congress.[3]

Whatever his perception when he entered office as secretary, Acheson was not concerned enough with the threat to alter existing China policy or to replace its architects. Although aware of the past power of China's supporters in Congress, he also knew that their ranks had diminished in the 1948 election and thought the question of aiding the Nationalists was rapidly becoming academic. Thus, when the China bloc renewed its campaign in 1949, Acheson chose to deal with the threat through a quiet, off-the-record lecture; his weapons were the overwhelming reality of Chiang's inevitable demise and his own considerable power of persuasion.

The first important China bloc attack came in a round robin letter fifty-one Republican House members sent the president on 7 February 1949. The two-and-a-half-page document recalled the wise policy of President Franklin Roosevelt in making "firm commitments" to Chiang Kai-shek "with full knowledge of the imperfections and limitations" of his government. This commitment, it complained, was abandoned in 1945 "in favor of a policy of insisting upon a coalition with the Communists as the price of American aid." The letter also contained seven loaded questions about current China policy and recommended that Truman appoint "a Commission of one or more eminent Americans, with top-level military, economic and political advisers, to make an immediate reexamination of the situation and report" to both Congress and the president.[4] Truman gave the round robin to Dean Acheson on 10 February.

The secretary soon learned that the main force behind the letter was Walter Judd. At Judd's request, Congressman Brooks Hays, a proadministration Arkansas Democrat, called Acheson on the following day. Hays relayed Judd's hope that the administration would not view the document as a "sniping" letter or think that the Republicans were trying to hurt the bipartisan foreign policy. All the signers believed in Acheson, did not fear helping him, and felt he would institute a "fresh start on China." Hays urged the secretary to talk to the group off-the-record about the administration's China policy. After the phone call, Acheson spoke to his aide who summarized the secretary's thoughts:

> The Secretary wondered if this might not be the time to give a direct answer to the letter. We have been holding the rug under the Nationalist Government, which has prevented us from really telling the story. He referred to General Marshall's testimony in closed session before the House Foreign Affairs Committee, which he thought was a masterful presentation of the matter. He thought that a re-draft of this was what really should go to the Congressmen, but that such action would definitely pull the rug out from under the Nationalist Government and probably leave us in a worse hole than ever as regards long-range benefits in China and the stopping of Communist take-over. I pointed out that with the Generalissimo absconded [to Taiwan with the government's gold reserves], the Cabinet having moved to Canton, and Li-Sun-Jen [sic] living in solitary splendor in Nanking attempting to negotiate a compromise with the Communists, it looked to me like the rug had already pretty well slipped on all four corners and in the middle. The Secretary agreed, but pointed out that pulling the rug now without some other hook on which to hang our hat would appear to leave the Communists in complete ascendency.[5]

After more discussion between the White House and State Department, Truman decided that Acheson should reply by holding a "very frank" off-the-record meeting with the Republican Congressmen.[6]

Acheson met thirty of the original fifty-one signators on 24 February in the Capitol. In a lengthy presentation, he reviewed the history of American wartime and postwar involvement in China. He assured his listeners that a Communist China would not immediately be a springboard for further Communist attack. It was, instead, a "morass." The United States could not foresee what would occur next "until some of the dust and smoke of the disaster clears away, and we can see where there is a foundation on which to build."[7]

The China bloc and lobby had prepared for Acheson's appearance. According to Chen Chih-mai, who reported on the forthcoming meeting to Ambassador Koo, "it was felt that those who had been discussing China affairs, such as Congressman Walter Judd, should stay more or less in the background, and let others 'carry the ball.'" Chen wrote that Alfred Kohlberg had been preparing for the meeting by "drafting pertinent questions and supplying information."[8]

A written account of the meeting appeared in *Time Magazine* the following week. Walter Judd, apparently, was unable to contain himself. "U.S. policy could almost be expressed in four words," he charged, "first, aid to China was 'unnecessary,' then 'undesirable,' and then 'too late.' Just what is being done? What are we going to do?" he asked. Acheson, who was suffering a bad cold—and rarely suffered long men he considered fools—stuffed his papers in his briefcase after further haranguing, muttered "we are not getting anywhere," and departed.

The meeting left the group with the correct impression that China policy was not going to change under the new secretary. It also left in the public record an overly simple version of Acheson's concluding remarks. According to accounts published later, he had described American China policy as simply one of "waiting for the dust to settle."[9]

McCarran's Bill

The 24 February exchange between Acheson and the House China bloc portended things to come but generated no payoff for either side. A more serious threat to the State Department occurred the next day when Senator Pat McCarran introduced a bill that would have, if enacted, mandated a massive aid program for Nationalist China. Regardless of how many speeches or letters China's friends might produce lambasting American policy, none could be as effective as one substantive act of Congress.

The history of the McCarran bill long predated the 7 February letter to President Truman. In 1948, two congressional committees each sent a well-known and specially hired staff member to China to learn what the United States might do to save the country from Communism after, presumably, Thomas Dewey became president. The Senate Appropriations Committee sent former Democratic Senator D. Worth Clark; the Joint "Watchdog" Committee on Foreign Aid sent former Ambassador William C. Bullitt. Bullitt, whose "mission" drew more press attention than Clark's, spent several months in China, where he assured the generalissimo that a Republican administration, prepared to send China massive aid, would replace the Democrats in 1949.[10] After returning from China at the end of 1948, both Bullitt and Clark filed reports calling for large-scale American military and economic assistance and the use of American military advisors in combat. Clark's plan did not contain a specific cost, except to mention a possible $200 million currency stabilization loan. Bullitt's program called for an $800 million loan.[11]

The State Department might have viewed these reports with greater concern had the Far Eastern Bureau been forced to contemplate the arrival of a Dewey administration or another Republican Congress in 1949. Since neither event came to pass, FE at first evinced no concern over the proposals (which had received good press coverage) and proceeded unperturbed with its own wait-and-see policy for mainland China.

These Republican-inspired committee reports, however, proved to be a springboard for Senator Pat McCarran, the incoming chairman of both the Subcommittee on State Department Appropriations and the Joint "Watchdog" Committee. On 28 January 1949, the Nevada Democrat issued a statement calling for a program of massive aid to Nationalist China financed by a $1.5 billion loan. He sent a copy of his program to the secretary of state with a cover letter stating that he assumed "the possibility that this statement might become of interest to the Department."[12]

At first it was not. The McCarran proposal and letter to Acheson ended up in FE, which was prepared to brush the senator off with a reply from a middle level bureaucrat. After some prodding from the Congressional Liaison Office, FE finally generated an Acheson-signed acknowledgement.[13] The department viewed McCarran's proposal with more concern, however, when it took the form of the bill introduced on 25 February. The measure called for a $1.5 billion loan: $300 million earmarked for economic aid, $500 million pledged to a currency stabilization program, and the balance for a military aid program supervised by American advisors. The Chinese would repay the loan with strategic material and by pledging the customs revenue at its major ports to service the debt. American advisors, in a gross violation of Chinese sovereignty, would be allowed to help rewrite Chinese tax laws and collect revenue.[14]

The Senate referred the McCarran bill to the Foreign Relations Committee. Chairman Tom Connally of Texas referred it to the secretary of state who passed it down to FE. The Far Eastern Bureau now had to take McCarran's proposal more seriously: if not as a practical program for saving China, then as a menace to its own policies. The bureau at once began drafting a firm response using Acheson's reply to the committee as its vehicle. The response, the product of a two-week drafting process, was a lengthy Acheson letter to Connally dated 14 March explaining why the McCarran bill was a bad idea. After noting that the Chinese government would not have the capacity to hold even South China in the face of a determined Communist drive, Acheson pointed out that an extension of $1.5 billion in aid over and above the two billion already given the Chinese since the end of the war would "embark this government on an undertaking, the eventual cost of which would be unpredictable but of great magnitude, and the outcome of which would almost surely be catastrophic."[15] FE drafted the letter as a definitive response not only to McCarran, but also to anyone else who urged a massive China aid program.

Before the Acheson letter reached him, Connally received another letter from fifty Republican and Democratic senators urging that hearings on McCarran's bill be held "as soon as possible" so that it might "be laid before the Senate with such amendments as the Committee may deem appropriate."[16] Taken at face value, the letter was a grave threat to the administration's China policy; fifty senators constituted a simple majority sufficient to pass a bill in that body. Once passed, it would be referred to a House that was itself unreliable on China policy.

There was, however, no cause for alarm. The day after he received the China bloc letter, Connally discussed it and the bill before a Foreign Relations Committee meeting in executive session with Acheson, convened to discuss another subject. Republican Senator Alexander Wiley of Wisconsin, one of two committee members who signed the McCarran letter, expressed embarrassment over having done so. "I do not endorse the bill," he explained. "I will say that I was solicited by Pat McCarran to sign it. The idea was that we would get the Secretary before us, and try to get an understanding of the Eastern situation." He was sure that "9 out of 10 who signed that petition did it with the same idea. They came to my office when I was busy, and I felt it was something we should at least get some information on."

A few days later, Wiley told the committee that he had "no apologies for signing this petition." He had never seen the bill and he signed the petition "because I was requested by Mr. Sourwine of the Judiciary Committee [staff], who is Senator McCarran's advisor."[17] It was soon known that other signators of the letter shared Wiley's point of view.[18]

Even the China bloc regarded the McCarran bill as a flawed instrument. Its sponsor was well known as a cynical politician and the leader of the Senate's "Silver Bloc," a position traditionally held by a senator from a state where silver was a major "crop." That more than one-third of McCarran's $1.5 billion would be devoted to supporting China's silver currency was not a point missed in Congress, the executive branch, or in the press.[19]

Aid for Formosa

While the McCarran bill was not the menace to the administration that it might have appeared to be in early March, it nonetheless threatened to sidetrack its own plans for the China aid program. On 15 March the administration requested an extension of the 1948 China Aid Act and submitted draft legislation that would achieve its purpose. The draft bill asked for two things: (1) that the time remaining to spend China aid money, an amount estimated at $58 million, be extended from 3 April to 30 December 1949; and (2) that the president be allowed to give aid to groups in China other than the "Government of China." The second provision soon became known within the State Department as the "flexibility clause," since it would allow the United States to give the money quietly to a breakaway Formosan regime that did not claim to be under the "Government of China."[20] China's government, it appeared at the time, might soon be a Communist-dominated coalition, the product of negotiations then under way between Acting President Li Tsung-jen and the Communists. The administration's objective was to obtain the permissive language without calling attention to its purpose.

House Hearings

In a series of executive session hearings scattered throughout March, the House Foreign Affairs Committee found two aspects of the proposed administration-backed legislation controversial. One objection was symbolic and not important to the State Department: the Republican members objected to the use of a bill separate from the legislation amending the European Recovery Program also then before the committee. When the original "China Aid Act" passed in the Republican 80th Congress, it was made part of the omnibus foreign aid bill that also funded the Marshall Plan. The Republicans considered this appropriate since they viewed Chinese and European aid as parts of a larger whole. The Democrats, who now controlled Congress, preferred that the two measures be separate, and their view ultimately prevailed in House committee.[21]

The second controversial issue was the flexibility clause, which amended the existing language by making "China" rather than the "Government of China" the aid beneficiary. Committee members Walter Judd and John Vorys suggested that the revised language was intended to allow the president to aid the Communists, a charge that administration witnesses denied with vague arguments. The continued aid, as one ECA witness put it, would support "certain areas which did not go along" with a possible future Communist regime.[22] Walton Butterworth, the State Department's spokesman at a closed 15 March hearing, gave a similar explanation. He came closest to mentioning Formosa in response to a question by Representative Helen Gahagan Douglas. The California Democrat observed that without more flexibility the law would "not permit them to give aid to islands which may be neither under the Communist nor the Nationalist government, . . . As far as I'm concerned," she continued, "I am not sure it is wise to give aid to those islands, but I think that is what Mr. Butterworth is getting at in this amendment. Am I right?" The FE chief answered, "Yes" without elaborating. Vorys pursued the point briefly but the discussion quickly turned to other topics.[23]

That afternoon Butterworth sent Acheson a memorandum mentioning the difficulties the ECA was having with the flexibility clause "which would permit this government, for example, to assist Formosa should the Nationalist government reach agreement with the Chinese Communists. I did not mention Formosa in my testimony," he noted with satisfaction.[24]

Ten days later the ECA returned to the committee with reinforcements, including Roger Lapham, fresh from his post in Shanghai. Lapham presented a detailed breakdown of the "intended" use of the $58 million: $8 million for the Joint Commission on Rural Reconstruction, $17 million "to make some capital improvement expenditures on Formosa," $31 million for food rationing in Shanghai, Shantung, and Swatow, and enough to liquidate in an orderly manner support programs in cotton, petroleum products, and fertilizer.[25] His statement was candid, but only insofar as he was stating his and ECA's intended use of the $58 million remaining in the China aid fund. He personally had little enthusiasm for the administration's unannounced accent on Formosa.

Lapham's testimony proved to be diverting. The only committee member curious about Formosa was Montana's Democrat Mike Mansfield, an administration supporter, who observed that "something is being built up there." Would, he asked, the Formosan aid program "form a basis by means of which a democratic China could again come into being?" Lapham replied that "Formosa is a limited area" and spoke briefly of the troubled island's recent history. Mansfield persisted and got Lapham to admit that were it "under non-Communist control, we could proceed to spend our economic aid in Formosa."[26]

Butterworth again represented the State Department. The previous day, 24 March, he had explained in a telegram to the American ambassador in Nanking that the department was supporting the bill "in large measure" for Formosa.[27] During the hearing, however, he chose to remain silent on this subject and apparently spoke only on other aspects of the bill and Asian policy in general.[28]

In the absence of a clear statement about the main purpose of the flexibility clause, China's friends on the House committee persisted in charging that the flexibility would allow the administration to spend the $58 million in Communist areas of China but lost their battle to have the clause deleted. The committee reported the bill on 28 March as a separate piece of legislation that allowed the remaining funds to be spent in China through 15 February 1950, and "to be furnished in such manner and on such terms and conditions as [the president] may determine."[29]

It was, however, a short-lived victory for the State Department. The China bloc continued the fight on the floor, and, in a compromise the China bloc forced on the House leadership to insure smooth passage of the higher priority European Recovery Program extension bill, the Democrats agreed to delete the flexibility clause from the reported China aid bill. When informed of this setback before the action was taken, Secretary Acheson reluctantly agreed to the deletion in hopes that the flexibility feature would be reinstated in the Senate bill and emerge intact from a House-Senate conference committee. Thus, without administration opposition, the House passed its bill amending the China Aid Act on 4 April with the support of Walter Judd and without the flexibility clause; aid was still slated specifically for the "Government of China."[30]

Muted Candor and Compromise

The Senate also agreed to an extension of the China Aid Act on 4 April when it adopted an amendment to the European aid extension bill that extended the China aid program. This amendment carried with it both the imprimatur of the China bloc and the flexibility desired by the administration. The Senate, better informed about the main purpose of the act, arrived at its bill by a slightly different route than did the House.

Unlike the House committee, the Senate Foreign Relations Committee invited both Secretary Acheson and the recently returned General David Barr to testify in executive session on granting further aid to China. Acheson, accompanied by Butterworth, opened his testimony on 18 March by quietly damning the McCarran bill. In a general review of China policy, he only once mentioned the department's request for extension of China aid then before the committee as a separate bill. The bill's purpose, he said, "was to permit the authorization to go to the end of the fiscal year, and the purpose of that was to continue these agricultural and other experiments and programs in South China, and also to have some leeway to prevent these coastal cities from suddenly disintegrating by not having any food." Butterworth later reiterated this point, but neither he nor Acheson apparently made any reference to the use of the $58 million in Formosa.[31]

The subject of Formosa finally came up when the Senate committee discussed the details of the bill during the following week. In an executive hearing on 24 March, Roger Lapham made the same presentation to the Senate committee that he had in the House. He said that an engineering survey group had recently recommended capital improvement projects totalling $67 million but that he and Hoffman decided the projects were not worth the risk. At the mention of these projects, Senator Arthur Vandenberg asked Butterworth if China and Formosa could be considered on the same basis. After a brief statement about the history of the island's ownership, Butterworth asked to go off-the-record. In his unrecorded discussion, he evidently explained the administration's hopes for Formosa and the need for flexibility to get around the requirement of giving the aid with the consent of the "Government of China." His statement called into question the whole rationale of the program that Acheson and Lapham had presented the committee—a program to be continued on the mainland to the bitter end and to allow the United States to place the blame for its termination on the Communists. At the conclusion of Butterworth's off-the-record statement, Democratic Senator J. William Fulbright of Arkansas, obviously confused by what he heard, asked, "If this bill is passed will this money be spent on this relief [on the mainland] or will it be conserved for use on Formosa?" Butterworth remained silent and allowed his ECA colleague to say that only approximately $17 to $20 million was earmarked for the island. While the committee members now understood the aid bill's major purpose, the Formosa cat never got out of the bag again, at least not in any official forum of Congress.[32]

The Foreign Relations Committee was skeptical about granting further aid to China under any circumstances and was unhappy with the complicated language in the administration's draft bill. At the committee's request, the ECA quickly produced simplified language that extended the aid program through 31 December 1949, with assistance to China to be furnished at the president's discretion. However, before Connally could submit it as an amendment to the European Recovery Program extension bill then before the Senate, Senator William Knowland obtained a copy of the ECA's simplified draft amendment and offered it on the floor with a gratuitous extra sentence stating that "the authority granted the President under this subsection shall terminate if in his opinion the government of the Republic of China becomes Communist-dominated." The Foreign Relations Committee discussed the purloined amendment briefly in a general business meeting on 29 March. Vandenberg urged Connally to relieve Knowland of "embarrassment" by offering the same amendment on the floor without the last sentence and with the committee's endorsement. Connally apparently intended to do this but, some time in the following three days, he discussed the amendment with Knowland and reached a compromise. It extended China aid through 15 February 1950 (the date in the House bill), and gave the president flexibility to spend the money in areas of China not under Communist domination.[33] Knowland submitted the compromise and won Senate approval for it on 4 April.[34] After conference with the House, the Senate version of the China aid amendment emerged attached to the European aid extension bill, and Congress promptly voted it into law.

The State Department had obtained the flexible legislation it wanted and also learned a lesson about the strength of the China bloc. In the cable he sent to Ambassador Stuart in Nanking on 24 March, Butterworth informed him that "sentiment in Congress this year, even more than last year, highlights the differences between the apparent strength of the advocacy of the large scale aid program and the actual support thereof."[35] Butterworth's confidence in the weakness of the China bloc may have been slightly tempered by the House's initial deletion of the flexibility clause, but probably not by much. The State Department, after all, had obtained the substance of what it wanted without revealing to many people the sensitive purposes on Formosa for which it assumed much of the $58 million would be used. Since it had no intention of spending the money in Communist areas, the Knowland amendment served the purpose of giving the China bloc only a hollow victory and the appearance of legislative clout. The administration's substantive victory was not well understood at the time—it was not intended that it should be—and it has been misunderstood by subsequent historians who dismiss it as a concession to a China bloc thwarted over the administration's rejection of the McCarran bill.[36]

The victory in Congress encouraged Dean Acheson to think that the department's China policy was secure. In a conversation with British Foreign Minister Ernest Bevin in the afternoon of 2 April, the secretary outlined his confident view of developments in China and on Capitol Hill. He said that the administration

> had given a great deal of thought to China. The Nationalists seem to be washed up and the Communists able to go where they wished. The Chinese are tired and disillusioned. Help to the Nationalists can have a contrary effect, since the Chinese might take the view it is only prolonging a war which must end. We had abandoned the idea of supporting the regime and were only extending to June 2 [*sic*] a further 58 million dollars under the China Aid Act. We thought the Moscow-trained Communists will be diluted, and that Chinese inertia and the corruption of the civil service will overcome them. After all the Chinese Communists must deal with the West to a certain extent, since Russia has no resources to offer. It had been difficult in this country publicly to withdraw support from the Nationalists, but the extreme supporters of Chiang Kai-shek in Congress were gaining a better appreciation of realities. The U.S. henceforth will pursue a more realistic policy respecting China.[37]

Acheson would soon learn that his confidence was premature.

4

Prospects for Chinese Titoism

While the State Department sought to thwart the congressional effort to make China policy a political issue, it continued throughout the spring and early summer to grapple in confusion with its three contradictory policies. None offered much hope for success. Formosa would not reform; the Nationalists on the mainland would neither collapse nor effectively fight the Communists; and the Communists would not publicly distance themselves from Moscow. Some Communist leaders did give private indications that the new regime might follow a neutral course in international affairs and, in effect, embrace a form of Titoism. Yet, they were to find the Truman administration unable, for both political and conceptual reasons, to respond to their overtures in an effective or positive manner.

The first three weeks of April brought little but abusive Communist propaganda about the West and pessimistic assessment from American diplomats abroad.[1] The Party radio broadcast a new denunciation of the North Atlantic Treaty on 3 April, warning that China would fight beside her "ally, the Soviet Union" in the event of war.[2] The American embassy in Moscow, which carefully followed events in China, saw little evidence of Titoist deviation. It cautioned, however, that the "permanent identity of Mao's and Kremlin's policies" was a "great question." The Nanking embassy's reports to Washington at this time reflected a similarly gloomy assessment.[3]

Consul General John Cabot in Shanghai, a city that would not fall to the Communists until 25 May, offered one of the few dissenting interpretations of Communist behavior in the early spring. They might be saying such foul things about the West, he suggested to the State Department, because the "Kremlin demanded it." In any case, "the rule that nothing a Communist says is to be believed cuts both ways . . . we should not uncritically overlook the other possibility that some Chinese Communist leaders have mouthed this propaganda with tongue in cheek to conceal their intention to be eventually masters in their own house."[4]

The Trade Weapon

The State Department had, in fact, designed its policy toward the Communists to test Cabot's hypothesis by using two forms of leverage it thought it had over the new regime: trade and diplomatic recognition. The trade policy held that China's need to maintain commercial ties with the West would force the new regime to reach an understanding with Western powers. Signs from North China in February and March appeared to support this assumption. Although the Communists' method of trade was disconcerting—they largely ignored Western merchants, banks, and consulates by trading for barter in Hong Kong—they did continue to trade.[5] After the People's Army captured the Western-oriented coastal cities of Central and South China, many observers assumed that China's need for foreign intercourse would increase significantly. Some American diplomats, however, challenged the trade policy, which foresaw only a long-term payoff, by pressing for the immediate use of economic pressure to force the Communists to recognize them and to tone down their propaganda.[6]

The State Department rejected the dissident view after some hesitation. The trade policy had not really been tested: it was designed to allow China to redevelop its commercial ties with Japan and the West and thereby strain the Sino-Soviet relationship; the commercial ties between China and the rest of the world, however, were still redeveloping. The policy was, furthermore, beginning to show prospects for paying off. On 30 April, Clubb sent Washington a cable reporting a contact he had made that morning with Chang Tsung-ping, an agent of a Party official, Yao I-lin, who would be China's future minister for trade and industry. According to Chang, Yao wished to establish trade contacts between North China and American-occupied Japan on a barter basis—Chinese coal and salt for machine parts, newsprint, and medicine.

Clubb also reported an interesting political note. During the discussion he had pointed out to Chang the bad effect of anti-American propaganda on possible future trade relations. Chang replied, according to Clubb, that Mao Tse-tung's political thinking was "moderate." The political situation was "complicated by thinking in lower Communist levels," which was "along more strictly Communist lines." He predicted, how-ever, that there would shortly be a political "veering to right."[7]

The Recognition Weapon

The State Department also kept its recognition policy under constant review. The policy's fundamental assumption held that the Communists wanted recognition enough to pay a price for it. Like trade, however, recognition also remained a largely theoretical question. Before the price could be quoted to the new regime, the department was confronted with the more immediate question of whether to keep in place or withdraw American diplomats already in China.

At first, there was uncertainty about what to do. In January, the depart-ment obtained President Truman's approval to keep Stuart in Nanking whenever the Communists took the city and to allow Lewis Clark to follow the Nationalist government to Canton. Butterworth supported this plan hoping that Stuart, because of his long acquaintance with many Communist leaders, could "contribute to the important objective of keeping open official and private channels of information, communica-tion, and influence in areas under Communist control."[8]

Ambassador Stuart also wanted to remain after the Communist take-over. On 10 March, he wrote Acheson requesting authorization to make a direct approach to the Communists after Nanking's fall. In "friendly discussions" he hoped to dispel Communist misapprehension; he would explain that while the American government recognized China's right to adopt a government of its choosing, the new regime would bring on China a "subtle and sinister form of despotism" if it imposed "the Rus-sian model." If they persisted in their purpose and met continued resist-ance, then Stuart wanted to say that the United States would probably "use every available resource . . . to restore real liberty to the Chinese people." American public opinion "would only be satisfied by convincing evidence of the basic freedoms of a constructive, friendly foreign policy."[9]

Stuart's letter arrived in Washington on 28 March, where its recommendations were generally in keeping with the line the State Department wanted to take. Although the question of his ultimate residence was still uncertain, the department sent him instructions agreeing to his suggested approach but requesting that he not threaten the "use of every available resource" to restore Chinese liberalism.[10] On 11 April, he was ordered to remain in Nanking, but the department qualified the instructions eleven days later by ordering him to Washington for consultation after the Communists had firmly established themselves. Butterworth drafted the revised instructions, as Deputy Under Secretary of State Dean Rusk explained to the secretary, "to help meet the domestic political situation in this country." Rusk agreed with Butterworth's concern and even doubted the wisdom of keeping Stuart in Canton at all.[11]

The ambassador made his first direct contact with the Communists abruptly on the morning of 25 April, the day after they seized Nanking. At 6:45 A.M., twelve Communist soldiers woke him as they entered his bedroom. The startled ambassador, who spoke fluent Chinese, jumped out of bed and asked what they were doing. "Just looking around, having fun, no harm, did I understand," Stuart recorded them saying. Two of his assistants rushed to his rescue and one was slightly wounded in the arm in a scuffle. The soldiers quickly evacuated the premises but the incident frayed nerves in Washington and was quickly followed by American protests to Communist authorities in Nanking and Peiping. Reports of the "outrage" in the American press did little to enhance the image of the Chinese Communists; "REDS . . . MOLEST U.S. ENVOY" read the morning headlines of the *New York Times.*[12]

Stuart soon got over the affront and began waiting for an opportunity to conduct personal diplomacy with the Communists. In the interim, he sent Washington his views on recognition in a 3 May cable urging that the United States adopt the tactic of "reserve, waiting for the new regime to make first approach." The "North Atlantic community," he suggested, should do the same. "Governments represented therein, and particularly those of Commonwealth, should not be permitted to jump the gun for temporary apparent commercial political gains which CCP may well attempt to dangle."[13]

The State Department agreed. As early as January it discussed "the recognition weapon" with the British along the lines Stuart suggested and, after receiving Stuart's cable, sent it to the field as a circular telegram along with instructions to solicit the reaction of friendly governments to a common front approach.[14] The replies, with the significant exception of a noncommittal British response, were cautious but positive.[15] With this modest encouragement, the Far Eastern Bureau formulated an ambitious recognition policy designed to protect Western interests in China and to turn the new regime away from the Soviet Union. In a telegram to Stuart on 13 May the department outlined three criteria it expected the new Chinese government to meet in order to obtain recognition:

1. de facto control of territory and administrative machinery of State, including maintenance of public order;

2. ability and willingness of government to discharge its international obligations;

3. general acquiescence by the people to the government in power.[16]

All three requirements were elastic, but the one most difficult for the Communists to meet would be the second. It required the new regime, in effect, to protect foreign property rights in China and thus forego fulfilling one of its revolutionary goals. From the American perspective, this cost may not have appeared high; China's new rulers were simply being asked to meet the normal standards required of any new government that wished to join the family of Western nations. Few American diplomats in either China or Washington were certain how the Chinese might respond to these criteria. The question was still academic in the spring since the Communists had yet to constitute a new government. It was not too early, however, to present the criteria for their leaders to contemplate. An opportunity to do so soon presented itself in Nanking.

Talks With Huang Hua

In early May a young Communist official named Huang Hua arrived in Nanking to assume command of the local "Office of Alien Affairs." That Communist leaders in Peiping selected Huang for this post was probably more than coincidence. He had been a student of Ambassador Stuart at Yenching University in the 1930s, had worked with Americans in the Dixie Mission, and was a classmate of Stuart's personal secretary and Chinese alter ego, Philip Fugh. The first contact with Huang came when

Philip Fugh called on his former classmate on 10 May. In a one-hour conversation, Huang asked Fugh about their "old college professor," but carefully said he did not recognize Stuart as an ambassador because he was accredited to the Kuomintang regime. Huang added, according to Stuart's report to the department, "that it would be up to USA, when time came, to make first move in establishment relations with People's Democratic Government." Huang also denounced American foreign policy and explained why the Chinese Communist Party considered the United States to be an enemy. He nevertheless agreed with Fugh that it would be well to call on their "old college President."[17]

Stuart's 11 May cable describing the first Fugh-Huang meeting impressed FE. Director Butterworth sent the telegram to Secretary Acheson and advised that it was "the first important report on the larger plans and intentions of the Chinese Communists and to me has the ring of authenticity. It is worth a careful reading and you might want to show it to the President."[18]

The first meeting between Stuart and Huang occurred on 13 May. The "friendly and informal" conversation at Stuart's residence lasted almost two hours. Stuart spoke of a "universal popular" desire for peace, of his conviction that much of the current tension was because of "misunderstandings, fears, [and] suspicions which could be cleared away by mutual frankness," and of particular American fears of the Chinese Communist Party's Marxist-Leninist doctrine. Huang complained about American aid to the Kuomintang and other "mistakes" in American policy but also "expressed much interest in recognition of Communist China by USA on terms of equality and mutual benefit" and he "expounded upon needs of China for commercial and other relations with foreign countries."

Stuart replied that the only "proper basis" for recognition would be China's observance of "accepted international practice with respect to treaties." It was customary for countries to recognize whatever government clearly had the people's support and was willing to perform its international obligations. He also hinted that most other countries would tend to follow the United States' lead on the recognition question.[19]

The first Huang-Stuart conversation did not produce any significant change in the Communists' public behavior toward Americans. Given the reports that "extremists" were "at present in ascendancy," this was not surprising. The Party's radio continued to broadcast statements accusing the United States of "aggression" and the local officials in Mukden continued to hold Consul General Angus Ward and his staff incommunicado.

Only Consul General Cabot in Shanghai maintained a consistent faith in the prospects for Titoism. "Vital question is whether break [with Moscow] will come in 2 years or 200. Our own policies may profoundly influence this," he cabled on 31 May.[20] The next day, the department received evidence suggesting that the break could come in even less than two years.

The Chou Demarché

On 31 May, Colonel David D. Barrett, an American assistant military attaché stationed in Peiping, met a correspondent of the United Press, Michael Keon. Keon, an Australian who had covered the civil war from both sides of the lines and had stayed on in Peiping after the city's capture, reported that he had spoken to Chou En-lai, who had asked him to relay a message to the United States government. Chou, Keon reported, had asked that the message be transmitted to the "highest American authorities on a top-secret level." He had warned that he would disavow the communication if it were to become public. To Keon, Chou had seemed "nervous and worried."

Barrett passed the message to Consul General Clubb who cabled a summary of Chou's message. There were serious disagreements within the Communist leadership on questions of industrial-commercial policies and international relations. There was not a split within the Party, but there was a liberal faction, headed by Chou, and a radical wing, headed by Liu Shao-chi. The first had advocated working with liberal elements in the Kuomintang (the Nationalist Party), arguing that without such a coalition "reconstruction might be so delayed that [the Communist] Party would lose support of people." After a big debate, the advocates of the "realistic coalition" failed. The Party, therefore, "must make most of bad job and obtain aid from outside."

Clubb then detailed Chou's attitude toward the United States.

> USSR cannot give aid which, therefore, must come from USA or possibly Britain. Chou favors getting help from USA . . . [believes] there is no real bar to relations between USA and other governments, [of] different political type. Unequivocally opposed to American aid to Kmt [Kuomintang] but feels this was given from mistaken motives altruism rather than American viciousness. Feels USA has genuine interest in Chinese people which could become basis friendly relations between two countries.

Chou, speaking for liberal group, felt China should speedily establish de facto working relations with foreign governments.

This question will be prime issue in struggle between two wings. Radicals wish alliance with USSR . . . while liberals regard Soviet international policy as "crazy." Chou feels USSR is risking war which it is unable [to] fight successfully . . . Chou desires these relations [with U.S.] because he feels China desperately needs that outside aid which USSR unable [to] give. Feels China on brink complete economic and physical collapse by "physical" meaning breakdown physical well-being of people.

Chou feels USA should aid China because: (1) China still not Communist and if Mao's policies are correctly implemented may not be so for long time; (2) democratic China would serve in international sphere as mediator between Western Powers and USSR; (3) China in chaos under any regime would be menace to peace [in] Asia and world. Chou emphasized he spoke solely for certain people personally and not as member party, that he was not in position make formal and informal commitments or proposals. He hoped American authorities remembering this would believe there were genuine liberals in party who are concerned with everything connected with welfare Chinese people and "peace in our time" rather than doctrinaire theories. As spokesman for liberal wing he could say that when time came for Communist participation in international affairs his group would work within party for sensible solution impasse between USSR and west and would do its best make USSR discard policies leading to war.[21]

Following transmission of the "Chou demarché," as it became known in limited circles in Washington and China, Clubb sent his own analysis offering two possible explanations. One was that Chou's group was seriously at odds with a radical wing "and may be straining toward Titoism." A second might be that the message was "one of high Communist policy" based on an assumption that a China aided by the United States would be better strengthened to assist the Soviet Union against the United States "in hypothetical future contingencies." Giving the department his own recommendation, Clubb restated his belief in the possibility of Titoism, but only after unpleasant economic and political events forced the Communists in that direction. It was too soon for the Party's rank and file to accept the development of Titoism since they had not "really appreciated [the] gravity [of] their economic and political predicament. . . . Until such time as there may be actual break with USSR [,] Communists must be assumed remaining in Soviet political camp." In response to the demarché—which requested no reply—Clubb recommended that the department give a noncommittal reply, stressing that the "full fruits of intercourse" could not be obtained without respect, mutual understanding, and cooperation.[22]

The State Department received differing assessments of the overture from other posts in China. Clark thought the message "smacks much more of tactics than strategy."[23] Stuart advised the department that it was an "extremely important indication as to possible American policy. . . . We must be careful not to overplay our chance while also taking full advantage of it." It indicated a struggle for power between the two men next in line after Mao and indicated that Liu was gaining ascendancy. "Chou's message is call for help. He would never have taken this risk otherwise."[24]

Several days after receiving the Chou demarché, the State Department received further encouragement in its hope for the growth of Titoism. According to a source available to Consul General John Cabot, Shanghai's Communist Mayor Chen Yi, an important party figure, told a meeting of local party workers that Soviet and satellite countries might not be able to offer assistance to China and thus "aid from US and British would be accepted if presented on basis of equality with no strings detrimental to Chinese sovereignty attached." Cabot's source "stressed this 'aid' meant loan, technical assistance of Marshall Plan nature, as distinguished from ordinary trade, which naturally also desired by Communists."[25] Commenting on Chen's speech two weeks later, Colonel Barrett in Peiping, who personally knew the Communist leadership from eighteen years service in China, suggested that it be read with "more than usual importance" given Chen's longstanding hostility to the United States and Britain.[26]

Huang Hua expressed a similar interest in American aid in a conversation with Philip Fugh on 8 June. According to Stuart's report, Huang told Fugh that the Party "could not follow [an] isolationist policy in China's reconstruction and that CCP would require particularly American help. . . . USSR could not give China required assistance since Soviet expectations had not yet been realized." Stuart added that Huang was believed to be a "Chou En-lai man."[27]

The news from other areas of China was less encouraging. Stalinists seemed to be tightening their control over Manchuria. In Harbin, the Chinese editor of a weekly magazine and one of China's best known writers came under political attack for suggesting in print that imperialism could come under "various colors," an implication that the Soviets might also be imperialists. "He does not understand that the Soviet Union, which is now engaged in liberating and helping the weak peoples, cannot possibly become an oppressor of other peoples," charged an article in the Communist *New China Daily.*[28]

Reports from Mukden, when they came, varied with the weeks. On 18 May, the department gave up its effort to communicate with the consulate general and officially closed the post. Ward and his staff, however, could not be informed of the news or extricated.[29] On 18 June, Communist radio charged that the American mission was a "spy organ," a charge the embassy in Nanking and the State Department quickly denied. The Communists, however, made no immediate effort to follow up on the charge and on 23 June the Nanking embassy received a telegram from Ward— his first to get through in six months—stating that he had successfully contacted local authorities and was discussing his departure.[30]

Mixed with continuing signs of anti-American hostility, the Chou demarché and other indications of latent Chinese Communist liberalism impressed the State Department, but not enough to alter the dominant belief that Chinese Titoism was a long-term proposition. The skepticism was evident, for example, in a State Department memorandum Acting Secretary of State James Webb gave President Truman on 10 June. Drafted for Butterworth by CA chief Philip Sprouse, the document contained the department's latest views on Chinese intentions toward the United States. In effect, it explained away recent signs of Communist moderation in commercial policy, noticed in Shanghai, as a result of a desire to "reduce the shock of the turnover on the economy" in the recently captured city. Sprouse explained recent moderation in press attacks on the United States as a result of a similar tone in recent Soviet press attacks; Communist China was just following suit. There was "no sign that the change is permanent, much less genuine."[31]

Skepticism about Chinese Titoism in the short term was probably only one of several factors shaping the State Department's deliberations on the Chou demarché. Another was American domestic politics. The policy of encouraging the eventual emergence of a Communist China free of Soviet domination still lacked appeal to either American military leaders or members of Congress who wanted the United States to do something more active to stop communism in Asia. The State Department also had to take account of the political reality that President Truman, much less Congress, would not allow the proffering of any American aid to the Mao

Tse-tung regime unless it drastically and publicly changed its attitude toward the United States. And—a matter of no small significance—any major change in policy would require approval of Secretary of State Dean Acheson, who was in Paris at a lengthy Foreign Minister's conference and was unaware of the telegram from Peiping.

On 14 June, Clubb received instructions from Washington. To guard against a verbal distortion of the message, he was asked to transmit the reply "on plain paper without signature or designation source." The message expressed America's "traditional friendship" for China and respect for her "territorial and administrative integrity." The United States wanted to maintain "friendly relations with China" in the social, economic, and political spheres "insofar as these relations based upon principle [*sic*] mutual respect and understanding." The propaganda barrage against the United States and the treatment of some Americans in China was counterproductive. While the United States welcomed expressions of friendly sentiments, Chou "must realize that they cannot be expected [to] bear fruit until they have been translated into deeds capable of convincing American people that Sino-US relations can be placed upon solid basis [of] mutual respect and understanding to benefit both nations."[32]

When Webb showed this reply to the president on 16 June, Truman approved and directed the department, according to Webb, "to be most careful not to indicate any softening toward the Communists but to insist on judging their intentions by their actions."[33]

While Clubb considered how to transmit the reply to Chou, the Communists gave Washington another public pronouncement to consider. This time the source was Party Chairman Mao Tse-tung. In a speech on 15 June (not reported to Washington until 20 June) before the Preparatory Committee on the New Political Consultative Conference, Mao was typically disparaging of China's enemies. He called for vigilance against the "imperialists and their running dogs, the Chinese reactionaries" who would not take their defeat lying down. After underlining this point in several paragraphs, he changed his tone slightly. "Everybody is our friend except the imperialists, the feudalists and bureaucratic capitalists, the Kuomintang reactionaries and their accomplices." China, he continued, was "willing to discuss with any foreign government the establishment of equality, mutual benefit and mutual respect for territorial integrity and sovereignty" if that government was willing to stop conspiring against it.[34]

The speech received mixed reviews from American officials in China.

Colonel Barrett saw it as an indication of Communist drift toward closer relations with the Soviets and a reason to abandon the effort to reply to Chou.[35] The Nanking embassy saw it as a restatement of previous sentiment, but interpreted Mao's expressed interest in establishing diplomatic relations with foreign powers as significant.[36] Clubb viewed the speech in an even more optimistic light. If "Chou approach represented will of important group, it should be exploited as perhaps open door to other important developments, and if Chou's approach was isolated or has been cancelled by group decision, [the] loss could be sustained. . . . Mao Tse-tung's speech makes present reply perhaps even more pertinent."[37]

The question of answering the Chou demarché, however, became moot; Clubb's efforts to pass the message along on 22 and 23 June were rebuffed. Chou was apparently not interested in receiving a reply to a message he had given the United States twenty-three days before, if indeed he had ever wanted a reply.[38] Colonel Barrett learned later in the summer that a spy in Chou's office had quickly leaked the original demarché to the Liu faction.[39]

"Almost an Invitation" to Peiping

In Nanking, Philip Fugh continued to call on Huang Hua, and, as a result of a suggestion Fugh made, these conversations took on a new importance. As Stuart explained to the department at the end of June, Fugh, earlier in the month

> asked casually, and not under instructions from me, if it would be possible for me to travel to Peiping to visit my old University as has been my habit in previous years on my birthday and Commencement. At the time Huang made no comment. However, 2 weeks later, June 18 to be precise, in discussing my return to Washington for consultation, Huang himself raised question with Fugh of whether time permitted my making trip to Peiping. Fugh made no commitment, commenting only that he himself had made this suggestion 2 weeks earlier. Neither Fugh nor I followed up this suggestion but apparently Huang did. Present message (almost an invitation) is reply.[40]

Stuart also began hearing from other sources of Communist interest in his traveling to Peiping, although he did not report them to the department. He received a telegram on 23 June from Chen Ming-shu, a member of the Kuomintang Revolutionary Committee cooperating with the Communists, cryptically indicating that the prospects for dealing with

Chou and Mao were good.[41] Several days later, Stuart received a "strangely phrased letter" from C. W. Luh, the chancellor of Yenching University, that assumed Stuart was to visit Peiping. Philip Fugh took the letter to Huang Hua. Huang told him, according to Stuart's diary, that "Mao and Chou would heartily welcome me." The Communist official then apparently checked again with Peiping and received further confirmation that Stuart would be welcomed. On the afternoon of 28 June Huang called on Stuart to relay a message he had received from Mao and Chou "assuring me," the ambassador explained to Washington, "that they would welcome me to Peiping if I wished to visit Yenching University." Stuart responded by noting that although he would like to go back to his old university, he thought travel to Peiping might be too strenuous by train. Huang said the trip could be made in less than three days and "that all facilities of railway would be put at my disposal."[42]

Stuart took almost forty-eight hours to report Huang's message to the State Department. Summarizing the background to the invitation, he mentioned only the conversation that he and Fugh had held with Huang. He regarded the invitation as a "veiled invitation from Mao and Chou to talk with them [while] ostensibly visiting Yenching. To accept would undoubtedly be gratifying to them." The opportunity would also give him a chance to describe American policy and its anxieties regarding Communism and world revolution. It would allow him to express the United States' "desires for China's future" and enable him to "carry to Washington most authoritative information regarding CCP intentions." The trip would strengthen "more liberal anti-Soviet elements" within the Party and "would be imaginative, adventurous indication of US open-minded attitude toward changing political trends in China and would probably have beneficial effect on future Sino-American relations."

"On the negative side," the ambassador gave a list of reasons against making the trip. They included possible embarrassment to the department because of domestic criticism, misinterpretation of the trip by the diplomatic corps, the appearance of a "peace making gesture," and possible enhancement to Mao's and the Chinese Communists' prestige, both nationally and internationally. Nonetheless, he "received clear impression that Mao, Chou, and Huang are very much hoping I make this trip, whatever their motives."[43]

Stuart's cable arrived at the State Department at 5:38 A.M. on 30 June. Sometime during the day it reached John Davies who found the "invitation" to be "extremely significant—even more so than the demarché made by Chou. (It may even be an explanation of why Chou turned down the approach from Clubb through an intermediary.)" Davies considered the objections raised in the telegram valid, but saw the trip as an occasion for Stuart to give the Communists a stern lecture. Butterworth also saw value in the trip, but thought the decision to go to Peiping rested on an assessment of domestic reaction. His formula for defusing it was to have Stuart fly first to Mukden to pick up Consul General Ward and his wife and stop off in Peiping on his way back. The problem Davies saw in this approach was that the Communists might find unacceptable the requirement that they free Ward. Davies's formula was to announce that "Stuart had not gone to Peiping to play footsy-footsy with the Communists but had gone there, as would be a fact, to read them the riot act."[44]

Davies conveyed his own and Butterworth's ideas to the secretary of state on 1 July in a memorandum first sent to George Kennan. Kennan passed it on to Deputy Under Secretary of State Dean Rusk, who showed it to the secretary. Acheson probably showed the Stuart telegram to the president during a private meeting at the White House in the early afternoon of 30 June. It is not known what, if anything, Acheson recommended as a response. It is likely, however, that both men read a story on the front page of the *New York Times* the following morning that helped shape their thoughts. Carrying a 30 June Shanghai dateline, it reported a speech given that day by Mao Tse-tung. The headline read: "MAO EXPECTS NO HELP FROM WEST: HAILS SOVIET AS CHINA'S TRUE ALLY."[45]

The speech was a body blow to anyone in China or the West desiring an early Sino-Soviet split. In his lengthy address commemorating the 28th anniversary of the founding of the Communist Party in China, Mao said it was childish to think that China needed aid from Britain or the United States. "In the world there is only one great imperialistic Power, i.e., the United States, left intact," he said. "She wants to enslave the world. She supplies Chiang Kai-shek with arms for the slaughter of millions of Chinese people." China, he said, would now "lean to the side of the Soviet Union." Stuart described the speech several days later as "very revealing," a speech with "clean, sharp lines." The United States owed Mao "a vote of thanks for his article . . . as an unprecedentedly clear exposition of just where top leadership of CCP stands." There was no need to read between the lines. He had dotted his "i's" and crossed his "t's." There was no better evidence available, he concluded, to support the "long view" of Chinese Titoism.[46]

At 5:05 P.M. on 1 July, President Truman telephoned Dean Acheson to inform him that he was opposed to Stuart going to Peiping. After that, the secretary approved a "Night Action" cable sent to Nanking an hour later:

> Following highest level consideration URTEL [your telegram] 1410, you are instructed under no, repeat no, circumstances to make visit Peiping. Principal reasons for negative decision are those contained URTEL.[47]

5

Renewed China Bloc Offensive

The State Department considered the mixture of Chinese Communist public propaganda and private overtures in an increasingly heated domestic political environment. The specter of internal Communist subversion, raised in well-publicized spy trials in New York and Washington, made even the appearance of a slight tilt toward Mao Tse-tung politically hazardous. Congressional investigation of influence peddling by presidential aide Harry Vaughn and other hints of corruption in high places further weakened the administration's hand. While not directly related to foreign policy, the corruption question diminished the president's authority generally.

The administration was also vulnerable because it needed Congress to obtain high-priority foreign policy legislation related to Europe, especially the bill funding the Military Assistance Program. Passage of such legislation would require the support of at least a portion of the China bloc in both Houses. The friends of China were aware of this leverage and they attacked administration policy with increased intensity through the spring and early summer. The State Department felt the pressure but was slow to react, preferring to respond with modest efforts at public education and perseverance, while its high command concentrated on European policy.

Spring and Summer Noise

Dean Acheson had discussed the public- and congressional-relations aspects of China policy routinely since he took office. Within a month of telling Marshall Carter that it was unwise to "pull the rug out from under Chiang " by discussing his difficulties in public, the secretary changed his mind. In a morning staff meeting on 8 March, he asked his senior advisors what the department should say in public. The group, an aide later recorded, concluded "that we should have a careful study made of the question of U.S. public opinion on China versus the feeling that a full airing of the question would have an adverse effect on the Chiang regime." Acheson doubted "whether we had to continue to shore up the Nationalist government to the extent that we had in the past." Discussion in the meeting "was all concerned with the public relations problems in this country."[1]

Acheson's response was his 14 March letter to Connally condemning the McCarran bill. Although drafted as a vehicle to rebut publicly the whole idea of further aid to the Nationalists, Connally failed to release it until a month later, when it only served as another target for the China bloc. Senator Bridges used the letter to accuse the secretary of sabotaging the "valiant attempt of the Chinese Nationalists to keep at least a part of China free" and called for a full investigation of State Department policy. Oregon Senator Wayne Morse, then a Republican, charged that the letter was a "sad and late admission of a fumbling and bumbling China policy." William Knowland vowed that the Senate would not allow the State Department to "sweep the situation under the carpet and forget about it." The only senator to defend the administration in this round was J. William Fulbright of Arkansas who was himself ambivalent about China aid.[2]

The next verbal salvo came from Senator McCarran, at home in Nevada, who issued a statement echoing three themes popular with the China bloc. Claiming that Bridges was "entirely right" in his attack on Acheson, McCarran charged that "when our own State Department peddles the Communistic propaganda line, as in the case of the department's assertion that Mao Tze-tung . . . is not a real Communist, it is time something was done about it." He disputed in detail the State Department's claim that the Nationalists had received $2 billion worth of American assistance since the end of the war and was also critical of the disproportionate emphasis the United States placed on aid to Europe. "If

Communism takes China completely," he warned, "Communism will take all Asia."[3]

The State Department had heard these charges for years and viewed them largely as the inspiration of the Chinese Nationalist embassy in Washington and its paid and unpaid American supporters. The Far Eastern Bureau's intelligence on the China lobby's activities was occasionally good. FE's director Butterworth learned, for example, that some important members of the China lobby had met on 16 April at the home of a member of the Chinese Nationalist Military Procurement Mission. This gathering, which included Chinese embassy officials, a Republican senator, and several lobbyists, was a meeting of Frederick McKee's "Chinese Emergency Committee." The committee, Butterworth explained to the under secretary in a brief memorandum, "is not supposed to include Chinese officials or citizens but is apparently in step with the Chinese Embassy." He reported the group's discussion of two major points. One was the $2 billion aid figure Acheson used in his letter to Connally; the figure led McKee to telephone McCarran in Nevada in order to give him the figures that the senator later used in his press attack on the State Department. The second point of discussion was that "FE and its constituent divisions were the repository of 'pink cells'." "As of possible connection," Butterworth concluded, Senator Knowland had asked the State Department "for biographical data on each officer in FE and its constituent divisions."[4]

The week after the "China Emergency Committee" met, Knowland revealed his request's purpose by introducing a resolution in the Senate calling for creation of a joint congressional committee to investigate American Asian policy.[5] In an accompanying floor speech he said that the Red Army was at that very moment crossing the Yangtze River; but that there was still hope. "If the situation in China looked very difficult right now it is not a bit worse than it was in Europe after Dunkirk." While Congress ignored Knowland's resolution, this and other recent China bloc activity called into question the validity of Acheson's assurance to Bevin that the extreme supporters of China were "gaining a better appreciation of realities." The Acheson letter to Connally—conceived of as an effort at public and congressional education—apparently convinced only the converted.

If the China bloc could not be enlightened as a group, then perhaps its members could be persuaded in pairs. Responding to an invitation from President Truman, Senators Bridges and Kenneth Wherry, the Republican floor leader from Nebraska, met with Truman and Acheson to discuss China policy on 28 April. Acheson spent most of the meeting answering questions on events in China. "Aside from such questions as whether I felt certain that advice I was getting in the State Department on the subject did not come from Communist sympathizers," Acheson recalled after the meeting, "the questions were directed to matters of fact . . . and to possibilities of policy which were discussed."[6] The senators seemed to be impressed but not convinced. Wherry commented later to newsmen that the briefing "was helpful in understanding things that I didn't understand before."[7] If Bridges' views mellowed, he did not indicate it to the press.

Acheson was still not satisfied with the public-relations aspects of China policy. On 3 May, he brought the subject up again, telling his advisors that he believed "very careful consideration should be given again to the question of what we should say on China." Butterworth, he thought, "was too rigid in regard to this question." Dean Rusk assured the group "that consideration was being given to this and that he would look into it further and would give Mr. Acheson a more complete report at a later date."[8] In two days the China bloc presented the secretary with more reason to view this question with concern.

"Pink Cells" in FE

On 5 May Acheson appeared before a subcommittee of the Senate Appropriations Committee, ostensibly to give testimony on an appropriation bill funding the State Department's operation in the next fiscal year. Since Pat McCarran was chairman and both Senators Bridges and Wherry were subcommittee members, the meeting was a potential forum for a China bloc attack. Two weeks before the event, a State Department official learned that such an attack would indeed take place; both McCarran and Bridges were, an informant told him, "laying for the Secretary's appearance." The target would be the aid figure mentioned in Acheson's letter to Connally.[9] The intelligence proved partly correct; there would be an attack, but it would be along different lines.

McCarran emerged as Acheson's chief antagonist. During the course of the public meeting, the senator referred to a *New York Daily Mirror* editorial discussing a "prevalent rumor" of a pro-Russian element in the State Department that was "actually working on a formula which will clean up all our current dealings with Soviet Russia, including a recognition of their conquest of China, by the round table de facto recognition of Mao Tse-tung."

What, McCarran asked, did Acheson have to say to that? "Senator," the secretary replied, "I might have a great deal to say but, exercising the greatest possible restraint, I will say that any report of any such rumors as is indicated in that editorial is completely, totally, and absolutely false." After McCarran assured the secretary that he was the administration's and Acheson's friend, the Nevada Democrat read another brief excerpt from the editorial. The secretary again forcefully disputed the rumor. "Do you think your Far Eastern desk is free from Soviet sympathy?" McCarran asked. "Yes, sir; absolutely," replied Acheson.

After a few questions by other senators on other subjects, Senator Bridges returned to the China question. In a maneuver implicitly linked to the McCarran "rumor," Bridges requested the "charts" of the top personnel "who had charge of the Division of Far Eastern Affairs and the China desk" since 1939. "I do not want to ask for anything to which we are not entitled but it seems to me that we are entitled to that."[10]

When the subcommittee reconvened the next day, Bridges refined his request. "I should like very much," he told Acheson, "to get the history of John Stewart Service, who at one time was arrested by the Federal Bureau of Investigation for giving information out to an enemy and who subsequently was reinstated by the Department. I understand he now holds a responsible position in the State Department." The senators also requested the files of John Carter Vincent, John P. Davies, and Butterworth.[11]

The State Department eventually furnished a list of its top personnel from its Far Eastern Office since 1945 but evidently refused to furnish personnel dossiers.[12] Although neither senator apparently pursued his request for personnel folders, Acheson's experience before the Senate Appropriations Subcommittee reinforced his concern about public relations. In his morning staff meeting on 6 May he again "raised the question of China and whether we should not possibly say something on it" in public and asked Dean Rusk "to make a special effort to get a first class evaluation on this matter." Later that day Acheson informed his cabinet colleagues that the department was studying the advisability of putting out a "White Paper" on the China situation.[13]

Korean Aid: A Surrogate China Issue

On 23 May, Dean Acheson left Washington to attend a month-long Foreign Minister's Conference in Paris. In his absence, the China bloc kept up its pressure by focusing on legislative vehicles that could be killed or amended to embarrass the State Department. One target ripe for attack was the economic aid bill for South Korea.

Split by hasty wartime agreements that created Russian and American occupation zones divided at the 38th parallel, Korea had become a tragic pawn in the Cold War. The United States had attempted to erect the southern half as a non-Communist, democratic, self-sufficient and secure Asian state. By January 1949, the U.S. Army had succeeded only on the first point and began pulling its troops back to Japan, turning its problem over to the State Department, the ECA, and the South Koreans.

On 7 June, President Truman sent Congress an ECA drafted bill requesting $160 million to continue the Korean economic-assistance program. Since the current authorization expired on 30 June 1949, the bill was arriving late in the legislative cycle. The delay in submitting the legislation occurred because ECA had assumed responsibility for the aid program from the Army only in January and because it took time to devise a legislative program that could be cleared with both the State Department and Bureau of the Budget (the latter trimmed ECA's original request by $22 million).[14]

The administration supported its request in Congress with an unusually large number of witnesses who presented a confused case for Korean aid. At various times they argued that the survival of a non-Communist government in South Korea was both important and unimportant to the United States. According to the State Department, the country's value lay in its symbolism. If the United States failed to do "all in [its] power, consistent with [its] world-wide obligations" to save this "outpost of freedom . . . countless millions of peoples in Asia will begin to doubt the practical superiority of democratic principles."[15] Summarizing Webb's rationale in a later hearing, one committee member suggested that South Korea might be a "clinic demonstration of our principles of civilization."[16]

The State Department position on Korea might have been stronger had it not been compared to that of the Army. The Army, by both words and deeds, called into question the whole purpose of the American effort in Korea. By 8 June, the date of the first hearing, the last American troops were completing their phased withdrawal from the peninsula. This move accorded with a general drive in the Truman administration to save money by keeping troop levels low, with a United Nations resolution calling for withdrawal of foreign troops from Korea, and with the Army's view that its troops would be safer elsewhere. American troops in Korea, one general explained, required significant reinforcements to be a useful deterrent, yet any such reinforcement would be incompatible with United States responsibilities elsewhere. "If we left troops in Korea we would be giving false hopes to those people because I do not think anyone would suggest we enter into combat with northern Korean forces, and we would not, as I understand our policy at the moment."[17] One committee member asked him if there was any strategic disadvantage in not having a toehold like South Korea on the continent of Asia? "It would be a very, very minor disadvantage," the general replied.[18]

This was not an overwhelming case for Korean aid to a Congress not yet in the habit of routinely granting assistance to small Asian countries. Several committee members asked why the money should be granted if South Korea were so insignificant. To this question the China bloc added its own twist: Why bother with Korea if the United States was willing to "let" China go Communist? Such aid would be, as one Republican charged, "too little and too late." He refused to support the bill "until the State Department clarified its Asiatic policy."[19]

On 30 June, the House committee reported the Korean aid bill authorizing $150 million in assistance for the next fiscal year. Connecticut Republican John Lodge attached to it a gratuitous amendment requiring the program's termination if the Koreans formed a coalition including one or more Communists. The committee rejected another Lodge amendment shortening the authorized aid period to 28 February 1950, and reducing the amount to $100 million. Five Republicans voted against the bill; four filed a minority report charging that "we labor with the mountain of Asia and succeed only in bringing forth the molehill of aid for South Korea." The minority claimed that it admired and respected the South Koreans, but considered their country a lost cause.[20]

The Senate Foreign Relations Committee reported the bill in a seven to one vote on 12 July 1949, after only four days of executive session hearings. The committee rejected a Fulbright amendment cutting the $150 million by two-thirds. When a committee staff member brought the John Lodge amendment to the committee's attention immediately after the vote, Senator Henry Cabot Lodge, John's older brother, brushed it aside. "Who proposed that?" he asked.[21]

The Korean aid bill quickly stalled in the House Rules Committee, which failed to grant a rule sending it to the floor. According to the State Department's analysis, the legislation's troubles stemmed from four sources: the failure of seven members of the Rules Committee, normally favorable to the administration, to support the bill; a general mood of economy in the House that made its passage on the floor unlikely; the need to deal with the higher-priority European Military Assistance Program (MAP) bill; and the opposition of the China bloc. In late August, Speaker of the House Sam Rayburn assured a State Department congressional liaison officer, A. B. Moreland, that the bill could not pass at that time. Moreland also learned that Ohio Republican John Vorys, the chief China bloc opponent of the legislation, had been willing to support Korean aid if China aid were included in the MAP legislation. Since a China amendment to the MAP bill had recently failed in the House, Vorys "served notice that he will go all out against Korea."[22]

The administration ultimately obtained interim funding for its Korean aid program when Congress passed two separate unauthorized appropriations of $30 million in the fall; Congress did not vote on the authorization bill until the next session.[23] The administration learned from the experience that the China bloc, when able to work with allies interested in economy, was still able to disrupt legislation not directly related to China.

MAP and the Chennault Plan

While the China bloc tampered with the Korean aid legislation, it also sharpened its knife for surgery on the European MAP bill, legislation Acheson thought vital to American security. Although Congress would not actually see the draft legislation until late July, the friends of China suspected that it would contain nothing for their cause.*

William Knowland took the lead in the effort to amend the MAP bill by making known his plans in April. Reviewing the 1948 China Aid "Act's" legislative history in a brief Senate floor speech, Knowland accurately observed that the aid provision was added to that year's Foreign Assistance Act "primarily at the insistence of Congress" and that Con-

*For detailed discussion of the MAP bill, see Chapter 8.

gress could claim sole responsibility for the addition of the $125-million military-aid fund. More aid was now needed. "With their backs to the wall the Government of non-Communist China will need additional aid if it is to preserve a part of the country free from Communist domination."[24] In a speech three weeks later, Knowland served notice that he would, "on behalf of myself and a number of other Senators on both sides of the aisle . . . be prepared to offer an amendment to the [arms] implementation legislation when it comes before the Senate to provide aid to the non-Communist forces in China."[25]

At least one member of the House China bloc was making a similar public threat and others could be assumed to be preparing amendments as well.[26]

The China bloc's threat to amend MAP was credible. With members of both Houses and parties objecting to the cost of the arms program, MAP's passage was not certain. If China's friends held the balance of power, it was possible that the administration might reluctantly back a China aid amendment in order to salvage its higher priority European arms bill. Success, however, was not guaranteed. The combination of forces compelling the administration to accept a China aid program in the 80th Congress was not duplicated in the 81st. Democrats were back in control; Republican ranks were smaller; and the State Department was prepared to oppose vigorously any further arms program for the Nationalists. In late July the issue was still in doubt. If congressional economizers were strong, the administration would need the China bloc's votes to save the European arms package. If the economizers were weak, the China bloc would fail.

To make a convincing case to Congress and the public, the China bloc needed to do more than criticize the Truman administration's past mistakes in China; a plan was required to convince doubters that a part of China could still be salvaged in the face of an apparently invincible Communist army. The friends of China obtained such a plan from retired Major General Claire L. Chennault, the famous commander of the wartime "Flying Tigers" in China and owner of a major portion of the Chinese airline, Civil Air Transport. Chennault was ideally suited to his lobbying role. The subject of a popular biography and a patriotic wartime movie, the general published an autobiography in early 1949 entitled *The Way of a Fighter*. Predictably, it did nothing to subtract from his reputation as a dauntless defender of China's freedom. Chennault's acquaintance with members of Congress and the administration allowed him, along with others, to lobby successfully for China aid in the 8oth Congress. In April 1949 he returned to Washington with a plan to save China and to lobby for more.[27]

Chennault's plan had two stable features and a third that varied, for awhile, from day to day. The first involved support for a collection of semiautonomous, anti-Communist generals who allegedly controlled vast stretches of China's interior. From the province of Kansu in Northwest China he drew a line through Szechwan ("an area irrigated by impassable mountains"), to Yunan and Kwangsi in the south—a "sanitary area of effective resistance" against the Communists if its rulers were effectively helped. The general wanted the United States to send military aid and American advisors to the area who would oversee operations down to the company level. A less advertised second feature of the plan, a requirement that the supplies be shipped via Chinese commercial airlines, made Chennault what the *Washington Post* described as "not a disinterested witness."[28]

The plan's third and less certain feature was its cost. To the Senate Armed Services Committee on 3 May 1949, Chennault estimated the cost at $700 million a year for two years. In a conversation with Treasury Secretary John Snyder on 1 June, he mentioned $500 million a year, an amount he later described as "an optimistic figure." Two days later the general wrote Snyder explaining that "the basic job can be done for less and if necessary a total cost of $150,000,000 a year would be sufficient to hold these areas." By the end of June, in a closed hearing before the House Foreign Affairs Committee, Chennault gave $150 to $200 million as his "total cost." In a long memorandum circulated in Congress and to contacts in the executive branch and the Chinese embassy, he estimated that to arm his "sanitary zone properly, the cost would be $350 million a year." On a "minimum basis," however, $200 million would suffice for both military and economic aid, "provided it was administered properly." There the figure finally stabilized.[29]

The general's personal lobbying effort was prolific. He peddled his plan to government officials, the press, and the China lobby in a series of hearings, private conversations, correspondence, and dinner parties beginning in the early spring and lasting until the passage of the MAP bill; by one estimate he talked to eighty-five senators.[30] Chennault also kept his name and his plan before the general public through numerous newspaper and magazine articles and as a guest on radio talk shows. Probably his most widely read article appeared on 11 July in *Life Magazine,* entitled

"Last Call for China—A Fighting American Says That a Third of Its Good Earth and 150,000,000 People Can Be Saved."[31]

General Chennault's plan was given careful attention in the executive branch as well as Congress. Under Secretary of State Webb learned that a friend of the general had been advising him to work with, rather than against, the State Department; pursuing this unlikely prospect, Webb arranged to meet Chennault on 10 May.[32] During the meeting the general gave only a brief description of his plan to Webb before he, Deputy Under Secretary Dean Rusk, and Chinese Affairs Division Chief Philip Sprouse, whom Webb had called in on the meeting, adjourned to Rusk's office. There, in the presence of a stenographer, Chennault went into greater detail. Rusk promised to give the plan "some close thought" and the general left to lobby elsewhere.[33] Shortly after this meeting the plan began to filter into the department from several sources. In late June, House Majority Leader John McCormick referred his copy of Chennault's memorandum to the State Department Congressional Liaison Office, which referred it to the Far Eastern Bureau. FE returned the document to the Liaison Office a day later with the notation, "We all have these."[34]

True to his word, Dean Rusk forwarded a summary of the Chennault plan to American diplomatic posts in China where the response was not enthusiastic.[35] Minister-Counselor Lewis Clark cabled Washington his blunt assessment from Canton: "Chennault plan should be profitable [for] commercial airlines, but detrimental interest US." He "could not justify prolonging suffering [of] Chinese people which would ensue" and observed that the plan "would also make Communist task easier by providing them with material to rally racial feeling in support of resistance to foreign intervention."[36] Butterworth was already on record as thinking the plan would only further strengthen the Communists since they would inevitably gain possession of any new American supplies.[37] Acheson also rejected the plan; in a 13 May cabinet meeting, when asked about Chennault's plan, he brushed it off with the observation that Chennault was a better soldier than a politician.[38]

Despite its flaws, the Chennault plan to save China proved a useful instrument in the hands of Knowland and his allies. In late June the senator used the general's Armed Services Committee testimony and an article in *Time Magazine* about General Ma Pu-fang, "the Moslem boss of China's northwest," to illustrate what could be done to stop the Communists. The article, which Knowland inserted into the *Record*, highlighted Ma's "highhanded but benevolent" qualities. He had built good roads in his province of Chunghai, sponsored extensive irrigation works, super-vised the planting of millions of trees and disallowed their felling with a "one head for one tree" policy, made education compulsory through the age of sixteen, and required all citizens to kill from five to fifteen flies daily. Ma and his sons were putting up effective resistance against four Communist armies in the vicinity of Sian with notable success. Without aid, Ma claimed that he could hold his province and even take back Sian. With aid, *Time* quoted him as saying, "I could mount an offensive that would take back Peiping."

Citing Chennault's testimony and the *Time* article, Knowland asserted that "very little help" in arms aid would allow "General Ma and the group in that area in China to probably hold out for a number of years." Thus, he continued, if the State Department and the Senate Foreign Relations Committee expected "us" to support their European policy, "they must be prepared to come before the Senate of the United States with an intelligent and sound policy in the Far East."[39]

The Moderates Attack Bipartisanship

China bloc and lobby attacks in the summer of 1949 did not stop with MAP or the Korean aid bill. Nor did they all occur in Washington. On 2 May, both Houses of the Texas State Legislature unanimously ap-proved a resolution calling on the United States to take immediate steps "to prevent Stalin from controlling China" and demanding the State Department dismiss those "men whose record show that they have helped to bring our country into its present peril by following the policy of treating the Soviet Union as a peace-loving democracy and the Chinese Communists as mere agrarian reformers who have no connection with Moscow." The resolution followed a speech William Bullitt made to both state Houses five days earlier blasting the administration's China policy. This flurry of activity in far-off Texas did not go unnoticed in Washing-ton; the *New York Times* reported the story and Knowland inserted the resolution and Bullitt's speech in the record.[40] Chinese embassy lobbyist William Goodwin boasted to his employers that it was the result of his work.[41]

The friends of China in Washington were also making more direct attacks on the State Department. Republican Congressman Robert Hale of Maine made a brief floor statement on 12 May echoing the theme of the Texas Legislature's resolution. "A few men never elected to office," he charged, had "decided to render futile the sacrifice of 200,000 American youths killed and wounded in the Pacific" and had attached themselves "to the cause of people who have proclaimed themselves to destroy us."[42]

Republican Senator William Jenner of Indiana attacked these "little men behind the desks in Washington" (as *Washington Post* columnist Stewart Alsop called them) at much greater length in a lurid floor speech on 18 May. "There are some in our midst," he charged, "who are overjoyed at the prospect of a Communist victory in China. This is what they have been working for for years, right in our own midst." Another group was preparing American public opinion to accept the Chinese Communists as something less than subservient to the Soviet Union. China was, furthermore, subject to "criminal betrayal" at Yalta. The meaning of this betrayal was potentially catastrophic, as Russia "will be able to take ten or twenty-five or fifty million Chinese Communists, train and equip them and ship them to the eastern frontiers of the European countries." "For myself," Jenner concluded, "I believe it is the duty of the members of the United States Senate to carry out an exhaustive investigation of the policies and personnel that have brought the Chinese catastrophe upon us."[43]

Despite their vehemence, China bloc attacks on the State Department in May and June did not obtain significant press coverage. While the State Department disliked them, partisan Republican denunciations of Asian policy were not new or especially disturbing. Yet, one attack, which received support from Republicans not usually identified with the China bloc, did stir up press comment and cause the State Department great concern. The occasion for the attack was President Truman's nomination of W. Walton Butterworth for assistant secretary of state for Far Eastern affairs, a position Congress created when it reorganized the department in the spring. The reorganization changed FE from an office to a bureau and elevated its chief from a director to an assistant secretary, a job that now required Senate confirmation. Butterworth, in effect, had to seek the Senate's permission to be reappointed to his old job.

As a China bloc target, Walt Butterworth had distinct advantages and disadvantages. When Acheson asked him to accept the elevation to assistant secretary, he resisted but ultimately accepted the opportunity to become, as he later explained to his staff, "the first in a long line of expendable Assistant Secretaries of State for Far Eastern Affairs." From the China bloc's viewpoint, Butterworth's greatest asset as a target was his long association with postwar China policy; his greatest defect was that any allegation that he was soft on Communism was laughable.[44] Opposition to his candidacy would have been only pro forma had it not attracted the support of Arthur Vandenberg, the "father" of bipartisan postwar foreign policy.

Senator Henry Cabot Lodge, Jr., a moderate Republican on the Foreign Relations Committee, outlined the problem the State Department faced with Butterworth's nomination in a 14 June committee executive session. "I personally do not share the [Republican] criticism of the China policy," he explained, "but I am realistic enough to know that a great many people are very, very critical of it, and I have had people speak to me who were not in the extreme pro-China group." Vandenberg vividly described the view of one of the "extreme" group: "Senator Bridges is one of those who just exploded when the name came in, and he immediately came over to me and, in language which I will not accurately reproduce, wanted to know if there was any possibility that he would be confirmed."[45]

The committee invited Butterworth to testify in his own defense on 21 June in another closed session. Vandenberg did not relish his opposition to the nomination and told the FE director that his critics were "relatively silent when asked to present any personal reasons why you are either not competent or eligible." The problem was "that our China policy is generally considered to have been a very tragic failure, and you, as the head of the division in the State Department responsible for it, have difficulty in disassociating yourself as a symbol of that failure." After Butterworth left the room, the committee voted to report his nomination; Vandenberg asked to be recorded as voting "present."[46]

The most vigorous discussion of the nomination occurred in a spontaneous floor debate on 24 June. Vandenberg defended his opposition to Butterworth's nomination by saying that it was time to bring in somebody with a "fresh point of view." Senator Robert Taft, who then rarely spoke on Asian policy, added to Vandenberg's statement by quoting from Joseph Alsop's column in the morning paper critical of the mess FE was making of American policy in Indochina. Was this evidence, he asked Maine's Republican Senator Owen Brewster, "that the Far Eastern Division is still operated today with a pro-Communist attitude in the region of Indochina?" Brewster suggested that it might be.[47]

From the administration's point of view, discussion then took a turn for the worse. Senator Vandenberg, whose support in foreign affairs was crucial to the passage of foreign policy legislation, proceeded to wash his hands in public of responsibility for Far Eastern policy. While the executive branch had been scrupulous in its consultation on some matters in foreign affairs, "there was no such liaison in respect to China policy. I wish to reiterate it, because I disassociate myself, as I have publicly done upon previous occasions, from the China policy which we pursued." The only olive branch he offered the administration was an expression of hope "that there will be no consideration of a recognition of a Communist government in China without complete preliminary contact and explanation of the subject with the Senate Foreign Relations Committee."[48]

As a capstone to the day's antiadministration activity, William Knowland secured the last of twenty-one signatures from both Republican and Democratic colleagues for a letter addressed to President Truman requesting that his "Government" make clear that it had no intention of recognizing a Communist regime in China.[49]

The early summer had not gone well in Congress for the Truman administration's Far Eastern policy. Perseverance and low-keyed efforts at public education were not paying off. Not only was the China bloc on the attack, but moderate Republicans were also backing away from association with China policy. European policy was exposed to the attack; there remained before the first session of the 81st Congress legislation ratifying the North Atlantic Treaty, appropriating funds for the Marshall Plan extension, and authorizing and appropriating money for the Military Assistance Program. Like the Korean aid bill, this and other legislation could be disrupted by an overlapping coalition of the China bloc, isolationists, economizers, partisan Republicans, and antiadministration Democrats. With events in China looking gloomy as well, the time had come for the State Department boldly to take the initiative both at home and in the Far East.

6

State Department Counterattack

Dean Acheson left for Paris in May worried about Germany and returned to Washington on 21 June, according to *New York Times* reporter James Reston, "worried slightly about China."[1] With Arthur Vandenberg's speech pronouncing bipartisanship in China policy dead, and with Mao Tse-tung's 30 June speech indicating that the prospects of Chinese Titoism were remote, the secretary soon learned that his worries were more than slight. Both he and his department concluded that the time had come to take control of events and they began to lay plans for a counterattack, both at home and abroad. By September, both efforts had failed.

Mid-Summer Chill

By mid-summer 1949, American influence in Communist China had plummeted to new lows and the State Department seemed incapable of reversing the trend. Consul General Ward and his staff remained incommunicado in Mukden and the Communists rebuffed American efforts to extricate them. The recognition policy was paying no dividends. The Communists had expressed an interest in obtaining Western diplomatic recognition, but not at the price Stuart quoted to Huang Hua in June. It also appeared that several non-Communist governments might eventually recognize the new regime when it was formally established, despite American efforts to maintain a common front.[2] The economic weapon was proving no more effective than diplomacy.[3] Not only were the British not willing to go along with a policy of controlling Communist trade, but the Nationalists began in June to jeopardize all trade with the mainland by instituting a surprisingly effective naval blockade of Communist-held port cities.

The United States took a hypocritical stand on the Nationalist blockade. Because it did not wish to acquiesce in the legally improper "port closure" (the term the Nationalists used) and because it wanted to allow Western trade with the Communists, the State Department deemed it necessary to protest the de facto blockade as illegal. President Truman, however, out of general pique with the Communist Chinese and political caution, ordered that the department do nothing that would make the blockade ineffective. The result was that the State Department formally protested the blockade without doing anything more to stop it and publicly admitted that the protest was pro forma. As a result, the blockade continued. It prohibited the Communists from developing a trade relationship with the West; and the Communists blamed their predicament on the United States.[4]

Symptoms of the decline of Chinese Communist-American relations began to appear in Shanghai, the city hardest hit by the blockade, even before Mao's 30 June speech. According to Consul General John Cabot, the Communists "found themselves involved in unexpected and unwanted snarls with foreigners."[5] The snarls worsened significantly after 1 July. One source of trouble was discharged laborers who had worked for defunct American businesses and official establishments and who demanded exorbitant severance pay. In the case of *The Evening Post,* and American-owned newspaper in Shanghai, the ex-employees besieged the apartment of the former editor, Randal Gould, scuffling with him and his wife. As a result of the altercation, a local court forced Gould to apologize to his former workers and to pay their final wages. The tribunal also compelled him to buy advertising space in another local paper to offer further apologies.

At the end of the month, the aggrieved employees returned and confined both Gould and an associate in the defunct paper's building. For several days the workers kept them on a diet of biscuits and water and demanded pay through 15 July. After further problems, Gould was finally able to reach a settlement and to leave China but these and other labor troubles in Shanghai discouraged American businessmen who had hoped to do business in Communist China.[6] While they blamed the blockade for crippling Shanghai's economy and understood the local authorities' sensitivity to urban labor, the Communists' unwillingness to protect their lives and property disturbed them. By August, many were ready to go home.[7]

While the State Department viewed the labor problems in Shanghai with concern, the mistreatment of its own personnel alarmed it even more. On 6 July, a delegation of former Chinese employees of the United States Navy besieged the Shanghai consulate general. The next day, Shanghai police arrested Vice Consul William Olive for making a wrong turn in his car and driving into a local parade. The police shuttled him between several station houses in handcuffs, "brutally" beat him, and threw him in a cell. After interrogation, the authorities forced him to sign one confession of guilt for his traffic violation, another for assaulting the police, and later, another statement denouncing the United States. The police finally released Olive on 9 July after forcing him to sign yet another statement vouching that he had been well treated and compelled him to make three waist-deep bows in front of photographers. The vice consul returned to the consulate emotionally shattered, with "soreness of all muscles and joints, twenty bruises, contusions, abrasions and some evidence of internal bleeding." The next day a local newspaper called the incident a warning to all American imperialists to abandon provocative action or suffer the consequences.

Signs of a hardening Communist attitude also began to appear in other cities in China, although the personnel confrontations were not as harsh. In mid-July, authorities in Shanghai, Hankow, and Peiping ordered United States Information Service offices closed and issued a similar order in Tientsin a week later. On 29 July, the situation in Shanghai turned critical again when the ex-U.S. Navy employees occupied the consulate's ground floor. The crisis ended on 2 August when the State Department and the Navy reached a cash settlement with the ex-employees.[8]

There was little encouraging evidence in July to contradict the evident deterioration of the Western position in China. In a conversation between Huang Hua and Philip Fugh on 2 July, Huang attempted to soften the impact of Mao's speech by likening its spirit and principles to the chairman's 15 June speech, but his effort was not convincing. In reporting the conversation, Stuart suggested that Huang was part of Chou En-lai's "liberal wing" and that Mao's speech disappointed him. Whatever his allegiance, however, Stuart predicted that Huang would soon adopt the dominant party line and become less cooperative with foreigners.[9] Two days later in another cable, Stuart speculated that his former pupil had lost face because of the ambassador's refusal to go to Peiping.[10]

Stuart's prediction about trouble with Huang soon materialized. On 12 July the State Department ordered the ambassador to leave Nanking in six days for the United States via Canton. Stuart objected to having to visit Canton (something Truman, prompted by Wellington Koo, personally requested) but soon found that he was unable even to leave Nanking.[11] The Chinese demanded that the members of the ambassador's party obtain "shop guarantees" insuring that they had left behind no debts. Although Stuart was exempted from the requirement, the State Department ordered him not to allow any of the departing group to offer guarantees. For several days the situation remained at an impasse that was made especially difficult because Huang Hua did not make himself available to discuss the question with embassy representatives. By the end of July the State Department and the Chinese Communists negotiated a settlement allowing the group, including Cabot and Olive from Shanghai, to leave. The embassy agreed to sign a guarantee for its personnel, but under protest.[12] On 2 August, Stuart and his party left Nanking to return directly to the United States. The highest ranking officer left in the embassy was Chargé d'Affaires John Wesley Jones.

Shortly before they left, both Stuart and Fugh held separate conversations with Huang Hua. In a 25 July meeting, Huang again complained to Stuart about American aid to Chiang and continued recognition of the Nationalists. He charged that the United States was behind recent well-publicized meetings between the "retired" generalissimo and the presidents of the Philippines and South Korea being held in Manila to form a "Pacific Pact." "Our personal relations were cordial," Stuart reported, "but I came away with [a] feeling of discomfiture."[13]

Philip Fugh saw Huang on 30 July in what Stuart considered to be a "very revealing discussion." Huang told Fugh that China now looked upon the United States as its enemy. He predicted that oppressed Americans would some day revolt and that Communist parties in countries around the world "knew they would win." Stuart wrote in his diary that Huang "revealed an ignorance of U.S. and a bigotry surprising in one otherwise so intelligent and in many ways friendly."[14]

Perhaps the most ominous symptom of declining Western influence in China appeared in recent reports of Sino-Soviet cooperation. During July, a Soviet mission arrived in Peiping that included economic, political, and military advisors.[15] Later in the month Ambassador Kirk in Moscow relayed to Washington a Soviet press announcement stating that a trade delegation from the "Manchurian People's Democratic Authority" led by Kao Kang, a pro-Soviet member of the Chinese Communist Politbureau, had recently concluded a bilateral trade agreement with Russia that swapped Manchurian food for a variety of Soviet goods. Communist propaganda organs in China quickly trumpeted the news as a great blow to the "imperialist" bloc. The American embassy in Nanking interpreted the agreement as "another link in [a] long chain of evidence indicating Chinese acquiescence in Soviet ambitions [to] sever Manchuria from China proper."[16]

Small Rays of Hope

While the Communists' public attitude toward the United States was manifestly hostile, some spokesmen for the new regime tried to soften the blows in private conversation with Americans. During July, Stuart continued to seek contacts with Communist leaders in Peiping, especially Chou En-lai. At one point, the ambassador, at the prompting of Philip Fugh, contemplated either violating his instructions and going to Peiping without authorization or proposing the trip again to the department. The purpose of the trip, he noted in his diary, would be to see Mao and Chou in order to facilitate his departure to the United States and to "inquire about treatment of [American] nationals: are they wanted? If not, say no —if they are they should be better treated."[17]

In the absence of direct communication with the party's leadership, Stuart used the service of Chen Ming-shu, a leader of the liberal Kuomintang Revolutionary Committee who was cooperating with the Communists and was an old friend of the ambassador. In mid-June, as Chen later recalled, the ambassador "commissioned" him to discuss his views on Sino-American relations with the party's leadership. To assist Chen, Stuart provided him with several documents that the embassy transcribed into Chinese for presentation to Chou and Mao.

When he returned to Nanking from Peiping on 12 July, Chen revealed that his mission of reconciliation was unsuccessful, although he tried to put a good face on it. Along with other statements of Communist principles, Chen gave the ambassador four written comments reportedly by Chou En-lai, shaped, apparently, to respond to questions the embassy drafted in June.

1) The Revolution has been forced upon us. The breaking of the peace originated with the U.S. Because the U.S. wanted dictatorial rule, she supported reactionaries. . . .

2) . . . America's many good points pertain to small matters, Soviet Russia's to large.

3) With respect to the question of Mr. Stuart himself, we must estimate virtue and measure power. Of course, he is a representative of imperialism—people in government carry out the policies of their government. . . .

4) When he [Stuart] says that China depends upon the American economy and that America does not depend on China, he is completely wrong.

While Chou's comments were not the standard Communist diatribe, they were hardly encouraging. Recapitulating the exchange in a 13 July telegram to the department, Stuart sadly "found no hint of any deviation from present political course set, including relations with USA."[18]

Consul General Clubb in Peiping was also in indirect touch with the Communist Party leadership. On 17 July he met, in the company of three other Chinese, with Lo Lung-chi, a Democratic League leader who would later serve the future regime in several high posts. Lo explained Mao Tse-tung's difficult position: "As leader [of the] Communist Party [Mao] must maintain [a] proper position vis-a-vis [the] USSR. Mao, however, as a Chinese leader may talk one way and act another, [and] would act in accordance the practical requirements of the situation." Speculation about Mao being a potential Tito was counterproductive. It was also a mistake for the United States to withdraw ECA support from China. If unconditional aid had continued "there would have been no further Communist interference." The strong anti-American attitude had resulted from Chiang Kai-shek's trip to the Philippines; the Communists felt the United States could have prevented the trip. On the question of recognition, Lo said the Americans would have to come forward; the Communists would not sue for it. Contrary to what he termed "unofficial statements" in April, Mao was not committed to join the Soviet Union in the event of war with the United States.

In reporting the conversation to Washington, Clubb guessed that Mao probably had foreknowledge of the meeting and that the Communists now had some regret that they refused to accept the department's reply to the Chou demarché. Clubb assumed that his conversation with Lo Lung-chi resulted from a Communist desire "in this indirect manner [to] reopen door again, [or] at least keep it ajar." He recommended that the department make "no response whatsoever."[19]

John Cabot, in his last weeks at his besieged post, was not able to send the State Department reports of private conversations with Communist officials speaking for the leadership, but he did offer strong criticism of the prevailing US-China policy. The decision not to allow Stuart to go to Peiping was "disastrous." The hypocritical policy toward the Nationalist blockade would cause resentment, make the United States appear weak, and frustrate the American trade policy. Cabot advised the department to send a plane or ship to Shanghai to evacuate all Americans willing to leave. This would reduce the potential for future "petty incidents" and allow for a freer hand in future American policy.[20] As he later explained, "The fewer Americans and American interests on which Communists can exert pressure, the better position we shall be in to sit back and wait for Chinese Communists to come to us."[21]

Before he finally left Shanghai, Cabot's mood was once again characteristically upbeat. In a long cable to the department he suggested that the Chinese Communists still did not "see eye to eye" with the Kremlin. "If Chinese Communists can make independent decisions their eventual cooling off towards Soviets seems probable." After detailing reasons why the Chinese would eventually follow a Titoist course, Cabot offered a warning. "If Communist moderation and tentative pro-Western moves are met by rebuffs, further pressures, trade limitations, and vitriolic publicity . . ., then Communists are likely to reason that modus vivendi with West is impossible, and advocates of that course have likely to keep silent or be driven from power." He advised the United States to "get out of China now" and sit on the side lines with dignity and allow natural forces to produce Chinese Titoism.[22]

In sum, few convincing signs reached Washington suggesting that the Communists would soon reverse their Russian orientation; most hard evidence pointed the other way. The American intelligence community strongly suspected that notions of a schism within the Chinese Communist Party were fraudulent ideas peddled by its Stalinist leaders in an effort to obtain Western aid and trade.[23] The State Department found it increasingly difficult to assert the Titoist hypothesis. Some Communists and Chinese liberals may have had regrets about the tilt in Mao's policy, but they were obviously powerless to reverse the dominant trend.

The State Department was thus left with the alternatives of pursuing a passive, long-term policy of encouraging Chinese Titoism or doing something positive to strengthen anti-Communist forces in China, or, as a third option, continuing to compromise between the two extremes. With Dean Acheson's concern about China policy growing, with the Republicans observing an open season on existing policy in Congress, and with the Communists clearly spurning the West, the State Department began to take a hard look at the second option.

Public Relations Offensive

Arthur Vandenberg's 24 June pronouncement that bipartisanship on Asian policy was dead—actually an obituary for something long deceased —should not have come as a surprise to the State Department. It was, nonetheless, a jolt. Ernest Gross, the secretary's congressional liaison officer, summarized the problem in a 28 June memorandum to Dean Rusk. There was no doubt, he wrote, "that time is becoming more and more of the essence on the whole China problem and I hope the Department will be able to seize and hold an initiative it has never possessed on the public and Congressional relations aspect of the matter."[24]

Perhaps as a direct response to Gross's concern, Acheson sent a letter to Senate Foreign Relations Committee Chairman Tom Connally two days later taking note of the recent Senate floor discussion about the prospect that the administration might recognize a Communist regime in China. Before any such move were taken, the secretary assured him that "the Foreign Relations Committee will be consulted concerning the facts involved and the course of action being considered."[25] The letter proved to be the opening shot in a two-pronged offensive the department was plotting to capture public and congressional support for its policies in Asia.

One line of attack was the China White Paper, a project the president authorized in May.[26] James Webb took charge of the project while Acheson was in Paris and delegated the editing of the document to FE. Webb, who was sensitive to the department's public-relations problems, followed the paper's development with concern, apparently unhappy with its progress in the Far Eastern Bureau. Shortly after Acheson returned from Paris, the under secretary and other senior advisors urged publication of the document as soon as possible. In a memorandum to Acheson on 28 June, George Kennan outlined the need for speedy publication. "The magnitude and strength of the Congressional offensive against the Executive's Far Eastern policy requires from us more than defensive expedients. . . . [T]he Executive should aggressively assume the offensive in what is rapidly developing into a major issue between it and the Legislature." The administration's Far Eastern policy had "never been adequately and forcefully presented to the public, largely out of deference to the Generalissimo. . . . The earliest possible publication of this paper should be the first step in our assumption of the offensive."

Along with the historical study's release, Kennan recommended publication of an "anonymous interpretative article on the Chinese situation" and a major presidential speech on Asian policy. The theme of the speech would be that the executive had wisely not taken a path of supporting Chiang that would have played into the Kremlin's hands. "The China policy of the administration," he claimed, "has been a triumph of good sense over a proposed gamble with our deepest national interest and security." Following the public-relations campaign, Kennan proposed that the department design "a series of carefully and closely timed actions" that would "demonstrate a positive and affirmative policy in the Far East. These acts will, of course, speak louder than any words and will serve to take the eye of both the public and Congress off the dreary record of the past."[27]

When Kennan told the substance of his proposal to Acheson, he was preaching to the converted. The secretary was already determined to publish the White Paper and, like Webb, was concerned over its progress in FE. He soon transferred its editorship to his confidant, Ambassador at Large Philip Jessup.

While it prepared the White Paper, the State Department devised a second line of attack, the creation of a group of outside consultants to advise the secretary of state on Far Eastern policy. The idea was not new to the State Department either. Dean Rusk proposed convening such a group in an 4 April 1949 memorandum to Webb, noting that a similar body had been formed the previous year on German policy. The panel Rusk proposed would: (1) be given classified documents and briefings by department officers; (2) have an opportunity to discuss policy with senior policymakers; and (3) have an "opportunity to reach any conclusions or recommendations which might come out of the group discussion."[28]

Dean Acheson at some point picked up Rusk's idea and decided to implement it. During his flight from Paris the secretary asked John Foster Dulles, an American delegate to the Foreign Minister's Conference and the Republican Party's best-known foreign policy expert, if he would head such a group.[29] When Dulles declined, Acheson also gave this job to Philip Jessup and began looking for two respectable Republicans who were in sufficient sympathy with the administration and who might serve as consultants. After some difficulty, he recruited Raymond Fosdick, former president of the Rockefeller Foundation, and Everett Case, president of Colgate University. Soon dubbed the "wise men" within the department, the two consultants were to be inducted at the time of the White Paper's release.

The department's master plan was for the White Paper to convince fair-minded people that past policy was correct and that further support of Chiang Kai-shek would be wasted. Fosdick and Case, under Jessup's supervision, would then take a fresh look at current policy, consult with various interest groups around the country, and point the way toward a new policy. If the two-pronged offensive worked, Congress and the public would be consulted, reconciled to the past, and reassured about the future. Such, at least, were the hopes of senior State Department officials in early July.[30]

"U.S. Policy and Action in Asia"

With the public- and congressional-relations offensive in motion, behind the scenes, the State Department's planners began generating proposals for policy actions in Asia without waiting for the benefit of advice from the "wise men." George Kennan and Dean Rusk in particular were impatient with FE's policies and offered their own alternatives. In a meeting with Webb and senior department officials in early June, Kennan "said that he had gone as far as he could [on several problems relating to Asian policy] without getting into the operating field of FE. He felt that someone other than himself should undertake the needling of FE." According to the meeting's record, Dean Rusk "said that he had already begun this [planning, needling, or both] and would intensify his activities along this line."[31] Shortly after Acheson returned from Paris, Rusk told the secretary that he was "developing a China policy on his own to check against, or for use as an alternative to, the current FE policy."[32]

Kennan was the first to offer a concrete proposal. On 6 July, he signed a Policy Planning Staff memorandum recommending that the United States take over Formosa by unilateral military force. The planning director understood the consequences of forcibly occupying the island. The action would provide the Chinese Stalinists with a "welcome propaganda foil" and would require "a considerable amount of pushing people around." Acting in such a manner would also cause moral problems among the American people and "would offend the sensibilities of many people in the Department on legal and procedural grounds." He nonetheless rejected the alternative of multilateral intervention as surpassing "the framework of experience and capabilities of many people, both here and abroad, who would have to participate in it." Despite advice he received that Formosa should be allowed to fall to the Communists, Kennan suggested that "we should take the plunge" with unilateral action if it had the proper support within the government. Basing his opinion solely on his instincts, he thought that unilateral occupation "carried through with sufficient resolution, speed, ruthlessness and self-assurance, the way Theodore Roosevelt might have done it, . . . would be not only successful but would have an electrifying effect in this country and throughout the Far East." Kennan ultimately withdrew his memorandum but may have conveyed its substance to the secretary verbally.[33]

On 8 July, Kennan forwarded another paper on Asian policy to several senior department officials, this a draft memorandum John Davies wrote entitled "Suggested Course of Action in East and Southeast Asia." While it was not a final staff recommendation, Kennan noted that it was the "sort of program we feel might . . . create a new and hopeful atmosphere in our East and South Asian policy." The Davies plan was intentionally provocative. It recommended a series of closely timed actions to be conducted with a "real sense of theatre," which, taken over a four-month period, would capture the waning confidence of the American public and diminish the nervous apprehension in East and Southeast Asia. One step was to "discuss frankly with and seek the approval of key congressional leaders for the course of action set forth below, telling them that in our opinion no lesser program is likely to be effective in containing Communism in East and South Asia." PPS–51, a controversial Planning Staff Southeast Asia policy paper, should, he urged, be implemented.* The White Paper should be released, coupled with a presidential speech outlining in "broad, affirmative, confident tones the future course of our

*For discussion of PPS–51 see Chapter 7.

[Asian] policy." There should also be dramatic acts of consultation with American allies in Asia and Europe; a Far Eastern tour by Ambassador at Large Philip Jessup; the establishment of a regional technical university in Manila; an American- Australian-Philippine security treaty; a Japanese peace conference and treaty; and military, economic, and technical assistance to Indonesia and Thailand.[34]

Dean Rusk soon surpassed the drama of the Davies proposal with his own memorandum in mid-July—the plan the deputy under secretary had promised Acheson after the latter's return from Paris. Entitled "U.S. Policy and Action in Asia," Rusk's recommendations overlapped the Davies program in several places: congressional consultation; "broadening" consideration of the present China problem into consideration of the problems of Asia; consultation with numerous allies; a trip by the ambassador at large to the Far East; and a security pact for the Pacific Ocean area (New Zealand was added to the group Davies mentioned).

In other points, the memorandum suggested consideration of significant departures from existing policy. For China, it urged: expressions of sympathy and understanding for the Nationalists, coupled with evacuation of all American officials and citizens from Communist areas; resignation of Ambassador Stuart; announcement of continued recognition of the Nationalist government; declaration of a non-recognition policy of Communist China; non-recognition of Soviet "special privileges" in Manchuria; and assistance to mainland non-Communist Chinese forces conditioned upon their demonstration of maximum self-help and upon international observation of the uses made of the assistance. Recommendations for other areas of Asia included: recognition of the South Korean government as the de jure government of a united Korea; pressure on France to "give full scope to basic demands" of Indochinese nationalists; a technical assistance program for Indochina; and support for the weak Bao Dai regime in Vietnam.[35]

On Saturday afternoon, 16 July, Acheson read the Rusk memorandum at his home and met with Rusk, Bohlen, Butterworth, Jessup, Gross, and Sprouse. The sketchy record of that meeting reveals only the questions the secretary had about Asian policy: What was the military situation in the free areas of China? What were the chances for the success of the Chennault plan (something he had been skeptical about only a month before)? What was the economic condition in Communist areas? How dependent was China on outside trade? Could the United States make it more difficult for the Communists to sustain themselves? Could the

United States penetrate the area to its advantage? What could be done in regard to Communist penetration of Southeast Asia? He wanted Jessup and his consultants to study these questions "with a view to reaching conclusions."[36]

The weekend discussion and the Rusk memorandum impressed Acheson. On Monday, he told the attendants of his morning meeting that he wanted a more positive policy in the Far East and that he planned to discuss the memorandum "U.S. Policy and Action in Asia" with the president that day.[37] When the secretary saw Truman in the early afternoon, he reviewed Rusk's proposals and placed particular stress on bipartisan consultation. "The president thought that the ideas were good and asked me to go ahead in developing them," Acheson noted later. Truman also agreed to call Tom Connally to signal the opening of the bipartisan offensive.[38].

During the same day, Acheson sent Philip Jessup a memorandum—at the ambassador's suggestion—requesting that he draw up programs for non-Communist areas in Asia and Southeast Asia. Jessup was to assume that it was "a fundamental decision of American policy that the United States does not intend to permit any further communist domination on the continent of Asia or in Southeast Asia."[39] There was nothing especially new in this charter, but it served at least two purposes. It gave Jessup's study group written instructions and thus, in a sense, made formal their assignment. It also probably gave Dean Acheson a sense that he was doing something positive about Asian policy, a feeling that apparently had been eluding him for some time.

The White Paper

On 19 July, the day after his meeting with the president, Acheson called on Senator Connally to advise him that the department would issue the White Paper the following week (it was not actually released until 5 August). He also reminded Connally of Vandenberg's 24 June floor statement criticizing the administration for a lack of consultation on Asian policy. Using this as a cue, Acheson offered to meet frequently with the Foreign Relations Committee to discuss Asian policy and, especially, the recommendations of the Jessup group and the implications of the White Paper. Connally agreed that this was a good method of maintaining bipartisan relations and thought that it was particularly a good idea "to get the Republicans in."[40] Three days later the secretary probably delivered the same message to Senator Vandenberg.[41]

Before the department finally released the White Paper, the document encountered opposition from several quarters. The whole idea of publishing it offended CA chief Philip Sprouse, a courtly gentleman from Tennessee who thought the document was somewhat impolite. On 19 July, he complained to Butterworth that "Aside from the highly questionable desirability of taking the *unprecedented* step of publishing a document of this kind (which will inevitably serve to pull the rug out from under the Chinese Government)," he felt compelled to raise several objections: the department had compiled the document too quickly; it might damage American policy toward Formosa; and it could endanger American officials remaining in China. Sprouse wanted its publication delayed. To serve the purpose of meeting congressional criticism, he suggested that the department furnish the document to Congress in confidence and make it public only when it could do no harm to the Chinese government.[42]

Butterworth gave his opinion about the paper in a 15 July memorandum to Acheson. He predicted that Vandenberg might object to its publication while large areas of the mainland remained out of Communist control and suggested that the department strike a deal with the senator: the department would delay releasing the paper until the Nationalists collapsed if, "in the interest of preserving and possibly extending the area of bipartisan foreign policy, . . . his party in Congress would refrain from *ex parte* attacks on the Government's China policy." He also warned that the document's publication might have an adverse position on "the Formosan situation."[43]

Another round of objections came from the military establishment. Louis Johnson and the Joint Chiefs of Staff worried that some of the documents published in the paper would reveal communication codes. The defense secretary also raised a question, "as a Cabinet member and not merely as the Military Advisor of the President," about the advisability of destroying the only group in China the United States could aid to oppose Communism. Truman and Acheson brushed these doubts aside; the president was an especially strong supporter of the project. Johnson later made it clear to Acheson that the military washed its hands of the whole affair.[44]

The last significant voices of opposition to the White Paper's publication came from the Chinese embassy and Pat McCarran. The embassy made a "personal representation" to the State Department asking it to reconsider. Hinting at a line of criticism the China bloc would take after publication, Senator McCarran publicly predicted that the document would "defend the department's do-nothing policy and seek to cover up its blunders and to excuse or condone, if not conceal, the department's long failure to do any constructive planning toward preventing the further spread of Communism in the Far East."[45]

The State Department released the China White Paper on 5 August. Titled *United States Relations with China with Special Reference to the Period 1944–1949*, it contained three parts: a summary "Letter of Transmittal" from Acheson (drafted by Jessup) to the president, a 400-page narrative history emphasizing the post-Pearl Harbor years, and an equally long documentary appendix. Taken as a whole, the White Paper emphasized Nationalist corruption and mismanagement and characterized American policy as, in Kennan's words, a "triumph of good sense." The "Letter of Transmittal" damned Communist China's leaders as Soviet stooges and threatened to help overthrow them. Jessup put the threat in remarkably blunt language.

> The Communist leaders have foresworn their Chinese heritage and have publicly announced their subservience to a foreign power, Russia. . . . We continue to believe that, however . . . ruthlessly a major portion of this great people may be exploited by a party in the interest of a foreign imperialism, ultimately the profound civilization and the democratic individualism of China will reassert themselves and she will throw off the foreign yoke. *I consider that we should encourage all developments in China which now and in the future work toward this end.*.[46]

The White House and State Department placed high hopes on the White Paper as an educational document that would quiet domestic critics. John Davies, for example, predicted in July that it would "go far toward justifying our policy toward China and quiet most of our critics." He also cautioned that it might "provide some fuel for the more extreme partisan critics of our policy in the Far East."[47] Davies proved to be half right; like Acheson's 14 March letter to Connally, the document only provided fuel for the department's critics.

The day of publication, Judd and Knowland cited the study as justification for their own criticism of China policy.[48] After looking through it, Senator Bridges pronounced it evidence that the "Chinese war was lost in Washington."[49] General Patrick Hurley, the former ambassador to China who had broken with Truman, called it "a smooth alibi for the

pro-Communists in the State Department who have engineered the overthrow of our ally . . . and aided in the Communist conquest of China."[50]
Walter Judd charged that the department had omitted sixteen crucial
documents that would have supported his criticism of China policy.[51]
McCarran, Knowland, Wherry, and Bridges issued a statement denouncing the White Paper as a "1,054-page white wash."[52]

Even moderate critics condemned it. John Foster Dulles described the
document as an attempt "to explain and excuse past failure."[53] Arthur
Vandenberg found only further evidence of "tragic errors" and took its
release as an occasion to call for the appointment of a new assistant
secretary of state for the Far East.[54] Nobody of stature in Congress spoke
out forcefully for the White Paper. The document apparently did nothing
more than convince the converted and fan the flame of the opposition.

Internationally, the White Paper did no noticeable good or harm to the
Chinese Nationalists; they were too far gone on the mainland and too
firmly in control on Formosa to be affected by its publication. In China,
the Communists interpreted it as an admission of imperialism. In a 15
August commentary, Party Chairman Mao Tse-tung reviewed the document's numerous "confessions" of guilt and highlighted Acheson's statement in the transmittal letter that American imperialism in China would
continue. By referring to the secretary's statement about "encouraging
all developments in China" that would "throw off the foreign yoke," the
chairman made his point without difficulty. The logic of the imperialists,
Mao concluded, was to "Make trouble, fail, make trouble again, fail again
. . . till their doom."[55]

To the Brink of Reintervention

While senior officials in the State Department worried about grand
strategy and domestic politics, conduct of day-to-day policy in FE began
to reflect the new hard-line attitude of Acheson and his advisors; the
policies the NSC adopted in March were sufficiently ambiguous to allow
such a shift in emphasis. Many of the moves were a compromise between
existing FE policy, which attempted to follow a middle course between
a policy of encouraging Titoism and the more hard-line policies Dean
Rusk proposed in his 16 July memorandum. In mid-August the department closed several diplomatic posts in China, including the consulate
general in Canton, and trimmed personnel in others.[56] This was a compromise between the recommendations of Rusk and Jessup, who wanted

all missions closed, and Butterworth, who objected strongly to "withdrawing American official personnel in China with precipitous and unseemly haste."[57] The administration was unable to evacuate all American citizens from China, as Rusk proposed, but the State Department did sponsor an American flag ship that sailed to Shanghai in September and withdrew all Americans with exit visas wishing to leave.[58]

In other moves, the department announced on 16 August that it planned to continue recognizing the Nationalists but did not go as far as Rusk's "declaration of non-recognition of Communist China."[59] The United States continued to support the Nationalists in the United Nations, although it was not prepared to use its full power to block their replacement with the Communists. The Rusk proposal for a "declaration that the U.S. no longer recognizes [the] right of [the] Soviet Union to special privileges in Manchuria" was not issued. Nor did the department implement most of Rusk's suggestions relating to other aspects of Asian policy; that was an area left to the Jessup group to study. The Truman administration, however, did apparently come close to implementing one key Rusk recommendation relating to the Chinese mainland—his suggestion that the United States grant military assistance to surviving non-Communist forces.

Like many of his recommendations in "U.S. Policy and Action in Asia," Rusk's call for renewed military assistance to China was not original and was only a suggestion for further study. Dean Acheson had rejected the idea in June but began to have second thoughts about it the following month as indicated by his request that Jessup's group study the Chennault plan.[60] By the end of July, the possibility of aiding surviving non-Communist forces also attracted the interest of Livingston Merchant, now the third-ranking officer in FE.

Like Rusk, Merchant was not yet ready to advocate such aid; he only wanted the question examined. "The evidence seems to me to be mounting that the Communists in China believe their own propaganda and really mean what they have been saying right along," he wrote Butterworth on 27 July. He doubted that the regime could qualify for de facto recognition even if the United States wanted to grant it; it was not a regime "which with any shred of dignity we can contemplate recognizing." While there might be a long-term hope in Sino-American relations, the question was what to do now. He recommended that the department make energetic efforts to urge private citizens to leave China, that several consulates be closed, and that remaining missions be reduced in size.

Finally, "and most important," he urged that an "intense reexamination" be undertaken "of the desirability, as a matter of policy, of encouraging fragmentation of China and embarking on the subsidization of individual leaders such as the Ma's in Northwest China, Li and Pai in Kwangsi, and the Gimo on Formosa."[61]

As Merchant wrote his memorandum to Butterworth, the prospects of any defensive line holding out against the Communists in the southwest, northwest, or on Formosa were not bright. On 18 July, after a brief pause, the Communists renewed their march south. In Kwangsi Province, the line of defense commanded by General Pai Chung-hsi, one of the Nationalists' better strategists, began to fall back toward Canton. In the northwest, the Ma generals were also retreating, despite their fierce reputation. In June, General Ma Chi-yuan, son of Ma Pu-fang, and Hu Tsung-nan, a Chiang loyalist, had turned a Communist attack into a rout and recaptured Lanchow in Kansu province. In mid-July, however, they proved incapable of capturing Sian, their former provincial capital.[62] On Formosa, the American consul general reported that the island "appears to be falling apart at the seams politically, economically, militarily and ripening for Communist take-over."[63]

With potential allies such as these, a heavy burden of proof fell on anyone advocating further large-scale American military or economic assistance to the Nationalists. One alternative some department officials considered briefly was direct hostile action against the Communists. In July and August Philip Jessup gave at least passing thought to the possibility of direct retaliation against the Communists, but recoiled at a bellicose idea thrown out by John Davies.[64] Davies, in a memorandum circulated in late August, suggested that the United States might begin a series of punitive air strikes against China. They would be "hit-and-run attritive raids and not attempts to capture and hold positions or impose a certain form of government on the country." The memorandum shocked Philip Sprouse who exclaimed that he "might be old fashioned, but this has to be read to be believed." Davies himself had misgivings and confessed that his "hair stood on end" when he learned that Jessup had seen it.[65]*

---

*A more accurate guide to Davies's thought can probably be found in a series of questions and answers he wrote regarding China policy on 19 August. He favored a policy of pursuing Titoism by "unequivocal neutrality on our part toward the internal affairs of China" and the avoidance of "a policy of deliberately creating chaos in China." Memo, "China Issues" under cover of slip, PLJ to Fosdick, 19 August 1949, 893.00/8–1949, RG 59, NA.

With Davies's proposal falling of its own weight, senior State Department planners divided on the question of aiding non-Communist forces fighting on the mainland. Butterworth had been against further aid in May when he dismissed the Chennault plan, and he had not changed his mind since then.[66] He made his views known to the Jessup group in a long 18 August memorandum laying out several policy options in China. One alternative was a policy that emphasized "unremitting hostility to the Chinese Communists, using the weapons of propaganda, economic policy and trade, and continuing aid to resistance groups in the hope of multiplying the internal problems of the Communist regime." Another was to accept the "probability of the control of China by the Chinese Communists" and to place primary emphasis on "measures calculated ultimately to drive a wedge between the Communist regime and the Soviet Union." Butterworth's advice to Philip Jessup, although not explicitly stated as such, was to recommend a middle course. While waiting for events in China to crystalize, the United States should "endeavor on the one hand to keep before the Chinese Communists the advantages and possibilities of cooperation with the West, while on the other hand give no real assistance to the Chinese Communists which would further the consolidation of their control or substantially lessen their internal problems."[67]

The department's diplomats in China also opposed further American intervention in the civil war. Lewis Clark, the highest ranking American official there after Stuart's departure, advised that the "land in the northwest can be written off as of no other than nuisance value." In the southwest, he saw only "slight possibility" of either Li Tsung-jen or General Pai Chung-hsi establishing themselves as heads of any durable government.[68] One faint note of optimism came from the American consul in Chungking. The Communists, he cabled on 19 August, were fighting a two-front war with increasingly long lines of supply over difficult terrain in the heat of the summer. While the bulk of the Nationalist soldiers were not well trained or willing to fight, "there are large forces being gathered under loyal generals which [are] capable of delaying [the] Communists." He thought that the situation could "string along for several uncertain months before the end becomes apparent."[69] A final Communist victory, however, was inevitable.

Nonetheless, President Truman gave the study of a possible aid program for the surviving mainland forces a dramatic boost. The president had largely remained silent in public about Communist China in the late summer. His only recorded comment, given in a news conference on 11 August, was in response to a question about a possible change in the administration's attitude toward Communist China. "The policy on China," he snapped, "is the same that it has always been. We have never been favorable to the Communists."[70]

By late summer, Truman was privately prepared to reverse existing China policy. On 24 August, he instructed the State Department "to explore in more concrete terms the possibility of aid to [Nationalist Generals] Li and Pai" who were attempting to hold a defensive line against the Communists above Canton.[71] James Webb responded by requesting the military establishment to "reexamine" the Chennault Plan by estimating its feasibility and effectiveness. Webb advised that any comment the Joint Chiefs of Staff made "concerning the military means which they consider would be necessary to achieve this objective, regardless of whether or not dealt with in the Chennault plan, would of course be most helpful."[72]

Truman's interest in Generals Li and Pai was prompted by a 23 August telegram Lewis Clark sent the department from Canton recounting a conversation he held that day with the two generals. Clark reported that they were confident that their three armies "plus the guerrilla outfits on the Anhwei-Honan-Hupei border" could form the "nucleus of victorious advance over communism provided they can obtain aid from US direct and not through any machinery controlled by [Chiang]." Both generals said that "they were anxious [to] welcome another General Stilwell to train and even actually command their troops; they all would give a warm welcome to American advisors."[73]

The two general's request for aid was the main subject discussed in the secretary's 24 August morning meeting. Acheson asked Dean Rusk "to follow this up and the point was made that Mr. Rusk was to keep a very close personal check on the Far Eastern Office in order that we could not be charged with failure to act."[74]

The next morning the secretary reaffirmed his desire to have a contingency fund for Asia in the MAP bill—something that Congress appeared willing to pass—and authorized a cable to the department's representative in Canton requesting more information about General Pai's plans and needs. The two subjects were intimately related; had the department decided to back Pai with military aid, the contingency fund would have soon been available to fund such a program. The inquiry to Canton was not meant to be an implied commitment to supply assistance, but, the department explained, "we may wish to send qualified officers to assess possibilities effective resistance if firm will to resist is demonstrated."[75]

Almost two weeks later, on 6 September, Chargé d'Affaires Robert Strong in Canton reported to Washington the "outline of a plan" Acting President Li's office had provided him four days earlier. The only good feature of the plan, Strong observed, was that it asked nothing of the United States. It called for the creation of ten new armies in six months supported by large-scale guerrilla operations. While the plan was "of no real value," Strong believed that if Pai adopted guerrilla tactics, his forces could hold out for a year and "with adequate supplies effective resistance may well continue much longer."[76] The Nanking embassy, commenting earlier on Pai's prospects for survival, gave him only a year of survival with American aid and advised against assisting him.[77] By the date of Strong's report, the chances of Li and Pai holding on had diminished further; the Communists were at the outskirts of Canton and the two generals, with about two hundred thousand troops, were preparing to fall back to Kwangsi province.[78]

With Generals Li and Pai steadily losing ground, the State Department's interest in supporting the Moslem generals in the northwest began to rise. On 26 August, Ma Pu-Fang suffered a setback when the Communists forced him to withdraw from Lanchow, the city his armies had recaptured in June. Ma, however, had left with his troops intact and American analysts blamed his difficulties on the failure of two other generals to render effective support, not on his or his troops' deficiencies.[79]

In spite of their difficulties, the Ma generals continued to evidence an impressive fighting spirit and control a large number of troops and square miles. "We called on General Ma [Hung-kwei] . . . and found [the] General interested in talking about only one thing—bullets," the consul in Canton reported in mid-August. "General Ma, gesticulating and signing in vigorous demonstration his professed feeling complete frustration, said he could not fight Communists without bullets."[80] After the defeat at Lanchow, a Ma Pu-fang representative in Taipei, Formosa, gave further evidence of the Moslem general's fighting spirit when he requested American military advisors and supplies in the event of a collapse of the mainland's central government.[81]

The administration was impressed but still not ready to throw American support behind Moslem armies that recently had been losing more battles than winning.[82] On 8 September, the department informed the consul general in Taipei that it was following "with interest [the] plans and capabilities [of] regional leaders to oppose COMMIES." While it was discouraged by recent developments, the department instructed that if he were approached again, he should express an interest in Ma's plans and capabilities but make no commitments.[83]

At high levels in the department, senior officials had, by Friday, 9 September, apparently reached a more hopeful assessment of the Ma's potential to survive. Some source in the administration, probably not the State Department, had recently circulated an unsigned "Top Secret" memorandum, arguing that non-Communist resistance on the mainland was not beyond hope of survival. It asserted that the "provincial troops in Northwest China are not yet defeated. With small but immediate aid they are believed capable of holding indefinitely, remote areas in North-west China which could be used later as bases for penetration into Siberia, Mongolia, Manchuria, and North China." The document touted the military prowess of the Ma's and Ou-U-san, the commander in Ninghsia. In positive terms, it also described the survival potential of Pai, Li, and other non-Communist generals in various parts of China. The document brushed aside the recent activities of Lu Han, the warlord of Yunnan, who had threatened to rebel against the Nationalists if he was not granted greater autonomy.[84]

It is not clear who saw this document (which ended up in the department's Office of Chinese Affairs files), but an increasing number of State Department officials apparently shared its encouraging assessment. In a meeting with his advisors on or near 9 September, Acheson may have decided to back the Ma's and possibly Li and Pai with military assistance. The evidence that he reached such a decision is circumstantial.[85] At 2:07 P.M. on 9 September, the department received a cable from Strong in Canton outlining Ma Pu-fang's desperate plight: an advisor to Li Tsung-jen reported that Ma had "less than 20,000 men left and, though still a tough fighter and still loyal [to] government, had decided [the] situation [in the] northwest is hopeless and plans [to] go [to the] Near East as emissary [of the] Chinese Moslems." Without help, the "northwest seems to be finished except for nuisance."[86] If there was a plan hatched within the State Department on the afternoon of 9 September, it probably would have been to rush support to Ma Pu-fang.

A crucial factor in any decision the department may have reached about aiding the Ma's or any other force in China would have been the availability of money to back such a program. At 1:00 P.M. on 9 September, the combined Senate Committees on Foreign Relations and Armed Services, which had been meeting together for over a month to consider the MAP bill, voted to adopt an amendment to the bill authorizing $75 million in unvouchered funds for an area defined as "China and the Far East," and it appeared likely on that Friday afternoon that the Congress would ultimately pass such an amendment.* This money would have allowed the administration to sustain a program of support for the Ma's for several months. The program could have begun immediately by the administration using various contingency funds available to the president and by diverting money from the extended China Aid Act. The $75 million from the MAP bill would have been available as soon as Congress passed the enabling legislation through a device in the bill that allowed the Reconstruction Finance Corporation to lend the administration a portion of the total authorization in advance of the passage of an appropriating act.

If Acheson and his advisors planned to back the Ma's, their scheme died the following Monday morning or shortly thereafter when the department received definite word that the Ma generals had given up the fight. At the end of the week the department received a report from Strong that Ma Pu-fang was "definitely intending [to] make [a] pilgrimage to Mecca in near future" and that he had completely lost his will to fight. In the same cable Strong reported that Ma Hung-kwei was not willing to engage his troops in combat and was either in or on his way to Canton.[87] Within a month the front around Canton collapsed and Nationalist General Lu Han of Yunnan province went over to the Communists.[88] The collapse of the Ma's left a strong distaste among Dean Acheson and his senior advisors for any more schemes of military assistance to forces on the China mainland. The $75 million would have to be spent elsewhere.

The administration had come close to reintervention in the Chinese civil war on the mainland but backed away at the last minute when it discovered that there was no viable force left to support. The State Department, in a burst of enthusiasm and despair, considered this hardline response to be a result of hostile pressure in both China and Congress. When it turned back from the road of reintervention—how far it traveled down the road is not certain—Acheson and his senior advisors

---

*Congress ultimately did pass such an amendment with the language changed from "China and the Far East" to the "general area of China." For the legislative history of this bill, see Chapter 8.

reluctantly returned to their earlier hope about long-term Chinese Titoism and began to devote more attention to Southeast Asia. Although plagued by chronic internal problems that would be exacerbated by the success of the Chinese Communist revolution, the subcontinent, at least, held a slim hope that it might be saved from Communism.

7

Southeast Asia Policy, Spring–Summer 1949

On 3 March 1949, the day the president and the NSC adopted three policy papers on China, the State Department's Policy Planning Staff discussed yet another Asian document: "U.S. Policy Toward Southeast Asia." Designated "PPS–51," the study represented a departure from the department's traditional view of the region, which concentrated on policies toward individual countries. The planning staff's effort to win department-wide approval for its paper—and a carefully considered Southeast Asian policy—would prove to be an impossible task.

Postwar Background

The planning staff examined a region of the world that the fall of the Japanese empire left in shambles. Japan did two things that broke European colonialism in Southeast Asia. First, it quickly defeated the European colonists at the war's outbreak and, in the process, destroyed the myth of the West's invincibility. Japan also stimulated Asian nationalism in some of its conquered colonies by granting the native populations a larger degree of self-rule than they had experienced under European masters; while Asian nationalists quickly soured on their Nipponese liberators, they did not lose their taste for independence. Left in the wake of

Japan's defeat were former colonies unwilling to accept the reimposition of European rule.[1]

Some metropolitan powers coped with postwar Asian nationalism more gracefully than others. The United States, fulfilling a prewar promise, granted the Philippines political independence on 4 July 1946. American economic, political, and military interests, however, continued in the islands after independence and, through 1948, the United States poured in over a billion dollars of economic and military assistance to keep the country's conservative government oriented toward the West. By 1949, the Philippines were politically stable, by Asian standards, but suffered from inept rule and a small Communist insurgency.[2]

Britain, after initial hesitation, granted most of her South and Southeast Asian colonies independence after the war. The consequences of decolonization were mixed. An independent Burma lapsed into a state of chronic civil war. After a period of initial conflict between India and Pakistan, the successors to British India observed an uneasy truce while quarreling over boundaries. The British chose not to withdraw from the multiracial Malaya where nationalism was diffuse among the country's heterogenous population. In all of these countries Communist elements were usually one part of a larger pattern of confusion. In chaotic Burma, the Communists were divided and fought among themselves as well as with other political factions; in Malaya, Communists in the Chinese community rebelled in 1948 but did not gain widespread support.

Siam, renamed Thailand in 1949, did not require a postwar grant of independence to be free. Although never a colony, it nonetheless suffered from internal political strife as well as problems with the French over the Siam-Indochina border. From the American perspective, Siam was stable but considered unreliable; the "wily" Thais were not a dependable bulwark against Chinese Communist expansion. As Dean Acheson explained to the Senate Foreign Relations Committee, the "Siamese are not very stout-hearted fellows" and could not be counted on to put up "rugged resistance" to Communist subversion.[3]

The two largest problems in postwar Southeast Asia were Indonesia and Indochina, where the Dutch and French attempted to reimpose colonial rule. Between the end of the Pacific war and the beginning of 1949, the Netherlands reasserted their control of the East Indies by a mixed policy of force and negotiations. After lengthy discussions with a native Republican government, the Dutch attacked the non-Communist regime in December 1948, disregarding both United Nations resolutions and an

American-backed truce reached in January 1948. After this "police action," the Netherlands' folly quickly became evident despite their capture of key Republican leaders. World opinion quickly turned against the Dutch, and even the United States Congress, which rarely noticed events in Southeast Asia, expressed its disapproval.[4]

French Indochina

The French, with active assistance from Britain and the approval of the United States, also reimposed colonial rule on their former colony. Initially, they only reoccupied southern Indochina, the center of prewar French economic interest. In accordance with a wartime agreement, the Allies gave China the task of restoring order in the north. In the process of implementing their mandate, the Chinese occupying army encountered the hastily erected native government of President Ho Chi Minh's "Democratic Republic of Vietnam" (DRV). Based in Hanoi, Ho's regime enjoyed widespread support in the north and was backed by a coalition of political parties known as the Viet Minh. The party's key leaders, including Ho, were Communists, but they claimed to be only nationalists interested in independence from France. The Chinese tolerated the DRV's existence because of the political leverage it gave them against France and allowed Ho's government to operate under its watchful eye.

In February 1946 the Chinese agreed to turn over North Vietnam to the French, a decision that left Ho with the choice of either fighting or negotiating with France. On 6 March 1946, Ho signed an agreement with French authorities allowing colonial troops to enter the north in return for French recognition of the Vietnam Republic as a "free state having its own government, parliament, army and finances, and forming part of the Indochinese Federation and the French Union." In May 1946 Ho and a Vietnam delegation went to France to negotiate a settlement. After the talks broke down, Ho signed a temporary agreement that looked toward future discussions at an unspecified date. When French forces in the north built up to a point that its commanders thought would allow them to liquidate the Vietnam Republic, they began to use military force. In December 1946 the Viet Minh, aware of what was coming, launched a brief attack against the French in Hanoi and then retreated to the jungle to begin a long war for independence and dominance by the Viet Minh.[5]

By the end of 1948, Indochina was in a state of siege, with French and pro-French Vietnamese forces controlling the major urban areas, and the

Viet Minh, concentrated in the north, controlling the countryside. It was evident to American diplomats that France was losing.[6] Since the French received economic assistance through the Marshall Plan, the Indochina war also indirectly drained American resources. According to the State Department's Far Eastern Office the cost "of continued disruption of the Indochina economy" was estimated at $900 million over a four-year period. The importance of this sum was increased by the probability that it would not "purchase peace but would represent an indefinite drain upon French resources."[7]

The French attempted to retrieve their declining position in Vietnam through greater military power. They sought Vietnamese political support by fostering a "genuine nationalist movement" under the sponsorship of the thirty-six-year-old former Vietnamese emperor, Bao Dai; Ho's nationalist movement was "false" since it was tainted with Communists. The major problem with the "Bao Dai experiment," as the French frankly called it, was that both they and Bao Dai approached it halfheartedly. After two failed attempts to strike an agreement with France, the ex-emperor (he had abdicated to Ho in 1945) signed an agreement with the French president in the Elysée Palace on 8 March 1949, defining the new relationship between the French and Vietnam. The agreement gave a "Republic of Vietnam" only a semblance of nationhood "within the French Union." The meaning of the French Union, which was never precisely defined, was suggested by the powers that France reserved to itself in the agreement: control of Vietnam's foreign policy, finance, and national defense. The French government also promised to ask Parliament to pass a bill that would reintegrate Cochin China with the northern provinces of Vietnam (France had separated this southern province from Annam and Tonkin in 1945).[8]

The 8 March accord was flawed in several ways. The French government that signed it was weak and several strong elements in the French Assembly opposed the agreement. In Indochina it faced opposition from colonials who did not want Vietnam granted independence, no matter how denatured. Non-Communist Vietnamese, on whose behalf Bao Dai signed the agreement, greeted it with apathy. Part of the problem was the man on whom its success depended. In 1932, at the age of nineteen, Bao Dai assumed the throne of a dynasty that had been in power for three centuries. An accommodating attitude toward any force that appeared to be dominant marked his reign. Under the prewar French he urged his people to work in "close and confident collaboration with the protectorate government." When Japan took over Indochina in 1940, he quickly adjusted to the new order and was kept on as a puppet. After the war he abdicated, briefly cooperated with Ho Chi Minh's government in Hanoi, and in 1946, returned to the French Riveria where he pursued his interests in sports cars, gambling, and the good life.[9] Even after Bao Dai signed the 8 March agreement, many observers in Paris, Washington, and Saigon doubted he could lead a Nationalist movement with the enthusiasm necessary to compete with Ho Chi Minh. Consequently, the Elysée accord remained unratified for many months in Paris and unimplemented in Vietnam. In the interim, the Viet Minh increased their strength in the countryside.

France pursued the Bao Dai experiment in the face of strong opposition and apathy because it needed American support. The United States, the French knew, would not endorse an effort simply to reassert colonial rule in Indochina and wanted evidence that France was pursuing some higher purpose. A Bao Dai government, however, feeble, gave the Americans something they could construe as a genuine nationalist movement; the only alternative was rule by Ho Chi Minh.

American Perception

The State Department, almost exclusively responsible for American Southeast Asia policy in the late 1940s, was slow to turn its attention to the region in the postwar years; its only major diplomatic effort undertaken in the area before 1950 was to mediate the Dutch-Indonesian conflict. The department was concerned about the region's deteriorating condition, its impact on the strength of Western Europe, and possible Soviet encroachment, but it was also disinclined to involve the United States in a major effort to reverse the course of events. Policy Planning Staff Director George Kennan expressed the dominant view when he wrote in February 1948 that the United States was "greatly overextended in [its] whole thinking about what we can accomplish, and should try to accomplish" in Asia. American power should instead be projected in Japan and the Philippines, "the cornerstone of a Pacific security system."[10] Kennan's strategic offshore philosophy was the prevailing view, not only in the State Department but also throughout the administration. The concensus was that an American "defensive perimeter" ran along a line from the Aleutians, to Japan, to the Ryukyus, to the Philippines, to New Zealand, and Australia. Few, if any, senior officials within the Truman administration believed that the containment line should be drawn across the mainland of Asia.[11]

As 1948 progressed, the State Department's concern over Russian influence in Southeast Asia increased along with the general rise in tension in the Cold War. By late summer, Charles Reed, chief of the department's Division of Southeast Asian Affairs (SEA), saw "every indication that Moscow is turning more and more attention to the Far East, particularly in Southeast Asia."[12] On 13 October, the department sent a memorandum to American diplomatic missions in Asia echoing this worry: the single goal of Soviet policy in the region, it held, was to substitute Russian influence for that of the West "in such manner and degree as to ensure Soviet control being as surely installed and pre-dominant as in satellite countries behind the Iron Curtain."[13] In December, the CIA characterized the situation in the Far East as being "favorable" to the Soviets; the American "ability to check and reverse this trend is presently hampered by the US being in a middle position between the demands of Asiatic nationalism and the policies of Western European states."[14]

Some observers studying the Communist threat saw a pattern of events dating back to a "signal" the Soviet Union sent to Southeast Asia and other regions of the world in September 1947. The forum was a European Communist party conference held in Wiliza Gora, Poland; the messenger was Andrei Zhdanov, a high Kremlin official and ideologue. The signal was a speech calling on comrades around the world to oppose imperialism. The world, Zhdanov said, was divided into two camps. On one side stood the "imperialists and antidemocratic" forces headed by the United States whose purpose was to establish dominance and "smash democracy." On the other side stood the people's democracies led by the Soviet Union. It was the duty of the democratic forces to close ranks and oppose the antidemocratic forces. In many Western minds, confirmation of the speech's sinister nature came when the conference created the "Communist Information Bureau" or "Cominform," a successor to the prewar Comintern that had spread Communist revolution.[15]

Events following Zhdanov's speech suggested coordination between the Soviet Union and Communist movements around the world. In December 1947, E. M. Zhukov, another Soviet theoretician, published an article applying Zhdanov's two-camp thesis to Asia. Three months after this article, a Communist-dominated "Southeast Asian Youth Conference" convened in Calcutta that went on record endorsing the two-camp thesis and condemning American imperialism. Not long after that confer-

ence, Communist-led insurrections occurred in Malaya, Burma, Indonesia, and somewhat later, the Philippines. State Department analysts
saw the conference as an occasion for Moscow to pass along the Zhdanov-
Zhukov doctrine and, they assumed, instructions to begin revolutionary
violence in Southeast Asia. Whether or not the revolutionary activity
could be traced directly to Soviet orders or from local assessments of
opportunities to seize power, or both, the sequence of events, coupled
with the pending Communist victory in China, forced the State Department to consider doing more to check Communist expansion in the
region.[16]

The State Department's strongest advocate for a more active Southeast
Asian policy was Charles Reed's SEA division. Yet, even Reed's recommendations for positive steps remained modest. The strongest counter-
measure he proposed to meet the increased Soviet challenge in August
1948 was an intensified propaganda effort, supplemented by American
business, missionary, medical, and educational activity. In addition, the
division urged that the United States "publicize our readiness to loan
technical experts in the fields of economic and social endeavor" (and thus
anticipated Truman's "Point IV" program by several months).[17]

One potential force checking a bolder American policy in the region
was FE director Butterworth. While he often acted vigorously on matters
pertaining to his jurisdiction, Butterworth more frequently directed his
energies toward blocking rather than encouraging American action on
the Asian mainland. "The conduct of foreign affairs," he said in a March
1949 speech on Asian policy, "is a marginal operation, of persuasion, of
the offer of benefit, at times the exertion of pressure in hope of changing
the direction to suit our national interest." The greatest force operating
against Communism and the West in Southeast Asia was nationalism. He
had "great confidence" in this force; it had "overcome any super-force
to date" and its spirit was "the most essential characteristic of Southeast
Asia today."[18] He was not opposed to modest measures of support for
friendly or potentially friendly states like Siam or Indonesia, but he lobbied against a "Marshall Plan" for Asia or American stimulation of a
"Pacific Pact" similar to the North Atlantic Treaty.[19]

Butterworth and Reed did not have sole control of Southeast Asian
policy within the State Department. At least three geographic offices, and
five divisions and independent units interested in economic policy, intelligence, and military assistance claimed an interest in the region. The
major cause of disharmony in this system was a traditional rivalry between

FE and the European office (EUR); the reason for conflict was usually either policy toward Indonesia or Indochina. Since these countries were at once European colonies and aspiring Southeast Asian nations, both offices and their constituent divisions, SEA and the Western European Affairs Division (WE), had joint jurisdiction over all policy recommendations going to senior department officials as well as all cables going to the field.*

The division led to frequent conflict at what was called the department's "working level." EUR and WE argued that Dutch and especially French orientation toward the West was of such importance to American security that the United States should not risk alienation by pushing them too hard to free their colonies. FE and SEA held that more, not less, pressure should be applied to the metropolitan powers to encourage their accommodation to Asian nationalism. By the beginning of 1949, FE was making some headway on the Dutch-Indonesia question; the United States cut off economic aid to the Netherlands after the "police action" in December and threatened to exclude the Dutch from the Military Assistance Program if they did not back away from the confrontation.

FE had less success with Indochina. It wanted a "wait and see" approach buttressed with occasional efforts to pressure France to back Bao Dai more forcefully. The office preferred to hold back support for the doubtful experiment until it demonstrated a more certain chance for success. EUR wanted to leaven FE's aloof policy with expressions of American sympathy for France's predicament and not apply much pressure on the grounds that the French government was granting as many concessions as it could in Indochina; the American embassy in Paris went so far as to recommend that the United States openly back the experiment on the grounds that it would fail without American support.[20]

By late spring 1949, the European and Asian offices reached a general agreement on Indochina policy. In a 17 May meeting, senior officials in WE and SEA agreed "that the US should not put itself in a forward position in the Indochina problem since there appeared to be nothing we could do to alter the very discouraging prospects."[21] The department

---

*Before the State Department reorganized on 3 October 1949, a geographic office was divided into divisions. The divisions of FE were CA (China), SEA (Southeast Asia), NA (Northeast Asia), and PI (Philippines). EUR had six constituent units. After 3 October, the regional offices became "bureaus" and the divisions became "offices." For a description of the department's organization, see U.S., Department of State, *Register of the Department of State, April 1, 1948* (Washington, D.C.: GPO, 1948) and later editions.

had already expressed the essence of this policy in cables to American diplomats in Paris and Saigon stating that the United States was willing to give Bao Dai diplomatic, economic, and arms support if France granted him the necessary concessions. The cable also noted that an aid program of "this nature would require Congressional approval."[22] Beyond this agreement, the two divisions argued vigorously over what constituted the necessary concessions and how hard the department should press France to make them. During departmental discussion of the Policy Planning Staff's paper on Southeast Asia, the consensus appeared to support the Far Eastern Office's hard-line view.

The Troubled Career of PPS–51

Perhaps because of orders from higher up, or a simple desire to earn their pay as shapers of policy, the Policy Planning Staff began drafting a Southeast Asia paper in February 1949. The study was a logical followup to the China paper that predicted the Chinese Communists would soon directly menace the subcontinent.

The "problem" PPS–51 identified was to "define U.S. policy toward Southeast Asia, including Indonesia, Indochina, Burma, Malaya, Siam and the Philippines." The "analysis" listed the characteristics that divided and united the region: many religions and varying degrees of political independence and political instability as opposed to a common racial background, economic backwardness, and the certainty "that SEA as a region has become the target of a coordinated offensive plainly directed by the Kremlin." The area was important because of its raw materials and its presence at a crossroads in global communication. If Southeast Asia were "swept by communism we shall have suffered a major political rout, the repercussions of which will be felt throughout the rest of the world, especially in the Middle East and in a then critically exposed Australia." With China falling to Communism, "SEA represents a vital segment on the line of containment, stretching from Japan southward around the Indian Peninsula." Japan, India, and Australia were the major non-Communist "base areas in this quarter of the world" and their security depended on Southeast Asia's denial to the Kremlin. The study identified "militant nationalism" as the most potent force in Asia. The problem facing the West was that the colonial-nationalist struggles in Indonesia and Indochina obscured the real enemy of Southeast Asia, Russian imperialism. With the Dutch and French following irrational colonial policies, the West had become its own worst enemy.

Given the great stakes involved in the success of non-Communist forces in Southeast Asia that were suggested in the analysis, the steps the report concluded the United States should take were modest. While it called for increased American activity in Southeast Asia, it contained no bold prescriptions for an American containment policy backed by large amounts of money, arms, technical assistance, or prestige; it suggested using all four, but only selectively and in small amounts. For the region, there should be multilateral consultation between the United States and the major friendly countries of South and Southeast Asia with India and the Philippines taking the lead. Economic interdependence between Southeast Asia, Japan, and the West should be encouraged along with American cultural and informational programs.

A two-page summary prepared for an under secretary's meeting on PPS–51 highlighted the paper's recommendations for individual countries: The United States should encourage Indonesian independence at the earliest feasible moment and "aid non-communist nationalist leaders to retain their supremacy and foster political and economic stability"; no dollar amount of aid was mentioned. With respect to Indochina, Washington "should frankly tell the French what we think about Southeast Asia," consult with the British and Indians, and "attempt to have the French transfer sovereignty in Indochina to a non-communist indigenous regime." There was no mention of material aid for the French or Vietnamese. For Burma, the department should consult with Britain and India and "wait until the smoke clears." In Siam, the United States should support the country's "resistance to Soviet and Chinese encroachment, and cultivate it as a center of stability and U.S. influence." Malaysia should be left to the British to worry about. The Philippines should be encouraged to play an active role in combating communism, be aided in developing its economy, and have benefit of a "major cultural and informational program." The summary also recommended that PPS–51 be forwarded to the NSC "for information" and that parts of it be shown to the Economic Cooperation Administration and the British.[23]

The planning staff presented the draft policy paper to an under secretary's meeting on 6 April with a misleading note stating that it had the "general approval" of seven bureaus and offices, including FE and EUR.[24] The staff had indeed written it in consultation with a number of offices, but the draft by no means pleased everyone. SEA chief Charles Reed was on record as objecting to the recommendations on Indonesia, complaining that they set forth operational steps best left to the discretion of the department's geographic offices. He disliked a paragraph calling for consultation with only the British and Indians on Indochina; the Philippines and Siam, he thought, should be consulted too. He also suggested a slight modification of the paragraph on Siam to allow for the possibility that "a Vietnam which is neither of a Soviet nor a Chinese inspiration" might encroach upon it.[25]

The paper fell flat in the meeting. Conselor Charles Bohlen, a man generally more concerned with European than Asian policy, argued against unilateral American efforts at encouraging nationalist movements in the area. He emphasized the need to work directly with Western powers and pointed out the "unwisdom of bringing the Australians, Indians, Pakistanis, *et al.*" in at the initial stages. The department's intelligence spokesman questioned the "timing factor" but suggested no specific changes. Butterworth had "no objection to it," provided a paragraph on Indonesia did not restrict American support of an interim government. Paul Nitze of the Policy Planning Staff thought the paper gave insufficient emphasis to the difficulty of creating orderly and effective native governments. Despite the reservations, the group decided to send the paper to Acheson, approved it "for general guidance in the Department," and ordered that FE proceed to implement its conclusions.[26]

At some point after the 6 April meeting, FE and other offices in the department raised further objections to PPS–51. After a discussion of general Southeast Asian policy in the secretary's morning meeting on 29 April, the planning staff altered two paragraphs in favor of FE's views of the proper policy. One change outlined the importance of inducing the Dutch and French "to adopt their policies to the realities of the current situation in Southeast Asia" and stated that "our first step should be, in conjunction with the British, to set forth to the Dutch and French in candor, detail, and with great gravity our interpretation of the situation in and intentions with regard to SEA." The other stated that "determination of future [American] policy toward Indochina should await the outcome of the [recommended] demarche."[27]

These changes, however, did not placate all of the critics, and George Kennan made a special plea to Acheson. Contrary to what the secretary had heard about it, Kennan said that the "paper *does* contain concrete suggestions for action at this time with respect to Southeast Asia." He urged Acheson to discuss its contents with the British and French in Paris and to approve it "as broad guidance to Departmental thinking on the subject as a strategic concept from which tactical planning by the operational offices should flow."[28] The secretary left Washington for the Paris Foreign Ministers Conference several days later without taking Kennan's advice.

Indochina Policy and the June Demarché

In the absence of a departmental statement on Southeast Asia, the formulation and execution of policy fell to the querulous geographic offices. SEA chose to implement the portions of PPS–51 it agreed with and ignored the parts it found objectionable. One aspect of the paper it dismissed without hesitation was the notion of a "regional approach." The only "universal cement" Charles Reed could find for the region was the "preoccupation of certain non-communist Asiatic countries with the danger of an eventual communist dominated SEA." Reed also thought that the United States should give up on Indochina and focus on strengthening Siam. His doubts about Indochina developed from service as American consul in Hanoi and Saigon before and after the war, and as SEA chief since April 1948. The two earlier French efforts to implement a Bao Dai "solution" left Reed unimpressed and he distrusted the renewed experiment in 1949. "Merely because [Bao Dai] offers at present the only possible non-Communist solution in Indochina is no reason, in view of his very dubious chances of succeeding, in committing the United States at this time to his support," he wrote in April 1949.[29] A month later he informed Butterworth that "The chances of saving Indochina" were "slim." The United States "should look to a strengthened Siam as a base from which to contain communism."[30]

Most American diplomats shared Reed's pessimism to some degree, but few were willing to write off Indochina without making an effort to save it. Butterworth and Reed's deputy in SEA were willing to support Bao Dai on the condition that France gave him a fair chance. Reed never pushed his argument very vigorously and accepted FE's conditional willingness to support the experiment by early summer. The key question in American policy thus became how hard to push France to give the exemperor his chance.[31] Since PPS–51 called for a stiff demarché to France on Indochina, FE concluded that it had a mandate to press hard.

The logical pressure point was the 8 March accord. The State Department saw it as only the beginning of a process leading to real Vietnamese independence. Yet, as of June 1949, the French Assembly had only recently taken the preliminary step of rejoining Cochinchina with the northern provinces, and the government still had not submitted the agreement for ratification. Responding to the tepid French followup to the agreement with Bao Dai, the Southeast Asian Division sought the approval of its European counterpart in the department to send the French government a frankly worded interpretation of the agreement and its implications for American policy. SEA, after a surprising clearance from WE for the strongly worded document, sent it to the American embassy in Paris on 6 June. Covering instructions, which Butterworth signed "for the Acting Secretary of State," requested that either Ambassador David Bruce or Charles Bohlen, then in Paris with Acheson for the Foreign Ministers Conference, present the demarché to the French Foreign Ministry as a statement of the department's thinking.

The fifteen-page note warned the French that they were playing into the hands of the Communists by not making the "requisite concessions" to nationalist demands in Vietnam. The accord's implementation, furthermore, would be only a first step; more concessions would be needed later if the United States were to view the effort with favor. Any American decision to support the Vietnam government would depend on "the extent to which the French Government has itself provided that Government with the political advantages upon which its appeal to the Vietnamese must be based."[32]

SEA attempted to alert the Paris embassy that the demarché was on its way and stress its importance as a cornerstone in American policy, but WE killed the warning cable.[33] As a result, the demarché and accompanying instructions arrived in Paris by courier without forewarning and the American embassy revolted. Ambassador Bruce, according to an aide, cried "poppycock" and, with the unanimous backing of the embassy's political section, sent his guest, Dean Acheson, the demarché, Butterworth's instructions, a draft cable Bruce proposed to send to Washington, and a cover note. In the note, Bruce expressed regret about bothering the secretary on matters unrelated to the Foreign Ministers Conference, but said that the presentation of the department's memorandum "would do a great deal of harm precisely at the time when encouragement rather than criticism is needed." Before this package reached the secretary, one of Acheson's aides showed it to Charles Bohlen who attached a note to the growing pile of documents stating that he "entirely agreed" with Bruce. While he was for doing something "appropriate to bring the French attitude in line with that of the United States," Bohlen could not support a "holier than thou" lecture coupled with suggestions that France was not about to follow.

Acheson instructed Bruce to send his draft cable to Washington protesting the demarché.[34] Sent 13 June, Bruce's cable requested that the department allow him to convey its "general views" in an oral resume. He explained that the presentation of the document would be counterproductive. The French government had gone as far as it could go and would not renegotiate the Elysée agreement. To lend weight to his "request," Bruce noted that the secretary of state had read the cable and concurred.[35]

The Paris embassy also scored another coup while Dean Acheson was its guest. In early June it learned that the French were planning to exchange instruments with Bao Dai in the near future that would put the 8 March agreement into effect; following this step, the ex-emperor would announce formation of a provisional government and France planned to notify foreign powers of this event and of Vietnam's ability to receive foreign recognition. The sequence of events did not indicate a departure in existing French policy, only a paper transfer of limited powers and a quest for foreign approval. It failed to constitute the vigorous backing of the experiment that SEA deemed necessary for Bao Dai to succeed. As a result, the division did not see it as an occasion for the United States to speak out in support of Bao Dai. From his vantage point in Paris, however, Dean Acheson decided that the department should issue a statement welcoming the creation of the new government. The statement, released on 21 June, fell short of the full diplomatic recognition that Ambassador Bruce desired, but did move closer to association with the questionable experiment. It called the formation of the Vietnam state a "welcomed development" and expressed hope that the 8 March agreement would "form the basis for the progressive realization of the legitimate aspirations of the Vietnamese people."[36]

According to Charlton Ogburn, one of SEA's senior officers, his division's Indochina policy had been "junked." In a 28 June memorandum to Reed, he complained that "FE is being put in an extremely vulnerable position" since nothing was being done to promote a non-Communist solution in Indochina. He mentioned a column Joseph Alsop had written attacking FE for its half-hearted Indochina policy and credited WE with responsibility for planting the story. The recent reverses were "the culmination of three years of consistent effort on the part of WE to set aside all considerations of our position in Asia and to keep a free hand for the

French." Consideration of the French government's weakness had "gagged" the State Department "beyond all reason in so many contexts that the thing has become a joke." Ogburn assumed that WE had all along anticipated that the Paris embassy would scrap the demarché.[37]

SEA's policy of watchful waiting coupled with pressure on France to support Bao Dai was not yet fully junked, as Ogburn feared, but it had taken a measurable step closer to the scrap heap. In an effort to define policy in the wake of Acheson's "captivity" in Paris, Ogburn drafted a memorandum outlining five policy alternatives for Indochina. The choices were: (1) to continue the wait and see policy; (2) to give tepid support to the Bao Dai government; (3) to promote a compromise with Ho; (4) to give "utmost" support to Bao Dai; and (5) to "follow a compromise course, endeavoring to give encouragement to the Bao Dai solution without committing the United States to support of the 8 March agreement or the Vietnamese government envisaged in it, and at the same time preparing for the time when it might be expedient to reveal publicly why we were unable to do more to save Indochina." Ogburn recommended the fifth option for lack of a better alternative. Drafted at Butterworth's request, SEA sent the options memorandum to its counterpart in EUR who refused to cosign it as a statement of policy.[38] Indochina policy would linger in this confused, half-committed state until the United States Congress stimulated the department to adopt Ogburn's option number four.

The Unexplored Alternative

When the State Department moved closer to endorsing Bao Dai on 21 June, it took one more step away from a rapprochement with Ho Chi Minh. By 1949 the department's attitude toward Ho was rigid. From evidence British and French intelligence provided in 1945, it knew that Ho had helped found the French Communist Party after the First World War, had studied in Moscow's "Toilers of the East" university in the 1920s, and had operated in Asia as a Comintern agent in the interwar years. With this background, the Vietnamese leader fit the stereotype of an international Communist agent.

There was, however, strong evidence suggesting that Ho was also a nationalist. In 1919, for example, he had approached the American delegation at the Paris Peace Conference in an effort to present Secretary of State Robert Lansing a petition requesting independence for the Vietnamese people. During and after the Second World War he had sent Western leaders a stream of appeals for postwar Vietnamese independence. He made a special effort to court the United States and, to his own advantage, cooperated with American OSS officers in nothern Vietnam in the last months of the war. Throughout his wartime and early postwar quest for Vietnam's independence, Ho brushed aside questions about his political ideology. All he sought, he said, was his country's independence. Ho's ambiguous record disturbed some American observers, but not enough for the State Department to have serious reservations about how to classify him. The department considered nationalism and Communism to be mutually exclusive and, by 1947, for the purpose of designing an Indochina policy, it considered him a Moscow-directed Communist.[39]

Doubts about Ho's true intentions nonetheless persisted and the Viet Minh leader would himself frequently add to the confusion. After he went underground in late 1946, Ho continued to seek American good will in the hope that the United States would not support the French effort to reoccupy Vietnam. In early 1948, he requested that an official American observer visit his camp, presumably to allow Ho to demonstrate his revolution's benign international intentions. SEA was not enthusiastic about the idea. If an American were to accept the invitation, one official reasoned, he might either find evidence that Ho was indeed a Moscow puppet and that past professions of friendship for the United States were a "hoax" or that Ho was an independent nationalist. If the observer verified the first possibility, "it would not change the policy of this government as our basic assumption seems to be that we cannot afford to assume that Ho is anything but Moscow-directed." If evidence were found to support the second possibility, it was unlikely that such a single report "would change the basic assumption of this government vis-a-vis Ho." It would, in short, "seem a poor investment to send an American." One alternative would be for the CIA to send a Chinese agent. "The value of information by a Chinese would depend on his keenness of observation," the officer wrote, "but he certainly would be in a position to add considerably to our sum total of knowledge of Ho's regime, particularly its ability to continue to offer military resistance to the French."[40]

The question of sending a CIA agent to Ho's Vietnam came up again four months later at a June 1948 conference American diplomats held in Bangkok. The department's representative at the meeting explained the problem: In the first place, we just couldn't do it because of our white skin. A white man would be very conspicuous in Indo-China. In order to have an effective intelligence officer, he would have to have a little brown blood. Then, we wouldn't be able to trust him.[41]

After Tito split with Stalin in the summer of 1948 (the Yugoslav leader left the Cominform on 28 June), the department did not revise its estimate of Ho and the Viet Minh. Indeed, SEA was slow to grasp the significance of the Tito phenomenon. As an approach to countering Soviet propaganda in the region, it recommended in mid-August 1948 that American propaganda emphasize "that a communist state is but a satellite of Moscow and with no scope for uncontrolled action or thought. We have plenty of ammunition for this attack in the examples of Yugoslavia, Czechoslovakia, Poland, Rumania."[42]

In the first half of 1949 the department's fixed view of Ho and growing attachment to Bai Dai withstood the challenge of the Vietnam leader's persistent assertion that he was not a Russian puppet. In a radio interview with *Newsweek* Magazine reporter Harold Isaacs, Ho was asked if his government was Communist. "Pure French propaganda," he replied, and noted that his government was composed of many elements. Did he fear that his country would become a satellite? "No, I have no fear," he answered. The magazine's editors suggested that Ho might be "more of a Vietnamese nationalist right now than a Communist stooge."[43] Ho attempted to reinforce this image in an interview granted the United Press in late May. In one question, which was submitted to him in writing, he was asked if he was or ever had been a Communist. "When I was young," he replied cryptically, "I studied Buddhism, Confucianism, Christianism [sic] as well as Marxism. There's something good in each doctrine. The Viet Nam Communist Party was dissolved in 1945. I have been in England, France, Russia, China and other countries."[44]

Along with Ho's direct testimony, the foremost French expert on Indochina offered the department a disquieting view of both Ho Chi Minh and Bao Dai. Paul Mus, director of the School of Overseas France in Paris, visited Washington in late April and paid a courtesy call on the department. Speaking to lower-level officials involved in research, Mus pointed out that the Bao Dai experiment had little chance for success. Ho Chi Minh, the professor was reported as saying, had "the complete support of the Vietnamese, except for a few hundred in Cochinchina presently backing Bao Dai." Even conservative and wealthy landowners who "know that Ho would kill them if he had complete power support Ho because of their desire for national independence." Describing Ho as "30% trustworthy," Mus considered him a nationalist above politics who "would become anything the situation made necessary." After independence Mus speculated that Ho's influence might decline and that Western diplomats would then "be in a position to exert a favorable influence on the development of democracy in the country."[45]

Such talk about Ho's ambiguity agitated American officials in Washington and posts in France and Vietnam. Reacting to the Harold Isaacs interview, the American consul in Hanoi reported on 11 May that members of Bao Dai's entourage were being led to think that the United States looked "almost favorably on Ho and considered him as much National-[ist] as Communist."[46] The department offered reassurance nine days later in a cable, drafted by Ogburn, containing a remarkably vivid exposition of SEA's views about Ho becoming a Titoist.

> In light Ho's known background, no other assumption possible but that he outright Commie so long as (1) he fails unequivocally repudiate Moscow connections and Commie doctrine and (2) remains personally singled out for praise by internatl Commie press and receives its support. . . . Question whether Ho as much nationalist as Commie is irrelevant. All Stalinists in colonial areas are nationalists. With achievement natl aims (i.e., independence) their objective necessarily becomes subordination state to Commie purposes and ruthless extermination not only opposition groups but all elements suspected even slightest deviation. On basis examples eastern Eur it must be assumed such wld be goal Ho and men his stamp if included Bao Dai Govt. . . . It must of course be conceded theoretical possibility exists estab National Communist state or pattern Yugoslavia in any area beyond reach Soviet army. However, US attitude cld take acct such possibility only if every other possible avenue closed to preservation area from Kremlin control. Moreover, while Vietnam out of reach Soviet army it will doubtless be by no means out of reach Chi Commie hatchet men and armed forces.[47]

When Harold Isaacs returned to the United States in late June, he called on Charles Reed, giving him the same story that Mus conveyed in the spring. "[The] only possible present action," said Isaac, "would be to contact Ho Chi Minh, find out what he wanted, and then accept his terms." The discussion became heated and Isaac left, leaving Reed unconvinced.[48]

While Ho, Mus, and Isaacs did not change the State Department's operating assumption about Ho Chi Minh, his ambiguity did trouble SEA. In April 1949 the division briefly considered promoting a French-

Bao Dai accommodation with the Viet Minh. John Davies and Reed drafted a brief paper describing a "possible method of solving the Indochina problem" that would "once and for all 'smoke out' Ho Chi Minh and determine whether he is primarily a nationalist or a communist." Their plan called for consultation between France, Britain, India, the Philippines and the United States. Following establishment of a common position, either India or the Philippines would call a conference on Indochina. France would be induced to grant Vietnam full independence and the foreign powers would establish an international mission in the country to monitor developments in the new states. The mission would remain for "some years" and function as the internationally supervised customs office had once functioned in China.

In the course of erecting this new system, the international mission would consult both Bao Dai and Ho Chi Minh. The group visiting Ho, "preferably composed of Asiatics," would point out that he "claimed to be a nationalist first and foremost," remind him of his appeal for international support to achieve Vietnamese independence, and assure him that France was willing to grant the country freedom. The mission would then "suggest to Ho that if he is the real nationalist he professes to be" he would "accept loyally the decisions and mandates of the government and the subsequent constituent assembly, et cetera, and bind himself unequivocally not to . . . subvert the true nationalism of his people" or a government that might emerge from the multilateral effort. The mission might even "suggest" that he leave Vietnam and "take up once more the philosophical studies to which he has devoted a great deal of his previous life, and it might even be suggested that there would be a pension adequate to support him in those studies."

Davies and Reed conceded that Ho might agree to such a plan and then try to subvert it. If he refused to cooperate at the outset, then the United States might be better off knowing "once and for all what we may expect from him and for what we should plan." Then it might be desirable to give France and the "nationalist Vietnamese" military help. One positive line of defense they suggested ran from Siam "down along the Mekong and cutting across Indochina to include Cambodia and Cochinchina."[49]

Reed sent the scheme to Butterworth, but the idea apparently never went much further. There is no evidence revealing what WE and EUR may have thought of the plan, if they saw it; if they did, the reaction was probably frosty. As the department's Europeanists demonstrated with their scuttling of the June demarché to France, they were not enthusiastic about leaning on the French government to do much of anything in Indochina.

By mid-summer 1949, SEA appears to have dropped all thought of seeking an accommodation with Ho Chi Minh. Ogburn dismissed the possibility of bringing the Viet Minh into Bao Dai's government in his June option paper. Even if the French would allow it and Ho were willing, the probability was, he wrote, that the Communists would quickly take over and "enlist Vietnam in the support of Communist China and the USSR. Such an outcome would . . . mean a failure of our policy and would reflect upon the Department's judgment." The consequences of Indochina falling to Communism might also cause a "chain reaction" in the rest of the subcontinent.[50]

The United States had three basic choices for Indochina policy in 1949: one was to do nothing; a second was to back the French; a third was to promote a compromise with Ho. The policy it pursued in the spring was a compromise between the first and second. The State Department ruled out the third as being too hazardous. There lay in it a serious domestic political risk in that a compromise with Ho might have invited an attack from the friends of China and other politicians willing to attack FE on the loyalty issue. Beyond that, the department did not want the Western position in Southeast Asia replaced by a revolutionary force directed by the Soviet Union. Given the subcontinent's strategic location, natural wealth, and relation to the economies of Western Europe and friendly Asian nations, such a takeover was potentially catastrophic.

Postscript

After the short life of the "international mission" idea and the stillbirth of the demarché to France, PPS–51 persisted in its fragile life. When the secretary returned from Paris, he gave it his approval and on 1 July 1949, the department dispatched the document to the NSC for its information. However, the paper's problems continued even after that. The Policy Planning Staff wanted it sent to the field as a general policy statement, but Charles Bohlen requested that the recommendations be deleted. On 11 July, Acheson sent it to the field with covering instructions advising that no action be taken on its recommendations. Thus, five months after its drafting, PPS–51 went to posts in Europe and Asia only "as a source of information and not the basis for any action."[51] It had become, in effect, a non-policy paper.

The fate of the Southeast Asia paper reflected, among other things, the triumph of both FE and EUR over the Policy Planning Staff. The two offices and their subunits preferred negotiating policy between themselves; they tolerated the planning staff, apparently, only when it supported their own policy line. The paper's fate also reflected the reality that Southeast Asia policy remained in the doldrums in spite of the growing concern that something needed to be done to prevent the region from falling under communist control. The policy remained adrift until the department, stimulated by fortuitous events in Congress, reviewed it again in the winter.

8

Money for "The General
Area of China"

The catalyst that stimulated an active American policy in Southeast
Asia was the Mutual Defense Assistance Act of 1949. The act authorized
funds for the Military Assistance Program (MAP), the first of many omnibus postwar military aid measures. While the 1949 act's main purpose
was to "implement" the North Atlantic Treaty's mutual assistance provision, it also contained an authorization for $75 million in unvouchered
funds to be used at the president's discretion in the "general area of
China." The purpose of the fund, at least as far as the China bloc was
concerned, was to finance overt and covert aid to Nationalist forces on
the mainland and Taiwan. Little if any money was spent for that purpose.
The effect the $75 million had was to stimulate planning for, and ulti-
mately begin financing of, a containment policy in Southeast Asia.

The Origins of MAP

The roots of MAP lie deep in Cold War history. The first major step
toward formulating an arms aid program for the non-Communist world
apparently came in a 5 March 1947 letter that Acting Secretary of State
Dean Acheson sent to Secretary of War Robert Patterson. Writing shortly
after formulation of the Greek-Turkish aid program, Acheson noted the

urgent need to study other regions of the world where American financial, technical, and military aid might be required.[1] Patterson turned the problem over to an ad hoc committee of the State-War-Navy Coordinating Committee (SWNCC), which produced a report six weeks later. The committee called for the formulation of a "comprehensive" arms sales and transfer program for countries in Europe, the Western Hemisphere, and the Far, Near, and Middle East. It noted that only limited legislative authority existed to grant such aid, and that much broader enabling legislation was required.[2]

By the end of 1947, SWNCC devised a legislative program to support a foreign military assistance policy. "The ideal," the committee reported, "would be an authority which would empower the President to provide to any foreign government, *with or without reimbursement,* such military assistance as appears to him to be in the national interest of the U.S." The committee realized, however, that the "ideal" presented political problems. Congress "would not be likely to grant the President a carte blanche authority under which he might be empowered to subsidize the world at the expense of the United States economic and industrial resources. It is therefore apparent that in the field of broad legislation a more limited objective must be sought." In detailing its "more limited objective" the report requested authority for the president to transfer arms to foreign governments when he believed it was in the national interest and when Congress had appropriated the money to pay costs.[3]

The Joint Chiefs of Staff soon drew up the proposed legislation that the secretaries of state and defense submitted to Congress informally as a "Title VI" to the omnibus foreign assistance bill of 1948. The title authorized the president to furnish military assistance to foreign governments when it "was determined to be consistent with the national interest" and when it was without cost to the United States or was paid for by congressional appropriations. In consultation with congressional leaders, the administration agreed to jettison Title VI to avoid impeding passage of other portions of the bill, including the European Recovery Program authorization.[4]

Advocates for using military aid as an instrument of foreign policy, a group apparently broadly based within the executive branch, remained determined to gain administration support for their proposal. They finally achieved their goal when the National Security Council and the president adopted the conclusions of an NSC paper in early July 1948 that called for the creation of a well-coordinated military assistance program to replace past, uncoordinated programs. The purpose of the aid was to "strengthen the moral and material resistance of the free nations," to "support their political and military orientation toward the United States," to augment American "military potential by improvement of our armaments industries," and to encourage American and Allied military collaboration in the event of war. The new program would be even larger than a combination of its predecessors and would require that Congress enact legislation along the lines of the ill-fated Title VI.[5]

The State Department and military establishment now had a mandate to develop a coordinated arms aid program. Before the NSC adopted its paper on arms assistance, SWNCC and its successor, the State-Army-Navy-Air Force Coordinating Committee, approached military assistance in an almost abstract manner. Earlier papers listed countries in order of priority for receipt of arms and stated general internal and external security objectives; but there was little detailed planning about the aid amounts to be given. As 1948 progressed, however, developments in the Cold War gave MAP planners obvious targets for their aid. The most likely were the members of the emerging North Atlantic Treaty, an alliance that both the United States and Western Europe wanted to strengthen. To develop the legislation creating a Military Assistance Program, the State Department, the Economic Cooperation Administration, and the military establishment formed a Foreign Assistance Correlation Committee (FACC) in December 1948.[6]

A Giant Contingency Fund

The FACC got off to a fitful start, but soon produced papers justifying an arms program to submit to Congress. The committee proposed legislation to "broaden the authority of the President to provide, suspend or withdraw military assistance in the interest of national security and the political interest of the United States" and to contain an indefinite authorization re-funded by annual appropriations. The FACC specifically designated for aid the future North Atlantic Treaty members, Austria, Iran, Greece, Turkey, Korea, and the Philippines. The committee classified the full list "Top Secret" because it included Austria, a country that Russia continued to occupy in part; publicity of an American intention to aid it would make Russian withdrawal more difficult to achieve. Administration officials openly discussed all other potential recipients, emphasizing the future members of the Atlantic Pact. In Congress, the legislation came to be known as the treaty's "arms implementation" bill.[7]

China had been on the list of possible arms recipients in 1947 and 1948, and received considerable amounts of American military assistance in those years through several legislative authorizations. The administration, however, removed China from the list in the latter part of 1948 because of doubts about Chiang Kai-shek's future. Yet, its planners were not certain that all non-Communist China would fall. Formosa might survive with some type of independent government; semi-autonomous armies in the extreme south and northwest might also survive for awhile. In view of these uncertainties, the FACC padded the bill with a contingency fund for China. The State Department's Chinese Affairs Division, however, thought it important that money for China "should be incorporated with other such requests so that the least possible attention will be drawn to it. There should be no reference to the possible use of such funds in any particular area of China—or even China if possible." Department officials also discussed using the fund in India, Pakistan, Afghanistan, Siam, Indonesia, Ethiopia, and, generally, "to take care of emergency situations which may develop."[8]

To meet the unpredictable needs of Austria, Asia, and other regions of the world, as well as the need for secrecy, the FACC incorporated an extra $100 million into the draft authorization bill. It left unspecified *all* recipient countries and asked Congress for what was, in effect, a $1.4 billion contingency fund to be used at the discretion of the president. The draft legislation allowed the president to send arms to any "nations which have joined with the United States in collective defense and regional arrangements" and to "other nations whose increased ability to defend themselves against aggression is important to the national interest." A "nation" was defined as "any foreign government or country, or group thereof; or any representatives or group of the people of any country" which the president might choose to designate. This was nothing less than the "ideal" authority the SWNCC rejected in December 1947 as politically unrealistic.[9]

After much anxiety, delay, and fanfare, the president sent the FACC draft legislation to Congress on 28 July 1949; but not without grumbling from within the State Department. The Far Eastern Office was dissatisfied with the amount of arms aid it was getting for its area of the world. Director W. Walton Butterworth complained to Deputy Under Secretary of State Dean Rusk that the $10 million earmarked for Korea, the $5 million for the Philippines, as well as a projected $30 million in the unenacted "Point IV" program for Asia, was too small given the size and importance of Asia. "Suffice it to say," he complained, "that this is an excellent example of *reductio ad absurdum.*" The Southeast Asian Division's Charlton Ogburn complained in a six-page memorandum that MAP was intended to send "arms to an area where in the first place it can do no good and in the second place is not needed. The situation in Asia is the reverse. There the arms could do good and there the arms are needed."[10]

False Start

Congress made short work of the first FACC draft legislation. Because of what quickly became known as the bill's "blank check" provision, a combined Senate Foreign Relations and Armed Services Committee, constituted especially to consider the arms bill, struck it down without a fight from the administration. The bill's chief antagonist was Senator Arthur Vandenberg. In a 29 July closed meeting of the Foreign Relations Committee, Vandenberg complained that the "whole thing is shot through with embarrassment. You take discussion of the . . . sentence . . . which permits the President, solely, in his own option, to give any arms he pleases to any country on earth on any basis he decides, which makes him war lord No. 1 of the earth. Now, it just can't be done." He made the same point forcefully to Acheson and Defense Secretary Louis Johnson in a 2 August executive meeting of the combined committee and, supported by other members, insisted that a new bill be drafted specifying the countries to be aided.[11]

An embarrassed Dean Acheson labored as best he could to defend the FACC draft that he apparently had not read. The loose definition of a nation, he explained to the committee off-the-record, resulted from the possible need of arms aid for Austria. (Elaborating on the reason for the "flexibility feature" before the committee several days later, he recalled that "there was a desire also to have a certain amount of flexibility with Southeast Asia. There will be problems with regard to the Philippines and Siam and places of that sort that would make some flexibility necessary.") Unable to persuade the bill's critics, Acheson returned to the State Department that afternoon, more angry with himself and the department than with Vandenberg, and ordered the drafting of a new bill. The next morning he told his senior advisors that "even a child would have picked up the weakness in the MAP legislation," and wondered aloud if he needed to read every future bill the department sent to Congress.[12]

While the FACC was quickly rewriting the MAP bill, Senator Knowland led the China bloc's attack on the dying first draft. In the 2 August executive session of the combined committee, which he attended as an Armed Services Committee member, Knowland complained that China was being treated "as a complete vacuum in this situation, although we have recognized the inroads of Communism and the danger of it in Korea and the Philippines. . . . I do not think we can be unrealistic and treat the map of the world as though China did not exist on it." Two days later, he introduced an amendment for himself and twelve other senators granting $175 million in American-supervised military and financial assistance to non-Communist China. In an effort to capitalize on the still sputtering loyalty issue, the amendment also required that the secretary of defense certify in writing that all American members of the accompanying aid mission were "loyal to the United States." When the administration submitted its redrafted MAP bill on 5 August, a draft that quieted criticism of the "blank check" provision, Knowland introduced a similar amendment five days later, reworded to match the new bill's language.[13]

The House China bloc was no less active than its Senate counterpart, although not as successful in obtaining press coverage. On 8 August, Republican John Davis Lodge cosponsored with a Democrat an amendment authorizing $200 million in aid for China to be administered in the same manner as aid to Greece and Turkey (that is, by American advisors). It would assist China "to throw off the foreign yoke," a phrase borrowed, ironically, from the China White Paper's "Letter of Transmittal."[14]

Except for two provisions, the new bill Knowland and Lodge were attempting to amend was stripped of its predecessor's flexibility. Recipient countries were named in separate titles: Title I authorized $1,160,-990,000 in aid for the members of the North Atlantic Treaty; Title II authorized $211,370,000 for Greece and Turkey; and Title III had $27,-640,000 for Iran, Korea, and the Philippines. Assuming that the administration wished to remain bound to the terms of the legislation, flexibility existed only to the extent that: (1) approximately $50 million was padded in Title I for Austrian arms, should Austria join the Atlantic alliance; and (2) there was a provision that allowed 5 percent of the money available in any one title of the act to be transferred to any other title of the act at the president's discretion.* Beyond possible expenditure of Titles I or

---

*Although the bill, as finally enacted, contained no reference to Austria, the State and Defense Departments submitted to the Budget Bureau for approval on 31 May 1950 an

II money on aid for Korea and the Philippines, there was no provision allowing aid for other countries in the Far East. Dean Acheson was aware of this deficiency and was prepared to offer a remedy.[16]

Disaster in the House

The secretary of state first revealed his position on an aid amendment for other parts of Asia in a public Senate committee hearing on 8 August. When a senator asked if Congress should appropriate a general sum for the Far East, Acheson replied that, since the whole subject of Asia policy was under review by Ambassador at Large Philip Jessup's study group, he could not justify such a request. However, if Congress wished to authorize it, "a comparatively small amount which could be used in the Far East at the discretion of the President would have considerable possibilities of usefulness."[17]

Three days later the secretary took the same position, although with considerable wavering, before a House Foreign Affairs Committee executive meeting. Acheson stressed that earmarking funds for China was unacceptable. However, if Congress gave the administration a modest amount of money, "which could be used in Asia, on a confidential basis, much might be done with it. We do not ask for it. If the Congress wants to do it, there are many ways in which that could be used in China and elsewhere." The amount he had in mind was $75 to $100 million. Such a fund, "would be quite ample to do whatever we can devise as a possible move. But as I said, I have no plans for it. I have nothing. I do not want the Congress to do that. If it does, I think it might come in very useful."

Two committee members expressed enthusiasm for this flexible approach. Connecticut Democrat Abraham Ribicoff regretted the absence of flexibility in the revised draft. "To my mind that was tough, realistic thinking." He proposed an amendment giving "the administration some

---

Austrian military aid program estimated to cost $85.5 million. It was to be funded under the authority of Title I of the Mutual Defense Assistance Act. The departments made the following comments in pleading their case:

> The [Act] does not specifically authorize the use of MDAP funds . . . for Austria. However, both the Secretary of State and Defense informed the House and Senate authorizing committees in executive session of the Executive Branch proposal to program [aid for Austria] as soon as Congress authorized . . . such aid. This authority would be sought immediately after the signing of the agreed treaty. The Committees thought it would be possible within a few days to amend the . . . Act to authorize such transfers to Austria. The Secretary of State is of such opinion that the Congress would not have any adverse reaction to the proposal to initiate supply action because the Executive Branch is doing exactly what was told the Congress and neither Committee objected.[15]

discretion, let us say, to sell arms to certain friendly powers if it is necessary," perhaps to Burma, Indochina, and India.

New York Republican Jacob Javits said that he might offer an amendment to add the phrase "any other nation" to the sentence in Section 3 that included Iran, Korea, and the Philippines. Was there any reason for not introducing such an amendment, he asked? Acheson, feeling perhaps that he had pushed his non-request for a contingency fund too far, replied with a confusing answer: "I do not think this is a reason you should not do it, but if you do do it, I think you will open in the Congress . . . the same row [that killed the first bill] and make the bill harder to get through. In my judgment it would be an unwise thing to do." Congress could act on aid to the Far East when it returned in January. Before he left the meeting, however, Acheson reiterated his willingness to receive a small confidential fund, a position John Lodge forced him back to by insisting on including some form of aid for China.[18]

On the following Monday morning, 15 August, the House committee considered the Lodge-Walter $200 million China aid amendment and killed it in a largely party line vote of eleven to seven. The committee only added to the bill a declaration that the United States felt it desirable for Asian countries to create a "self-help and mutual cooperation" organization that might receive some unspecified form of American assistance. In the afternoon session, it reported the legislation with the full $1.4 billion authorized. Administration supporters obtained this only after voting down another amendment submitted by James Richards (D-Georgia) and John Vorys (R-Ohio), among others, to cut the European arms authorization in half. Both the China bloc and the economizers, an overlapping group, vowed to take their amendments to the House floor.[19]

Lodge attempted to reach a compromise with the Acheson position by using the good offices of Philip Jessup, who was actively lobbying against China aid, and Ernest Gross, the assistant secretary of state for congressional relations. After inconclusive telephone conversations between Lodge and Gross, Representative Walter Judd, the real force behind the Lodge amendment, telephoned the assistant secretary to make a deal. Judd offered to support an amendment authorizing $150 million in China aid and $25 million for other Asian countries. He stressed, however, that it would be important for the department to inform Democrats that the revised amendment met with the administration's approval.[20]

The following day, 16 August, Acheson and his senior advisors reviewed what was now known as the "Judd-Lodge" amendment in their morning meeting. After lengthy discussion, Acheson stood by his position taken before the House committee on 11 August. He was willing to accept a "confidential fund which could be used in the President's discretion in the Far East to support the independence of areas threatened by Communism." The fund might possibly be half of the $200 million Lodge proposed. "I made it clear that this was entirely up to the Congress," he explained. After this meeting, Acheson visited the president and obtained his approval for the department's position on the contingency fund.[21]

Following instructions from Acheson, Gross telephoned Lodge that same day to reject the Congressman's overture. Lodge expressed his regret, but nonetheless introduced a revised amendment on the floor authorizing $75 million for China and $25 million for Southeast Asia to be administered by an American military aid mission. After a lengthy debate and frequent invocation of the names of General Claire Chennault and other authorities on China, the House voted the proposal down 164 to 94.[22]

Shortly after defeating the Lodge amendment, the House shocked the administration by slashing the funds for the European portion of the bill, a move that would have implications in the Senate for the China bloc's fortunes. In what Acheson later described as one of its "beserk moods," the lower body accepted by 238 to 122 the Richards-Vorys amendment cutting the European arms authorization in half. Many of the amendment's supporters were also friends of China who had once voted with the administration on European aid. The subheadline on the first page of the next morning's *New York Times* told the story: "Leadership Taken Unaware—Deserted by GOP Who Usually Help—Hope Put in Senate Restoration." The hope for restoration, however, appeared to rest more and more in the hands of the Senate China bloc.[23]

The First Knowland Offensive

While the House was preparing to deal its blow, the Senate China bloc was preparing its own. Knowland had begun his drive to obtain China aid amid radio broadcasts, press conferences, circular letters, floor speeches, and, in the combined committee, with a well-publicized effort to bring General Douglas MacArthur back from Japan to testify on the MAP bill. In identical letters sent to the secretaries of defense and state on 6 August, he urged that MacArthur and Vice Admiral Oscar Badger, the senior naval commander in the Western Pacific, be recalled to testify "on

the Far Eastern phase of the problem which is global in character." While
the China bloc knew that the general would not return, its members also
knew that the publicity associated with the effort to recall him would
publicize the amendment.[24]

When the administration proved unresponsive to his recall motion,
Knowland brought the question before the combined committee in the
form of a motion and immediately ran afoul of the frequently ill-humored
committee chairman, Tom Connally. Connally, the MAP bill's chief
spokesman, did not suffer his political opponents gladly even on his best
days, and he had not been having many good days since Vandenberg had
forced the redrafting of the first MAP bill. He had an especially low
tolerance for William Knowland, the lowest-ranking member of the combined committee, the leader of the China bloc, and one of the State
Department's most vocal critics. It was "unfair," Connally charged in a
heated executive session on 10 August, for Knowland to inject "that
thing" into the committee's deliberations.[25]

Meanwhile, from the "greatest living American in the Far East," the
first comment was a terse "no comment" with the elaboration that his
views on Pacific policy were "fully on file with the Department of the
Army." Expanding on this statement several days later, MacArthur
adopted a more characteristic tone. "Needless to say it is difficult for me
to ignore the heartwarming and friendly overtures to return to my native
land, for which it is natural for me to long just as would anybody else in
my circumstances. But an impelling sense of duty in a position of highly
critical responsibility leaves me no other recourse."

The general's disinclination to return, as reported in the Friday morning papers and read to the committee by Connally, did not dissuade
Knowland from pressing forward. A "committee of the Senate of the
United States is entitled to get the best firsthand information they can
regarding the situation which is very much at issue," he insisted. With the
votes of two Democrats and all the Republicans, Knowland forced Chairman Connally to invite formally the two commanders in the Far East to
testify before the committee by a vote of 13 to 12. Connally called the
resolution's adoption a "shameful act," a characterization his colleagues
compelled him to withdraw. After the meeting, when a reporter asked
him for a copy of the resolution after the vote on 12 August, the chairman
gave it to him with disdain, snapping "Certainly, I shall have no further
use for it."[26]

As expected, the general declined the invitation, opting to remain in the more tranquil Far East. Admiral Badger, however cabled that he would return to Washington to testify around 6 September.[27]

The Department Counterattacks

Over the next three weeks the combined Senate committee largely ignored the China question while it disposed of other aspects of the bill; congressional discussion of China continued outside the committee. On the day after the disastrous House vote, Walter Judd launched his sharpest attack on the recently released China White Paper. On the following Sunday, Senators Pat McCarran, Styles Bridges, William Knowland, and Kenneth Wherry issued a joint statement denouncing the document. The State Department's high command discussed the attacks at length in a meeting on Monday morning, 22 August, and decided that the time had come for the secretary to strike back at the White Paper's critics, especially Walter Judd.[28]

Later in the day, in a related move, Ernest Gross urged Dean Acheson to compromise on the European portion of the bill. Gross explained that there were three groups in the combined committee: one group, lead by Tydings and Connally, supported the full $1.16 billion authorization for Europe; the second group, led by Vandenberg (and John Foster Dulles from outside the committee), were for a straight $1 billion; the third group, led by Georgia Democrat Richard Russell, supported the 50 percent House cut. Gross advised that the first and second groups be united on a nine-month, $1 billion military aid program. After accepting Gross's advice, Acheson communicated his retreat to Louis Johnson and Tom Connally in afternoon phone calls. In talking to Connally, Acheson also asked if the senator could meet with him alone in the next day or so. An appointment was made for the following day. With the European aid problem made more tractable by compromise, Acheson was in a stronger position to deal with the China bloc and ready to secure adoption of his Asian contingency fund.[29]

Tuesday, 23 August, began with the morning papers carrying stories describing the efforts of John Foster Dulles to reach a compromise on both the amount of aid for Europe and the question of China aid. The New York senator told reporters that he had put a China compromise before Ambassador Jessup and received some indication that the department might agree to give arms to non-Communist forces in China.

With talk of compromise in the air, Acheson met Connally in the afternoon and, it is likely, gave him a State Department draft amendment for the Far East. The next day Connally let the press know that he and the administration were now willing to allow a $100 million contingency fund for the "Far East" to be attached to the military assistance bill, a position consistent with Acheson's position before the House Foreign Affairs Committee.[30]

Both the China bloc and the administration appeared to be moving toward a compromise. While Acheson counterattacked the critics of the White Paper on Wednesday, State Department spokesmen informed the press the next day that the department was willing to have the word "China" attached to the phrase "Far East" in a description of the area where the president might, at his discretion, use the contingency fund.

On Friday, 26 August, Knowland appeared to be joining the spirit of compromise when he offered the committee new language for his amendment; the compromise offer was taken after a meeting Thursday night with Philip Jessup and several China bloc members. The new language gave the president authority to spend $210,640,000 for military assistance for non-Communist China, Korea, the Philippines, and "any other nation in the Far East." Of that sum, Knowland later explained, $175 million was for China, $17.64 million for Korea and the Philippines, and $18 million for "any other nation." As a further concession, China aid would be used only at the president's discretion. After receiving this amendment, the committee passed over the question while it disposed of other parts of the bill.[31]

The committee considered China aid next when a subcommittee, composed of Senators Connally, Vandenberg, Tydings, and Republican Chan Gurney of South Dakota, and attended by Ernest Gross, convened on 30 August to fix the amount of European aid. After settling on $1 billion, the senators turned to China. Tydings was thoroughly opposed to the pending amendment and observed that Knowland was "primarily interested in getting the principle of China aid inserted." Perhaps, he said, in order to get maximum support for the bill, it might be "wise to put in $50 million for China to be expended only if, as, and when the President deemed it wise to support and stabilize the Chinese situation." After Gross said that the State Department "flatly opposed" Knowland's amendment, Connally offered language that, he said, the secretary of state had suggested: "In consideration of the concern of the United States in the present situation in the Far East," the amendment read, "X" dollars were authorized to be appropriated to "accomplish in that area the policies and purposes declared in this act." It would be deemed "inadvisable to specify the nature of such expenditures."

"The idea of the State Department, Acheson among them," Connally explained, "is they are willing to agree to some substantial sum strictly to be within the control of the President and without mentioning China or without mentioning any arms aid to China, leaving it up to the whole area of Asia, so that he can help here or help there. But that is as far as I understand."

Tydings saw the amendment's value lying in the support it might gain for the entire bill. "We are in basic agreement on this bill," he said. "Our problem now is whether we want to go ahead and fight the Chinese combination—and I believe we would win . . . or whether we want to give them this money under these conditions where it may never be spent at all and go out of our committee pretty near unanimous." Connally said that he was "against the whole Chinese thing" but was willing to go along with $50 million. Senator Tydings objected to such a large sum and Ernest Gross said that Acheson preferred a smaller amount.

Arthur Vandenberg was troubled with constitutional scruples. "We are," he said, voicing his only recorded objection, "the victims of our own form of government at this point. I have no doubt in the world that the President of the United States, handed $100 million, without the necessity of even accounting for half of it, could by intrigue and manipulation raise unshirted hell in the Far East and do $5 billion worth of damage to the cause of communism, and that is what I would like to do, but I do not know how you would do it under our form of government."

"A small, unvouchered, confidential fund," replied Ernest Gross. "He has had it before. In wartime it went up over 100 million." "Wilson had more than that," added Connally. "OSS was financed in part that way," continued Gross. Furthermore, if it were necessary to win the agreement of Senator Knowland, the secretary would not object to the mentioning of China. Tydings suggested that the words "present situation in the Far East" be changed to "present situation in China and the Far East." Connally agreed to this alteration. Tydings and Connally also thought it was wise to keep the use of the fund secret. Connally explained that the State Department wanted the "money to be secret so they can bribe some of these war lords and others." Vandenberg ended the discussion with the prediction that the Connally amendment would not placate Knowland.[32]

While the question of the China amendment was left unresolved, the subcommittee had made significant progress. As a result of its decision on $1 billion for European arms aid, the full committee was no longer seriously divided and thus open to China bloc exploitation. In the week following the subcommittee meeting, both Tydings and Connally assured Acheson that not only could they kill the Knowland amendment, but they could come up with a $50 million contingency fund for Asia as well.[33]

A "Sop" for Knowland

Senator Knowland's final offensive began when Admiral Badger arrived in Washington in early September. It was a time of confusion over the administration's position on a Far Eastern amendment and of heightened ill feeling between Connally and Knowland. The confusion arose when Connally, contrary to the State Department's and his own earlier position, told the press that he would not allow the word "China" to be attached to the phrase "Far East" (making it "China and the Far East") as the stated recipient in his amendment. In spite of repeated efforts by his staff and Ernest Gross to assure him that the reference to China would not compel the administration to spend money there, the chairman continued, as Gross put it, to "slip a cog" on the subject for several days. The further decline in the Connally-Knowland relationship came after a sharp floor debate between the two men in which Connally claimed that Chiang Kai-shek had "absconded" to Formosa with $138 million of gold.[34]

Badger's 8 September appearance before the committee in executive session added little that was new to the debate. The admiral, who wanted to send aid to China, offered only another version of the Chennault Plan and his testimony played more into the hands of Connally than Knowland. After the meeting, Connally discussed the testimony with reporters and linked it to his own administration-drafted amendment that had recently appeared in the press. The admiral, he said, had recommended putting $75 million in the president's hands to be used at his discretion. When reporters noted the similarity of this idea to Connally's amendment, the chairman agreed while avoiding a direct comparison. Knowland told the press simply that Badger's testimony had "helped the China case" and that the administration had not yet offered his group anything "firm."[35]

The day after Badger testified, the committee passed by 12 to 7 Connally's amendment (Connally having settled on the amount Badger had recommended) authorizing $75 million for the president's discretionary use "in China and the Far East." Knowland made it clear that he was not satisfied. "In this case," he complained, "he could spend it in Borneo and the Congress is foreclosed from knowing where it was spent or under what conditions." After the meeting, he condemned it as "a mere sop, a mere gesture." The prospect now loomed that he would file a minority report, take his fight to the Senate floor, and perhaps damage the bipartisan coalition the administration had hoped to have behind the Senate bill.[36]

On Monday morning, 12 September, the combined committee conveyed its last meeting. Before it reported the bill, Arthur Vandenberg healed what had seemed to be an irreparable breach over the China issue. He recommended that the wording in the Connally substitute be amended to read "China" instead of "China and the Far East," and that the funds be spent in "that general area." With his changes, the amendment now read:

> In consideration of the concern of the United States in the present situation in China, there is hereby authorized to be appropriated to the President, out of any moneys in the Treasury not otherwise appropriated, the sum of $75,000,000 in addition to funds otherwise provided as an emergency fund for the President, which may be expended to accomplish in that general area the policies and purposes declared in this Act. Certification by the President of the amounts expended out of funds authorized hereunder, and that it is inadvisable to specify the nature of such expenditures, shall be deemed a sufficient voucher for the amounts expended.

The committee quickly adopted this change by a vote of 17 to 6, with Connally voting a contentious "no" and all the Republicans and most Democrats voting yes.[37]

Senator Knowland at last expressed satisfaction, telling reporters that while the amendment did "not accomplish so much as I hoped, it definitely does change the trend of our policy toward China. It is a recognition of the importance of China." Connally did not see it this way. In his press conference after the meeting a reporter asked if the new language changed the sense of his amendment. "Not a bit," Connally replied, "We hope it changes Senator Knowland. We offered it to get his vote . . . we put in that general area simply as a sop to try to get some votes."[38]

The Connally amendment, as further amended, became Section 303 of the MAP bill. Floor debate began on 19 September and lasted four days.

With the controversy taken out of the China amendment, the senators spent little time discussing it. Tom Connally, as floor manager, explained on the first day that the "broad grant of authority" in the China provision was to allow the president "swiftly [to] take whatever action seems to be necessary either with respect to China itself or other countries, in that general area, such as Burma, Indochina, India, and other countries." The president would have "complete freedom of action to deal with the protection of our interests in that part of the world in any way he sees fit."[39]

In an unusual duet, Senator Knowland agreed with Connally's definition of the "general area of China" and observed that the term was more restrictive than "Far East." That wording might have allowed use of the funds in the Dutch East Indies. Connally replied that the "general area of China" was a little more restrictive than the "Far East." Nothing in the measure, he said, "would permit the use of any of these funds in colonial areas. The Senator from California has referred to Indonesia. Of course, the President and the Congress can instantly cut off any money before it is used on projects of that character; and before any money is used for such purposes, there must be general agreements." Senator Claude Pepper added that the committee did not wish to limit the fund's use to China.[40]

The next day Senators Vandenberg and Dulles made brief, favorable references to the China provision.[41] The only discordant note came from Senator Guy Gillette who quoted a recent Walter Lippmann column likening the "offer to contain communism in Asia for $75,000,000 a year" to the deal offered by "the man who had the bright idea of selling the Brooklyn Bridge to widows and orphans for a downpayment of $2.75." Nobody responded to Gillette's brief criticism and the Senate passed the bill with Section 303 remaining exactly as the combined committee had reported it.[42]

When the House-Senate conference committee took up the differing versions of the MAP bill on 26 September, Connally once again interpreted the phrase "general area of China" as an unimportant alteration of the original language of his amendment. It was "just a dodge of language which in effect would mean the Far East," he explained. "Well, a lot of them kicked and bucked and snorted about the Far East. . . . So we struck out the Far East and inserted 'that general area', meaning China and that area around it, for instance, Burma, India, [laughter]. If their purpose is to stop the advance of communism, why, they might have to do something in Burma."

John Vorys, a House conferee, made the China bloc's only attempt to alter the amendment by eliminating "this blank check secret business" and by making the amendment's purpose conform to the intent of the China Aid Act of 1948. When he asked if the State Department favored a "$75 million slush fund for the Far East," the ubiquitous Ernest Gross requested a chance to make a statement for the record. Speaking "directly and personally" for the secretary of state, he stressed that, whereas the department had not asked for the authorization, it would not oppose it if Congress, on its own initiative, gave the president such a grant of power. "It might prove very useful as a confidential fund as the months ahead unroll. It might be used in other areas of the Far East which are affected by the developments in China. That would include such areas as Burma, [or] the northern part of Indochina, if it becomes desirable to suppress communism in that country."[43]

The conference committee adopted the amendment as passed by the Senate with only John Vorys voting against it. Congress passed the Mutual Defense Assistance Act of 1949 on 28 September without any further debate on Section 303 and with the full $1 billion voted for the North Atlantic Treaty states. On 6 October, the president signed the bill into law. At the administration's request, Congress appropriated without controversy the $75 million for Section 303 in a bill that passed on 28 October.[44]

With the exception of Senator Gillette's brief criticism, available records do not disclose in any step of the legislative process a congressional effort to probe the confidential fund's possible uses outside of China. Some congressmen raised fleeting and ambiguous questions about the wisdom of granting the president such broad discretionary authority, but they did so mostly behind closed committee doors and did not pursue them. Most of the public and executive session debate leading to Section 303's adoption concerned the question of aiding non-Communist forces within China's borders. The "compromise" found senators and congressmen, who had haggled at length over the amount and use of aid for Europe, handing the president $75 million (and perhaps more, via the 5-percent transfer clause) to spend in Asia as he saw fit. It suggested that Congress either did not understand what it was doing or, more likely, was willing to delegate responsibility for Asian policy, with all its puzzlement, to the executive branch. Perhaps it was both.

Historians writing about the "general area of China" fund have generally dismissed it as an insignificant sop the administration gave the China bloc that had little impact on China or Asian policy in general. Some contemporary observers, however, saw it was important. In a brief *News-*

week article in September, the magazine mentioned the amendment the Senate committee had recently reported. It rated the legislation as a "historical development in American foreign policy." Although Truman and his predecessor had emergency funds that could be spent in secret, there had never been such a "broad grant of power" given a president in peacetime. When Congress passed the bill, it was predicted the fund would "for the first time make possible clandestine support of promising anti-Communist regimes or individuals in Asia. In that respect it holds an important key to new U.S. policy in the Orient."[45] The prophecy was deficient only in that it did not foresee that the fund could be used for overt as well as covert aid.

9

Dividing the Pie

After passage of the MAP bill, Congress quickly disposed of some matters relating to Asian policy and left others unresolved before adjourning on 19 October 1949. The Butterworth nomination, which had been delayed until after publication of the White Paper, finally came to a vote on 27 September. The administration won an easy victory, 49 to 27. The "general area of China" compromise had taken much of the heat out of the issue. In a Senate Republican Policy Committee meeting held a week before the vote, Senator Vandenberg indicated his willingness to make a motion to recommit the nomination, but he pointed out that not to oppose it might be preferable "since the majority had met with success in getting the $75,000,000 appropriation for China in the Military Assistance Program." Vandenberg and nineteen other senators failed to show up for the vote.[1]

The Korean aid bill remained bottled up by the House Rules Committee but Congress did advance $60 million in two interim appropriations for the program before it adjourned.[2] Speeches by China bloc members were few in number and subdued in tone. A number of congressmen and senators journeyed to the Far East during the adjournment. Knowland went the greatest distance by traveling with General Chennault to beleaguered Chungking to confer with Chiang Kai-shek. Knowland and other friends of China would return to the second session of the 81st Congress with renewed enthusiasm for their cause and first-hand reports to support their special insight about the problems of the Far East.

By late October, however, Congress was out. The administration was left with $75 million to spend, bleak prospects in China, and a deteriorating situation in Southeast Asia. The State Department spent most of the rest of the year trying to sort out what its China policy should be and whether to spend the money there or elsewhere.

Peking Seeks Recognition

In China, blatant anti-Americanism subsided somewhat after July but by no means vanished, and the fundamentally hostile Communist position toward the West remained. The American President Line ship *General Gordon* arrived in Shanghai under State Department sponsorship on 23 September and left in the early morning two days later carrying 420 Americans. The Communists and the Nationalists cooperated in the unprecedented voyage by allowing the ship to dock and depart unmolested. The authorities in Shanghai, however, withheld exit permits for eighteen Americans in charge of important businesses; Ward and his staff were still unable to leave Mukden, and throughout China the Communists continued to make life difficult for Americans who remained.[3]

On 1 October, after convening a Political Consultative Congress composed of both Communist and non-Communist political elements, the Communists established a formal government. On the same day they renamed their capital "Peking"—the pre-Nationalist name of Peiping—and sent notes to foreign missions requesting diplomatic recognition. The American consulate general received one also, addressed to "Mr. O. Edmund Clubb."

> Sir: Mao Tse-tung, Chairman of the Central People's Government of the Peoples Republic of China, on this date issued a public statement. I am sending this public statement to you, Sir, with the hope that you will transmit it to your country's Government. I consider that it is necessary that there be established normal diplomatic relations between the People's Republic of China and all countries of the world. Chou En-lai (signature and seal), Minister of Foreign Affairs of the Central People's Government of the People's Republic of China, Peking, October 1, 1949.[4]

The State Department's first response was to issue a statement that the United States continued to recognize the Nationalist regime and to assure Congress that it would be consulted before changing this policy. It also indicated that the department was in no hurry to alter this policy.[5] The request forced the Truman administration to consider several factors: advice from diplomats in the field; assessments of the success of its common-front policy to extract maximum concessions from the Communists; and estimates of probable domestic political reaction if it "abandoned" the Nationalists before their actual demise.

The diplomat to whom the State Department listened most carefully about Communist affairs in China was O. Edmund Clubb. Clubb had continued to transmit reports to Washington in the fall indicating that the new rulers of China were not irretrievably in the Soviet camp. On 24 September, an emissary from Democratic League leader Lo Lung-chi called on the consul general to relay a long message from Lo who had recently held a conversation with Mao Tse-tung. Through the emissary, Lo stressed that the United States would have to choose between the Nationalists and Peking. As Clubb reported, "Lo considered Mao's attitude regarding general question Sino-American relations moderate, that Mao [was a] realist, not Communist extremist," and the United States could not expect China to "change quickly its attitude toward USA." Lo expressed an interest in obtaining American economic assistance for China and passed along a friendly suggestion. Referring to Acheson's statement in the White Paper's letter of transmittal, Lo said that it "would be helpful if Americans refrained from open announcement [of] support [for] Chinese democratic elements." Lo's own position would have been stronger had Acheson not issued his letter. He noted, for instance, that "there was to have been setup [a] foreign relations committee headed by Chou En-lai with Lo and [Democratic League member] Chang Tung-sun participating but that project had been abandoned after issuance [of the] White Paper." Assessing Lo's message, Clubb took the same frosty attitude he held during his last contact with the Democratic League leader in July. "His basic proposal is USA should not expect return for anything given. . . . Lo seemed indulging himself in favorite Chinese pastime of eating cake but proposing have it too."[6]

After the Communist invitation to establish diplomatic relations, Clubb reflected on the formation of the new government and the latest Lo overtures in an 8 October cable to Washington. He recommended that the United States maintain a noncommittal attitude for the present, "but through present crack in door early endeavoring show some interest in the planning, intentions, and policies [of the] regime." He wanted the Communists to "get [a] glimpse of concrete benefits to be obtained through commerce (without slightest hint USA would give charity) and good relations with non-Soviet countries." Finally, if the new rulers of China seemed "willing [to] adopt more reasonable attitude and [to] indicate readiness [to] follow usual standards international behavior," then the United States should "recognize that government and maintain relations with it even as with USSR and East European countries."[7]

Several days later, Clubb cabled an even more encouraging assessment. There was good reason to believe that "Communist leaders truly desire American recognition and regularization relations for both political and economic reasons which this office has previously outlined." In support of this he noted "that, coincident with bid, since October 1, press has carried little anti-American material (except few special features)." While the decline in hostile propaganda might simply be the result of press attention devoted to establishment of the new government, there was also another explanation: "some real shift in Communist propaganda line to aid People's Government's bid for recognition." Clubb observed that in his 19 July conversation with Lo, the Democratic League leader had indicated that the Communists would not sue for recognition. Chou's message to Clubb on 1 October had obviously reversed that policy. "If Communists willing make concessions, reason would . . . be rooted in political and economic exigencies: They need at least moderately good relations with USA in more ways than one."[8] American diplomats in Moscow and London also conveyed similar advice.[9]

Support from a selected group of American business leaders chosen to consult with the State Department and the apparent failure of the "common-front" policy toward recognition reinforced the advice that the department received from its diplomats. The Chinese note on 1 October stirred the British to respond with a demarché that verged on de facto recognition.[10] The department also soon learned that other non-Communist governments might recognize the Peking regime in the near future but decided to remain steady on course.[11] With a Nationalist government still alive in China, and with strong opposition to recognition in the general public, in Congress, and in the White House, it instructed Clubb to answer Chou's note with a polite acknowledgement and a query about Angus Ward and his staff.[12] On 12 October, the department cabled American foreign missions that its views on the subject of recognition had not changed since June.

Announcement of establishment Chi Commie "Govt" long anticipated development and does not in US view lend any special
urgency to consideration question recog by non-Commie countries.
Development does however point up necessity interested friendly
Govts, in their own interests, maintain common attitude respecting
question.[13]

While the Communists established their government in Peking, the old
regime's position in the south deteriorated at an accelerating pace. The
Nationalists abandoned Canton on 14 October and the remnants of the
old regime fled to Chungking. Pockets of resistance held out in the
southwest and northwest, but there was no personality capable of rallying
support. As one State Department report to the president in mid-November put it, "disintegration is apparent in all fields and is likely to increase
in geometrical progression."[14] On Formosa the situation continued to
look grave. "Without US military occupation and control," the CIA predicted in October, "Taiwan, like the rest of China, probably will be under
Chinese Communist control by the end of 1950."[15]

Bleak Southeast Asian Prospects

Elsewhere in the Far East, the two major Southeast Asian countries in
crisis still concerned the State Department. The Indonesian situation
remained stable but could erupt again at any moment and destroy the
negotiations begun in August at the Hague. The prospects in Indochina
were bleaker. On 19 October, the CIA informed the president that "with
the forces now available, the French can do no more than maintain the
present stalemate. . . . If present circumstances continue basically un-
changed, the Vietnamese nationalists will probably be able to drive the
French out of Indochina within two years" with catastrophic results. The
loss of Indochina to the Communists "might be the critical breach in the
non-Communist crescent around China, which now consists of India, the
Southeast Asian peninsula, Indochina, the Philippines, and Japan. The
US interest in preserving this crescent intact is therefore threatened by
the current trend in Indochina."[16]

None of these developments in the latter part of 1949 departed
dramatically from trends that American policy planners had observed
earlier in the year. State Department plans to reverse the West's declining
position in Southeast Asia were still modest by late August. Along with
the half-hearted acceptance of the measures prescribed in PPS–51 to save
the subcontinent, the department in May agreed in principle at the under

secretary's level to an aid program of about $400 million that the United States would provide to the International Monetary Fund, the Export-Import Bank, and other agencies for technical and economic assistance to the region.[17] The Southeast Asian Affairs Division also held discussion in the spring about small amounts of military aid for Indonesia, Thailand, and perhaps Indochina—if the Bao Dai experiment appeared to have a chance of succeeding—as something that might be desirable.[18]

Discussion of economic and military aid for Southeast Asia, exclusive of the Philippines, was, however, hypothetical before 12 September. Prior to that date, the MAP contingency fund was in peril, and the prospect for passage of a separate bill funding Southeast Asia aid was not bright. Thus, when the combined Senate committee reported Section 303 of the MAP bill, the money it authorized began to influence the thinking of officials charged with planning Southeast Asian policy. Congress had given the administration a pie that could be cut many ways. And, even if the initial slices were small, they were large enough to whet numerous appetites at home and abroad and to stimulate the creation of a policy of military containment by proxy in Southeast Asia.

Foreign Requests for 303 Funds

Before the Truman administration introduced MAP in late July, several existing and prospective Asian governments expressed an interest in obtaining military assistance under the omnibus arms bill. Interest in arms aid rose when Congress began considering the bill in August and, before its final enactment, the administration was faced with an international chorus asking "Where's mine?"

The Chinese Nationalists filed the earliest and the largest request. Anticipating the enactment of a China bloc amendment to the MAP bill, and as part of an effort to encourage its passage, on 15 August, 1949 the Chinese embassy gave the State Department a memorandum requesting $287 million for a program "of a short term character" to assist Nationalist forces fighting the Communists.[19] Informally, Ambassador Wellington Koo showed the request to Senators William Knowland and John Foster Dulles to allow them to counter any assertions in a Senate debate that the Nationalist government had not even sought aid.[20] Koo and his agents lobbied for passage of the amendment and, after the combined committee reported the 12 September "compromise," the ambassador began pressing State Department officials for prompt expenditure of the $75 million in China through the country's recognized government.[21]

Another high-ranking Chinese official in America who took a proprietary interest in the $75 million was Dr. Kan Chieh-hou, the "Personal Representative" of Acting President Li Tsung-jen. Kan, whose constituency was somewhat different from Ambassador Koo's, sent a letter to President Truman on 30 September congratulating him for signing the MAP bill (a premature gesture since Truman did not actually sign it until six days later). Kan noted that the measure included an appropriation of $75 million "for aid to China" and that he had acquainted both Rusk and Butterworth with "all the details of how best to utilize the new appropriation." Having done this, he explained, "I shall refrain from burdening you with same." In a conversation on 16 September, Kan had spoken to Rusk and Butterworth, urging that a commission of three or five Americans be sent to China with complete authority to spend the fund. If it were channeled through Acting President Li rather than the "retired" Chiang Kai-shek, Kan assured them that Li would "take over" Formosa. On 12 October, he followed up his letter to Truman with another urgent appeal for "the immediate allocation of the funds already voted for by Congress and for your immediate release of these funds."[22]

Other appeals for American aid came from both Formosa and mainland China, transmitted by Acting President Li, Li's son, the Nationalist Foreign Office in Chungking, other officials of the fractured Nationalist government, and semiautonomous warlords scattered throughout Northwest and Southwest China.[23] General Lu Han, the warlord of Yunnan, was pessimistic about the success of resistance to the Communists in the southwest. According to the American vice consul in Kunming, Lu believed that the $75 million would, if supervised by a United States military mission, effectively stop the Communists. Without it, he observed, "everything would be over in a few months."[24]

From Southeast Asia and Europe came other requests for 303 funds. In May and June 1949, an Indonesian police official in the United States sought assistance in the form of police equipment for his emerging nation.[25] In July, the Thais expressed hope that small amounts of arms and equipment would be available under the MAP program to help them combat Communist infiltration from Malaya.[26] French officials conveyed their interest in American help in a Foreign Ministers meeting on 15 September, three days after the Senate committee reported the MAP bill. After MAP's final passage, officials in Bao Dai's regime also began to evince interest in obtaining military assistance.[27]

Before granting any of these requests, the United States government had to decide how it wanted to spend the money. The first consideration was whether it should be dispersed to anti-Communist forces surviving in China, to Formosa, to fragile countries and colonial areas in Asia threatened by the Chinese revolution, or to all three. It took the Truman Administration three and a half months to reach a decision.

The Administration's Plans

One of the first direct connections between the 303 fund and Asia policy was explicitly drawn in a 13 September meeting of Far Eastern experts held to brief Acheson for a meeting with the British foreign secretary. It was also apparently the first large meeting the secretary held with his advisors since the Ma generals of Northwest China had quit fighting.

A centerpiece in the discussion was a 2 September telegram from the Nanking embassy recommending a future China policy. The cable reviewed three conclusions that could be drawn from recent history: the Chinese Communists were here to stay "for some time"; any successful movement to resist them would have to be "purely Chinese"; and there was no current prospect that an anti-Communist leader might arise who could successfully challange the new regime. Given these premises, a new policy "should be to prevent China from becoming reinforcement to Soviet power." To achieve this end, the United States "must wait for development [of] Chinese Titoism, meanwhile doing nothing to encourage growth of strong Communist China." A policy of outright hostility toward the country's new rulers or support of subversive activities "would be unlikely to contribute toward detachment of China from USSR because it would conflict with, rather than make use of, Chinese chauvinism."[28]

Most of those attending the session, including the consultants, FE representatives, and Ambassador Stuart, "were in general agreement with the line of policy stated in the telegram." Acheson had reservations about the cable's recommended policy of "dignified aloofness." He thought "there would be some difficulty in applying the policy . . . in view of the attitude of U.S. public opinion and Congress. For instance, there was the question of the use of 75 million dollars of discretionary funds in the MAP Act."[29] By the afternoon the secretary was impressed enough to read the telegram to Bevin as a memorandum on the China situation that "expressed our views so clearly."[30]

After 13 September, the State Department considered the use of 303 funds at two levels: at an operational level, where officers in sub-bureaucracies sketched programs for the fund's use; and at the high-policy level, where the question of how to use the money recurred in numerous forums. The money was, by its mere existence, nudging American Asian policy in a more activist direction.

Detailed planning for the fund's use began in late September, when Livingston Merchant of FE was asked, in his words, "to conduct a preliminary survey of the claimants and uses to which these funds could be most effectively put."[31] Merchant first studied the nature of the gift from Congress. An early step was to ask Ernest Gross, still in charge of the department's Congressional relations, about the precise meaning of the phrase "general area of China." The "Far East," Gross replied in a 21 September memorandum.[32] Another FE officer reported the same day that the Congressional Liaison Office felt "there was very little doubt that the [Senate] Committee intended to put all or a substantial part of the fund into China." However, it was "further clear" that its use "in the contiguous areas such as Indochina or Burma or other countries in the area" was permissible as well.[33] Reassured, Merchant turned to the department's Legal Office for a ruling on foreign governments that the administration might aid. There were no limitations, replied the Legal Office on 5 October.[34]

With this affirmation about the broad scope of the legislation, Merchant requested that the constituent units of FE provide "horseback" recommendations for possible expenditures of the fund.[35] The geographic divisions were quick to discover uses for the money. The China division replied that it could not recommend a program of military assistance to China at that time but, in case it did at some future point, the division foresaw the possible need for $40 million.[36] After consulting other units of FE and the Office of Near East, African, and South Asian Affairs (NEA), Merchant made a preliminary estimate of how the money might be earmarked. He listed $25 million set aside for possible "covert military assistance to provincial leaders in China," $8 million for the French in Indochina after ratification of the 8 March accord, $8.5 million for Siam, $12 million for a possible supplement to MAP and already scheduled for Korea and the Philippines, an undetermined amount for an increased propaganda program for China, and an undetermined amount for Burma. He specifically excluded India, Pakistan, and Malaya, all in

NEA's domain, from the list.[37]

On 17 October, Merchant circulated his estimate in the department and the next day Dean Rusk convened a meeting to discuss it. The meeting concluded with Rusk instructing FE to prepare a memorandum to Acheson selecting "the two or three most urgent projects" to be supported.[38] Butterworth responded by producing three memoranda. The first urged that the question of overt aid to China "be met squarely without delay." After a lengthy explanation about why overt aid would be wasted, he turned to covert aid. "It is believed . . . that some part of the funds should be reserved for possible use in supplying *covert* military assistance to promising resistance groups within China if and when an opportunity to do this arises and for remedying specific military supply deficiencies on Formosa if this becomes necessary and desirable."[39] A second memorandum dealt with the question of covert aid to non-Communist Chinese.[40] A third paper noted the need for the United States to assist "in every possible way" the ability of governments in the "general area of China" to put down "internal revolt" and resist "external Communist pressure." The funds "now available under Section 303 afford an extraordinary opportunity for the United States to act quickly in the light of this situation." Butterworth concluded by outlining the programs that FE supported: $1.01 million for propaganda in China, $10 million for "police equipment" in Indonesia, $5 million for Thailand, $1.22 million for river patrol boats in Burma. While Indochina had been deleted from an initial list, the Southeast Asia Division hoped that the region might receive military aid after France implemented the 8 March accord and after other Asian states recognized Vietnam.[41]

The FE position on 303 fund use did not rest well with Assistant Secretary of State George McGhee, the head of the Near East and South Asia office. McGhee was unhappy that the two largest countries in South Asia were excluded from direct American aid. In discussions with Merchant, Butterworth, and Rusk, he reserved his position and, on 24 October, he appealed his case to Acheson. Both the Congressional Liaison and the Legal Offices, he argued, had interpreted Section 303 as granting wide discretion to the president to spend the money. "India is the keystone to our developing policy in the whole of the general area envisioned by the Act"; nor should Pakistan or Afghanistan be eliminated from consideration either. While at present he could only recommend aid to Burma, he wanted the door kept open to spend money in other areas in South Asia. His appeal was in vain.[42]

Acheson Remains Hard Line

As 303 fund programming proceeded in the department's working level, the policy review process that Philip Jessup and the consultants started in August began generating recommendations. Departing from the dominant hard-line tone of recent operational discussions with respect to China, the group sent Acheson a memorandum on 2 September outlining "Tentative Findings on United States Policy in the Far East." The brief paper sketched a program of "psychological warfare" that was necessary if the United States were "to take the initiative and to appeal to the imagination." Its finding that "Asia and the Far East present a single problem and should be covered by a single policy" contradicted FE's conclusion that Asia was not susceptible to a single policy. Other parts of the document endorsed a number of old ideas (presidential statement on the Far East, a statement on Southeast Asia by the Western foreign ministers, an Asian trip by a high-ranking American official, creation of a Pacific-States union, enactment of Point IV, enactment of a discretionary fund), and urged the pursuit of Titoism in China. The memorandum drew considerable criticism. Jessup's effort to follow it up by drafting a flowery declaration to be issued by the United States, Britain, France, and the Netherlands was picked to pieces in FE and eventually killed by EUR.[43]

The consultants' memorandum did not immediately alter Acheson's hard line views on China policy or have any other perceptible effect on American policy. Not even the briefing on 13 September convinced Acheson that the policy of pursuing Titoism in China was worth much investment. After the collapse of the front in Northwest China, the secretary still remained interested in aiding non-Communist forces in China. In a conversation with Governor Dewey on 21 September, recounted in a memorandum drafted by Jessup, he candidly revealed his thoughts. After discussing the recent mistakes and defeats of the Nationalist army, Acheson pointed out that "the various centers of resistance in south, southwest, central and northwest China [called] attention to the fact that in each instance the local forces were capable merely of guerrilla resistance." It was possible for the United States "to render certain types of assistance to some of these resisting elements," he explained and "pointed to the fact that, if Congress passed the $75,000,000 confidential fund . . . we would have sufficient funds to accomplish the limited kind of operation which was called for."[44]

Acheson continued to take a hard line before an executive session of the Senate Foreign Relations Committee three weeks later. "This Chinese Government is really a tool of Russian imperialism in China," he told the committee on 12 October. "That gives us our fundamental starting point in regard to our relations with China." He endorsed the existing trade policy, which was, he pointed out, influenced by Japan's need for a foreign market. Although the United States protested the Nationalist blockade of the China coast for reasons of international law, he favored the obstruction as being "helpful to the West generally in creating problems for the Communists in Shanghai." When asked about the prospects for Chinese Titoism, the secretary allowed Jessup to summarize the department's position. There were, Jessup said, "a good many elements which would suggest that possibility. We do not think it is safe to bank on it. But it is clear that in the Tito situation that [it] was brought about by Russian action and the internal situation in Yugoslavia and not by any action of the West."[45]

Acheson also briefed the committee on possible uses of overt and covert aid. Early in the hearing he had explained his reason for opposing overt aid: "It will solidify the Chinese people against us in favor of the Communist government, and will be vastly expensive and in the long run it will be futile." Later he noted that the administration had considered groups in China it might assist: "The great difficulty is that by the time you have about made up your mind that somebody is a pretty 'stout fellow' and is going to stay with you, he is over on the other side." Asked about General Claire Chennault's plan, he said that it was "very unwise." The administration was "investigating every possibility of giving some sort of support as quiet as possible to any group we really wanted to stand firm and maintain their position. But, as I said, by the time we had just about concluded that our friends, the Ma's—they are the favorites of everybody, including General Chennault's—and the two brothers have decided to go to Mecca on a pilgrimage."[46]

October Policy Review

Two weeks after conferring with the Senate committee, Acheson met with a large group of advisors to review the findings of Jessup, Fosdick, and Case in a two-day Far Eastern policy discussion marathon. Jessup opened the first session on 26 October with a general argument about the American need to side with Asian nationalism in order to "recapture" the revolutionary movement from the Communists. He called for an expanded American propaganda effort and for assistance to help the "free" countries in the region become "demonstration projects" of the non-Communist way of life. After diffuse discussion, which was prevelant throughout the seminar, the conversation turned to China.

Jessup admitted that he had no startling new ideas on the subject. As revealed in the notes Charlton Ogburn took of the meeting, Acheson soon sharpened the focus by raising the question of future overt and covert aid to China. He inferred that everybody felt that use of "the President's $75 million discretionary fund for open assistance to the anti-Communist forces in China would be a bad idea" and asked "whether, first, the support of covert operations would be profitable, and second, whether such support could, in fact, be rendered correctly."

There were no conclusive answers. Ambassador Stuart and Raymond Fosdick doubted if any covert-aid project could be kept secret. Acheson wondered if they were receiving adequate information from non-Communist China, recalling that the "two Generals Ma had been widely acclaimed as highly dependable Moslems and the next thing that happened was that they went off to Mecca on a pilgrimage."

In the course of the discussion, Dean Rusk endorsed a policy of granting covert military aid to the Chinese. While counseling against granting it to organized military groups, he supported giving covert aid "in whatever form and in whatever case offered hope of fomenting dissatisfaction with the Communist regime." The United States "might provide arms for some guerrillas as a form of payment and . . . should employ whatever means were indicated in the specific cases in the furtherance of our interests—arms here, opium there, bribery and propaganda in the third place."

Butterworth questioned the consistency of rendering technical assistance to the Communists—as some of the discussants had suggested—while at the same time stirring up trouble. Fosdick stated reservations about following Rusk's program while recognizing the new regime. Rusk "believed that recognition of the Communists need not deter us from encouraging dissatisfaction with their regime. He regarded recognition as a useful lever for us to apply in prying openings in the 'Iron Curtain.' "

Rusk's views notwithstanding, the consensus was that covert aid to the mainland would be unproductive. As Acheson saw it, "our engaging in the covert supply of weapons and of stirring up guerrillas must be regarded as a short-term operation which would have to be undertaken quickly if at all—before recognition of the Chinese Communists—since the only purpose would be to slow up their advance. There would be no use in our undertaking these operations just for the sake of doing something." Someone noted that arms might be supplied "only for the purpose of winning bases for propaganda dissemination." Acheson agreed and "observed that the question was now being reduced to the scale of small policy decisions. He felt that if any operation of the kind under consideration were recommended, the burden of proof would lie with the proponents." Butterworth said that this was FE's position and that he wanted to discuss some borderline cases with the consultants; later he mentioned $1 million in 303 funds for a program of covert dissemination of propaganda.

Butterworth stayed in the background throughout much of the early discussion and spoke more to raise questions than to offer opinions. Later, however, he waded in, informing all present what existing policy was and should be, and controlled the discussion for the rest of the meeting. "Mr. Butterworth," Ogburn records,

> stated that our policy in China is based upon the fact that the ingredients of the situation in China are certain in themselves to make trouble for any Chinese regime. It was incumbent upon us to see that these ingredients operate against the Chinese Communists without risking the issue by ourselves undertaking to contribute minutely to them through acts of doubtful wisdom. Since the process will be slow and undramatic it will not appeal greatly to the American public in view of our national psychology, but it offers more promise than any other course.

Rusk observed that "we might utilize our potentialities for creating trouble as a bargaining weapon with the Chinese Communists in negotiating on recognition." Butterworth dismissed this by saying that "we would be in a doubtful position if we promised to cease illegal acts as a *quid pro quo.*" Speaking later, Acheson said that he did not regard recognition "as a major instrument for showing interest in the Chinese people or for winning concessions from the Chinese Government."

Butterworth also spoke out forcefully on other questions. He opposed large-scale trade with the Communists that might require significant American financing until the larger question of Sino-American relations was resolved. On the Formosa question, he said that the military establishment might soon recommend using American force to deny the island to the Communists. The issue involved was

> our whole moral position in the world. If, after giving assurances of our scrupulous regard for the territorial integrity of other nations and of our staunch desire to defend their sovereignty, we should, in the process of gathering together a Grand Alliance of smaller states, then take occasion to pick up a tangible asset for ourselves without regard for these assurances, the confidence we expect of the smaller nations would be destroyed. It was impossible to carry on a broad foreign policy on such a basis.

Philip Jessup agreed.

Butterworth then led the discussion away from Formosa to make two points. First, he dismissed a Jessup suggestion that Indonesia be made an American "demonstration project." That was something for the Dutch to do after granting Indonesian independence. Second, he pointed out that the European Bureau had prevented the United States from making forceful statements about emerging nations in Asia. John Davies suggested that EUR "should not exercise a veto on our policies toward the Far East." The two-and-a-half-hour discussion ended with Acheson observing that after the conclusion of current Dutch-Indonesian negotiations, "we must move more in the direction of FE's interest rather than in EUR's." He had "detected no progress toward a successful solution of the Indochina problem and felt we might have to push the French harder."[47]

The secretary met with the consultants in a smaller and shorter meeting the next day. Much of the discussion concerned the dispute between the consultants and Butterworth over the value of an "area approach" to Asia or, as Jessup put it, "a new frame of mind on the part of the Department." Such an approach would allow regional planning, "electrify both Asian and American opinion," and provide the basis for a fruitful approach to Congress in a request for foreign aid. Butterworth saw in this little but the potential for uplifted hopes in Asia that inevitably would be dashed, and he persisted that there was more that separated the countries of the Far East than joined them. Acheson sided with Butterworth. Although he had earlier endorsed the concept of an area approach in private conversations outside the department, he said that it needed further clarification and that the Policy Planning Staff, in any case, should

be giving the department a unified view of the area. Acheson also criticized a proposal, implicit in Jessup's comments, for more economic assistance to Asia. He observed that "the United States Government was
operating under a heavy deficit. What was called for in our foreign policy
was the application of more brains and fewer dollars."

When Jessup continued with a review of American policy toward individual countries, there was little further mention of American aid. For
Japan, the consensus favored an early peace settlement. They discussed
the status of India at some length, but without conclusion. In Korea,
Jessup believed that the United States should not commit its armed forces
to guarantee the country's integrity. He also noted that the department's
legal office doubted the president's $75 million could be spent there and
wanted to do something to prevent Korea from "going down the drain."

Discussion concluded with the "most difficult problem of all—Indochina." The consultants, he said, had thought that the question might be
referred to the United Nations. In response, Butterworth explained that
FE did not want to submit the Indochina question to the United Nations
before that body had resolved the Indonesia question. He reasoned that
a United Nations incapable of solving the Indonesia question would be
doomed to failure in dealing with Indochina. Acheson asked if Indochina
was in the forefront of FE's concerns; Butterworth assured him that it
was. The secretary then observed that "it would be necessary to have a
closer look at Ho Chi-minh, whom he recalled that Nehru [the Indian
Prime Minister had been a recent visitor to Washington] had considered
the only figure in the country." Butterworth "supposed that we should,
but opposed participation by the United States in any arrangement which
might bring the Communists into control of Indochina." Rusk suggested
that Ho's participation in an Indochina government might be brought
about by the United Kingdom, India, and France. Shortly after this, the
meeting adjourned.[48]

The Policy Review Payoff

The day after the second meeting, Acheson gave the participants of his
morning meeting his impression of the two-day policy review session.
The record of the meeting does not reveal what he said, only that his
views were "for the advice of the group in the room and not to be general
conversation pieces in the Department." It is not likely that they were
positive. Acheson, as he later wrote, never had much patience "with a

type of nonsense particularly prevalent in the State Department known as 'kicking the problem around.' "[49] The consultants had "kicked the problem around" for three months and had offered little that was either new or usable. Jessup had placed major emphasis upon the "area approach" to Asian policy, but it was not a new idea and FE ignored it. The general policy objectives that the consultants outlined predated their arrival at the department. Their recommendations for country policies suggested little that had not been thought of before. The concept of "demonstration projects" in Asia requiring large expenditures of American resources was not acceptable in the political climate of 1949, when all requests for aid to Asia were subject to China bloc attacks. A proposed American endorsement of a Pacific Union also fell on unreceptive ears.

The review process did have value, however, even if Acheson did not appreciate it on the morning of 28 October, 1949. Jessup and the consultants, during their brief service as a group, met with many members of Congress and citizens interested in China policy who might otherwise have attacked the administration had they not talked to the men the secretary of state had charged publicly with formulation of a new Far Eastern policy. The consultants performed that task well. Their top secret policy review also reaffirmed the Chinese Tito hypothesis, which was under attack even within the State Department. It also reduced the chance that a significant portion of the 303 fund would be squandered on covert operations designed to make life more difficult for the Chinese Communists. As the 26 October meeting revealed, there had been two schools of thought on China policy: Rusk's hard line approach of harassing the Chinese; and Butterworth's approach of dignified aloofness. Prior to the meeting, Acheson had leaned more toward the Rusk position; by the time it ended, he appeared to be backing away. By supporting Butterworth on China policy, Jessup and the "wise men" both helped soften China policy and saved the 303 fund for other purposes.

Whatever Acheson's views about the fruits of the Jessup group, he also found it useful for one more key purpose, that of winning presidential endorsement for the State Department's Asia policy. In mid-November, the secretary arranged a meeting between the consultants and the president to discuss their findings. It proved to be important because Truman, under the influence of the military and his own strong feelings, was rapidly moving toward a much harder position than even the one Rusk recommended.

10

Policy Showdown: NSC-48

The State Department's reaffirmation of Far Eastern policy was not identical to the larger process of policy formulation within the executive branch. Once the State Department had completed its policy review, it was still necessary for the department to convert, or at least obtain the acquiescence of, the president and the military establishment. The task was not easy. Both Truman and the Pentagon had special views on China policy and took a proprietary interest in the 303 fund.

The military establishment—reconstituted as the Department of Defense in October—began programming 303 funds faster than the State Department. The day after the joint Senate committee adopted the amendment, Major General L. L. Lemnitzer, assistant to the secretary of defense for foreign military assistance, urged the Joint Chiefs of Staff to examine how the $75 million might be spent in China.[1] The JCS turned the problem over to their Joint Strategic Survey Committee, which filed its recommendations on 6 October. The committee devised a plan of limited military aid to China and a program of special operations to obstruct Communist control; it apparently did not approve plans for sending the money elsewhere in China's "general area." The plan's purpose was "to contain Communism within North and East Central China rather than at China's Southern border and thus minimize Communist penetration from the North into Southeast Asia." With the emergence of capable leadership, the money might assist non-Communist Chinese to retain a foothold in the south, prevent the Communists' consolidation of China, aggravate Communist China's economic and political problems, and interfere with air and sea communication. The aid should be "direct" if possible, or channeled through "special operations" if necessary.[2]

The 6 October plan formed part of a larger Defense Department effort to take control of the $75 million. During the MAP appropriation bill hearings in the Senate, Defense Secretary Louis Johnson startled Under Secretary of State James Webb, appearing for the State Department, by indicating that he and the president had reached an "understanding" about how the money might be used.[3] After Webb told Acheson of Johnson's assumption, the secretary of state asked President Truman, who controlled the fund. Truman replied that he was the final judge of how the money would be spent and that recommendations for its use should be presented to him, cosigned by the secretaries of state and defense, through the Bureau of the Budget.[4]

The President's directive did not deter the Defense Department from making plans. In late October or early November, Johnson sent directly to Truman—apparently without State Department clearance—303-funded CIA plans for covert operations in China, and during a trip to Paris in October, he offered the French government some of the money for use in Indochina without informing the State Department.[5] In mid-November, Livingston Merchant learned from a member of Johnson's staff that *"various groups over in the Department of Defense were working on possible plans for the expenditure of part or all of this money."*[6]

Pulling Back the President

It is likely that any plans the defense secretary had for harassing the Chinese Communists fell on fertile ground in the White House. The President had long been on record as wanting "to make things just as tough economically for the Chinese Communists as possible." When Truman discovered that two American tankers were possibly destined for Manchuria in early September, his "immediate reaction [was] . . . that the Maritime Commission should stop it." Butterworth ultimately thwarted the Truman proposal on the grounds that the oil would get there by other methods and that stopping the American flag traffic would hurt American shipping, but he did not change the president's bias.[7] In a 16 September cabinet meeting Truman attacked the root of the trade policy by giving Acheson a copy of NSC–41 along with his opinion that the policy was outdated and needed revision. Acheson assured him that the policy would be reexamined at once.[8]

Two weeks later Truman broached the subject again, but from a slightly different angle. In a 1 October meeting with Webb, he noted a recent shooting incident involving two American flag vessels caught in the Nationalist blockade and "indicated strongly," Webb wrote later, "as he has previously indicated, that he wished the blockade to be effective and that he desired the Department to do nothing to be of assistance to those vessels." After the under secretary explained that the department was innocent of such assistance, Truman "stressed again the fact that his policy was to permit the blockade to work effectively, to which he expected strict adherence."[9]

By the time the State Department finished its reassessment of NSC–41 on 4 November—a reendorsement furnished six weeks after Truman requested it—the president had become even more aggressive.[10] On 24 October, the Communists arrested Angus Ward and four staff members for beating a former Chinese employee of the consulate general. After a trial with a predictable verdict, a "People's Court" sentenced the group to deportation on 22 November. Before Ward and his group left Mukden, the Communists arrested a vice consul on his staff, tried him for espionage, and ultimately released him.[11]

Before the affair's resolution, however, the president seriously considered extricating Ward by force. In public, his comments were restrained but pointed. When asked at a 19 October news conference if the United States would recognize the Communists under any circumstances, he replied, "I won't go into that. I hope we will not have to recognize it." A week later, Truman again deflected discussion of recognition at a press conference, but on 31 October he indicated the extreme nature of his views in private to Webb who was acting secretary while Acheson was out of town.[12] Referring to the Ward case, he suggested that a plane might be sent to Mukden to bring the consular staff out and indicated that "he was prepared to take the strongest possible measures, including some utilization of force if necessary, and if he was sure it would be effective."[13]

During the same meeting Truman also offered Webb some of his own ideas (or perhaps those suggested to him by Louis Johnson, the CIA, or the China lobby) about using the 303 fund. The president produced a

map of Russia with colors indicating a large belt of "Moslem and Buddhist peoples" in southern Russia whom he considered "fundamentally
antagonistic" to the Soviet regime. "He wanted us to try to develop some
plan by which part of the $75,000,000 might be used to penetrate these
peoples if such was feasible through covert activity," Webb recorded.
This was to be done by working with like religious groups contiguous
with the Soviet Union's southern border. In analyzing the situation, Truman also indicated on the map that it was in the "Slovak [sic] populations," extending east to west along the trans-Siberian railway, that the
present regime had its greatest support. When he returned to his office,
Webb turned the suggestion over to the CIA.[14]

Two weeks later, Truman was prepared to go even further. At a 14
November meeting with Webb, he said that he wanted the department
to explore the possibility of blockading coal shipments between Tientsin
and other ports in north China that might travel down the China coast
to Shanghai. The move would teach the Chinese that the Americans
meant business and it would gain the United States respect abroad. Webb
asked the president how far he would be willing to go to back such a move
if the Chinese refused to obey orders from the American Navy. As Webb
later related, Truman said that "if we meant to go into this matter we
should be prepared to sink any vessels which refused to heed our warning." To stimulate the department's thinking on the subject of harassing
Communist China, Truman also gave Webb an unsigned, undated memorandum recommending a $40 million *a month* program to aid non-
Communist forces deep in China and on Formosa and Hainan Island.[15]

It is difficult to determine from available documents which idea hor-
rified the State Department more: the idea of an American naval blockade
of China or of a $40-million-a-month military aid program that, among
other things, would have exhausted the 303 fund in less than two months.
While FE quickly prepared the State Department's negative response to
both propositions, Dean Acheson and the consultants took the occasion
of their meeting with the president on 17 November to set him straight
on China policy. In their meeting, long planned for the consultants to
convey their findings to Truman, they stressed their frequently stated
views about the "area approach" and the folly of attempting to overthrow
the Chinese Communists.

The meeting impressed Truman. He admitted afterward to Acheson
that he gained new insight into the reason for the Communist victory and

he "found himself thinking about it in a quite new way." In a Truman-Acheson meeting later in the day, the secretary underlined the department's recently reaffirmed China policy. He told the president

> that if we had had a little more time this morning I should have liked to have had the discussion center on what seemed to me to be a pretty basic issue of policy on which I thought the Consultants minds were very clear. Broadly speaking, there were two objectives of policy. One might be to oppose the Communist regime, harass it, needle it, and if an opportunity appeared to attempt to overthrow it. Another objective of policy would be to attempt to detach it from subservience to Moscow and over a period of time encourage those vigorous influences which might modify it. I pointed out that this second alternative did not mean a policy of appeasement any more than it had in the case of Tito. If the Communists took action detrimental to the United States it should be opposed with vigor, but the decision of many concrete questions would be much clarified by a decision as to whether we believed that we should and could overthrow the regime, or whether we believed that the second course outlined above was the wiser. I said that the Consultants were unanimous in their judgment that the second course was the preferable one.
> The President thought that in the broad sense in which I was speaking that this was the correct analysis and that he wished to have a thorough understanding of all of the facts in deciding the question. He believed that today's meeting had greatly helped him.[16]

Truman's new frame of mind relieved pressure on the State Department. On 7 December, the Chinese themselves relieved even more when they allowed Ward and his staff to board a slow train south to Tientsin and ultimately a boat to the United States. On the same day, the Division of Chinese Affairs summarized existing policy in a memorandum for Ambassador at Large Philip Jessup as he prepared to take a trip to the Far East. It was a terse recapitulation of the China policies formulated nine months earlier. The memorandum mentioned the possibility of supporting anti-Communist groups, but not as a likely alternative; it also reendorsed NSC–41 and Formosa policy. The prospects for the island's survival in non-Communist hands, however, were not bright. Unless its rulers undertook enlightened and vigorous reform, the paper predicted "Formosa likewise will eventually fall to the Communists."

The memorandum also devoted a paragraph to the recognition question, which, like everything else, was "under active study." It was a masterful example of advancing a position without explicitly endorsing it.

The policy of a common front was crumbling. While some people might find in American recognition a surrender to the regime, "other quarters would doubtless construe it as an encouraging sign of US determination to come to grips with reality." Generally, nonrecognition would serve no useful purpose, could lead to other Ward-type cases, and might be detrimental to remaining American interests in China.[17]

In nine months the State Department's China policy underwent several changes. In the first half of the year the department considered either harassment of, or limited accommodation with, Communist China. For awhile it moved in both directions simultaneously. After July, it leaned toward harassment; by late October harassment appeared pointless. There were no significant anti-Communist groups in China, and Formosa appeared doomed. After Ward's release, the policy of aloof accommodation and pursuit of long-term Titoism became marginally more viable within the United States. Yet, it was still not popular or secure. Although Truman had recently expressed sympathy with the department's views on China policy and tended to take the advice of Dean Acheson above other advisors, his mind was subject to reconversion. His natural instinct, like that of many Americans, was hostile toward regimes that denounced the United States and allied themselves with the Soviet Union. And, if his natural instincts should fail, the president had Louis Johnson and a Defense Department to point the way toward a hard line. Thus, not until the State Department decisively defeated the Pentagon could its China policy be secure.

Formosa Review

In selling its views on Far Eastern policy, the defense establishment employed three important levers of power. One was its dominant representation on the National Security Council. Although a new congressional act struck the three service secretaries from council membership in October and altered the balance of forces within that body, the NSC remained a forum that allowed the defense secretary to offer ad hoc comments—"from the military point of view"—on Asian policy. The Pentagon could also use the council's staff to study questions that might otherwise have fallen within the domain of the State Department.

A second lever in the Pentagon's hands was its responsibilities connected with the Military Assistance Program, an oversight duty it shared with the State Department and ECA. In Asia, it could attempt to direct the use of the 303 fund in areas it thought proper.

A third was the military's right to assign strategic value to various parts of the globe, a task the JCS performed with ponderous deliberation. The military used its assessment of Formosa to influence China policy in early 1949 and continued its interest in the island after the NSC and the president overruled the JCS request to allow the Navy to station "minor fleet units" there in March. After that, the chiefs dropped the subject of "fleet units" but continued to weigh Formosa's strategic significance in the second half of the year.

The State Department remained ambivalent about Formosa policy through 1949. In light of the island's deteriorating situation—which did not respond to existing policy—Acheson and his advisors were uncertain whether they wanted to let it fall into Communist hands or to seize it. On 11 July, Acheson ordered the department to review NSC–37/5, the paper supposedly guiding Formosa policy, and to tabulate all events that had transpired since its approval; following this, a decision should be made about what policy to recommend. The recommendation, he ordered, should ignore the question of whether or not the military had the "where-withal to enforce any policy arrived at." Before the State Department reached its conclusions, however, Acheson wanted JCS advice on how essential the island was "from a strategic point of view."[18]

The Joint Chiefs responded to Acheson's request for guidance on 17 August, restating their earlier opinion that Formosa's "strategic importance" did not "justify overt military action" to save it. They qualified their judgment by noting that it was based on their assessment of the American military's inability to occupy the island and meet other commitments around the world. No mention was made of granting military aid or stationing "minor fleet units" at the island.[19]

Following this delphic clarification, the department's senior officers grappled with Formosa policy without reaching a definitive position. They found some cheer when a capable Chinese military leader assumed command of Formosa at the end of August but did not find that conditions on the island improved significantly thereafter.[20] Livingston Merchant summed up the "illogic" of the situation in a conversation with British diplomats in early September.

(1) Formosa is completely self-supporting; (2) the Nationalists on Formosa have a well-equipped army, air force and navy; (3) the Communist forces have no air force or navy; (4) the Nationalists on For-

mosa have an abundance of foreign exchange; (5) it would appear on the surface that the Nationalists under good leadership could establish themselves in an impregnable position for an indefinite period; and yet (6) there is every evidence that the Communists will be able to gain control of the island.[21]

While evidence suggesting Formosa's ultimate fall accumulated, more hints that American support of the island was chaffing the Communists in Peking also reached the State Department. According to reports reaching Consul McConaughy in Shanghai via Democratic League leader Lo Lung-chi, "Mao was adamant" that there could be no improvement in relations until the United States quit supporting the Nationalists and stopped "her designs on Taiwan." Although the consul could not confirm this report's validity, he did "know that locally manifested Communist hostility to American policy is more and more concerned with Taiwan."[22]

In early October, the State Department submitted yet another Formosa paper to the NSC. Noting a CIA prediction that the island would fall to the Communists before the end of 1950, the analysis painted the by now standard grim picture and suggested alternative courses of action. The department recommended reaffirmation of existing policy with one modification: large-scale economic assistance (called for in NSC–37/5) would be withheld until conditions improved significantly; in the interim a modest program of economic aid then underway would continue. The department also requested authorization to inform Chiang Kai-shek that "the U.S. Government *will not* commit any of its armed forces to the defense of the Island," and that future decisions about American economic aid depended upon how well his government performed.[23] As a result of discussions in a 20 October NSC meeting, the language of the proposed demarché to Chiang was changed from "will not" defend the island to a less firm "does not intend to."[24] The alteration was a minor setback for the State Department, a subtle change that indicated a slight weakening in American resolve not to back Chiang with direct military force. The revised language also indicated a difference of opinion between the State and Defense Departments that would separate them even more dramatically in the near future. The issues would not only be the Formosa question, but also the use of the 303 fund, the larger question of which department determined Far Eastern policy, and the personality conflict between Louis Johnson and the high command at the State Department.

Louis Johnson and NSC–48

Louis Johnson was not secretary of defense long, before he made known his view that the United States should do more to "stop Communism in Asia." Within the administration he was openly critical of the State Department's China policy and charged that it was based on unsound information. His own sources, he claimed, were more reliable.[25] He was also critical of the government's ad hoc approach to Far Eastern policy. In order to stimulate creation of a broader approach, one of his aides, Najeeb Halaby, urged him on 8 June to sign a draft memorandum to NSC Secretary Admiral Souers that would "support studies already initiated in the NSC staff and request their correlation into a broad proposal of what we should do to stop communism in the Far East." Johnson modified the memo slightly and sent it to Souers two days later. The secretary explained that he was increasingly worried about the advance of Communism in Asia, and while he was aware that "several departments of the government" were watching the situation carefully, he did not think that was enough. "It occurs to me . . . that this day-to-day, country-by-country approach may not develop a broad program in our best long-range interests." He therefore recommended that the NSC staff develop a "carefully considered and comprehensive plan" to contain Communism in Asia. Souers designated the proposed study "NSC–48" and circulated the memorandum to other council members.[26]

The defense secretary evidently liked what he had started. Rumors soon surfaced in Washington that Louis Johnson had compelled Dean Acheson to pursue a more active China policy. In a column in mid-July, Drew Pearson alleged that the NSC had overruled Acheson on China policy and that Johnson had been the victor. The State Department denied the meeting ever took place; in the Pentagon, however, Assistant Secretary of Defense Paul Griffith confirmed the story to Ambassador Koo.[27]

Johnson's confidence in his power ran high. On 12 July, Under Secretary Webb sent him a letter requesting the loan of a "highly competent and experienced general officer who might be consulted by our own principal officers about the strategic situation within China" on the understanding that his advice would not constitute a military establishment commitment toward a China policy.[28] With the support of President Truman, Johnson replied in a letter to Dean Acheson (he would not write and rarely spoke to under secretaries) with the bureaucratic equivalent of a polite "hell no." He reminded the secretary of his 10 June memorandum to the NSC. While his department would furnish the State Department with specific documents, Johnson thought that State "should proceed urgently with the formulation of proposals and submit them to the National Security Council" where the major questions concerning American foreign policy should be discussed. "There will then be a basis on which the *President* can decide what our foreign policy with respect to China and the Far East will be."[29]

The defense secretary, however, was soon brought down a notch when Truman rejected his advice—and accepted Acheson's to publish the China White Paper.[30] Nevertheless, the State Department still had to deal with Johnson's NSC project. In early September he sent another note to Admiral Souers urging that the study "be now treated as a matter of priority."[31]

The State Department's dim view of NSC staff work, so evident in 1948, did not improve in 1949. It continued to think that the staff was in over its head. One paper reinforcing its opinion was a staff report on United States policy toward the Soviet Union (NSC–20) in the spring of 1949. After the under secretary of state informed Admiral Souers of its displeasure with the report, Souers admitted that the staff's accomplishments had not been impressive and agreed that it would not, as a rule, undertake to draft papers of its own.[32] Louis Johnson's mandate of 10 June to review Asian policy as a whole forced the NSC staff, in effect, to break the rule.

The first draft of the NSC Asia paper reached the State Department in mid-October. It did nothing to inspire further confidence. Jessup and the consultants examined it in New York and requested that a member of their staff, Walter Wilds, call FE to express "the most grave reservations regarding certain of its conclusions." Livingston Merchant took the message and assured Wilds that FE also had grave reservations.[33] Stephen Brown, an officer in CA, wrote a solemn memorandum to Philip Sprouse stating that he had read the document with care and could only say "that I have never seen, in my eighteen months in the Department, a more imposing collection of logical absurdities."[34] The document described the major American objective in Asia as the development of friendly nations and the reduction of Soviet influence. It offered a "positive program" that would achieve those ends: the formation of a regional, noncommunist association in which the United States would participate, military assistance to the region, acquisition of "title to Formosa and the

Pescadores," to be later turned over to the trusteeship of the Pacific association, a systematic program of covert and overt bedevilment of Communist China, and a Japanese peace treaty. Also recommended were unspecified economic measures and a mobilization of all "instrumentalities of government which may be effectively utilized."[35]

A second NSC draft dated 25 October also met the displeasure of Assistant Secretary of State George McGhee who oversaw American relations with South Asia. "The over-emphasis of North and East Asia reveals itself many times," he charged. He objected especially because it relegated his sphere "to a secondary and even minor role."[36]

The Bureau of Far Eastern Affairs, the principal bureau concerned with NSC–48, found the first NSC staff draft painful, and two subsequent ones unacceptable as well. In late October it began writing its own version, retaining as much of the language of the less important analysis section as possible, while almost completely overhauling the conclusions: the section that threatened to become "national policy." In making its revision, FE attempted to use language from existing NSC papers prepared in the State Department. By 25 November, FE produced a draft for consideration at a special intradepartmental meeting.

The 1 December Meeting

On 1 December, representatives from fifteen sub-bureaucracies attended a meeting chaired by Dean Rusk to discuss FE's substitute draft. Focusing mostly on the document's seven pages of conclusions, the participants read nothing that startled them. The "basic security objectives" in Asia were: the development of stable, self-sustaining nations; "containment and where feasible reduction of the power and influence of the USSR;" and the "prevention of power relationships in Asia" that would threaten Asian stability of American security. With these goals pegged, there followed a review of country and regional policies: the United States would view with favor the creation of an association of states in Asia, although it would take no part in forming it; it would keep an open mind about bilateral and multilateral security arrangements in Asia; in accordance with the conclusions of a 1948 NSC document, the United States should conclude a brief peace settlement with Japan, with or without Soviet or Chinese Communist participation and consistent with future American security interests; in Korea, American economic, technical, military, and political support would continue in accordance with an

NSC decision of March 1949. The paper also recognized the possibility of a Communist takeover of the entire Korean peninsula and concluded that, "to the extent that it may be practicable, the U.S. policy in Korea should take this possibility into account by preparing to minimize the impact of such a development on the position of the US in the Far East."

China policy stuck to previous NSC documents with equal fidelity. The fundamental objective of American policy was discreetly to exploit "rifts" between the Chinese Communists and the Soviets "and between the Stalinists and other elements in China." Trade was to be allowed in nonstrategic goods. Military and political support of a non-Communist regime was disallowed, unless "such regimes are willing actively to resist Communism with or without United States aid and unless such support would mean successful resistance to the Communists." Contact was to be maintained with all elements in China. The paper endorsed the tactic of using nonrecognition as a diplomatic instrument and foresaw the possibility of future recognition. On the Formosa question, it quoted the JCS August affirmation to the NSC that "the strategic importance of Formosa does not justify overt military actions" and endorsed existing policy.

The paper concluded with brief references to India and Indonesia, and paragraphs touching on trade, Point IV, investment, tariff policy, and the value of cooperation between non-Communist Asian states. There were no specific directives on Southeast Asia, which was discussed in the analysis, and no reference to the 303 fund. The draft was old wine in a new bottle.[37]

Speaking early in the 1 December meeting, Butterworth expressed his hostile view of the entire project: the paper added nothing to present policy in the Far East; it existed only because the secretary of defense wanted it. Rusk, who dealt directly with the NSC staff and consultants, assured the group that no previous policy would change without specific statements to that effect. In relating the views of the NSC military consultants, he mentioned their desire to "strengthen" the Formosa section and said that he had agreed to deal with the island in a separate paper.

John Ohly, the deputy director of the State Department's Office of the Mutual Defense Assistance Program and a recent deputy to Louis Johnson, "suggested that something be included in the paper on the military aid question and the use of the $75 million fund." The officials, according to the summary of the meeting, agreed "that although much of this was to go for police equipment rather than strictly military material, some reference should be made to the problem."[38]

The State Department's 5 December redraft did not differ significantly from its 25 November predecessor except in the deletion of the section on Japan, the deletion of the paragraph allowing for the write-off of Korea, a new reference to the need to urge the French to support Bao Dai, and the addition of language about the $75 million fund's use. The last addition read: "The funds available under Section 303 of the MDA Act should be utilized immediately to strengthen the Indonesian constabulary. Similarly the use of these funds should be considered with respect to other countries in Southeast Asia."[39]

Rusk was not happy with the latest draft but he presented it at a secretary's meeting on 6 December and at an under secretary's meeting the next day.[40] The latter meeting started out congenially, with several officers expressing their approval of the paper, but fell into dissension when a representative from the Office of German Affairs expressed general unhappiness with it. John Ohly then strongly objected to the 303 fund's use in an area as distant from China as Indonesia. He opposed starting programs requiring additional funding; he thought that the State and Defense Departments were too far apart on how the money should be spent; and he wanted a clearer idea about other projects for the fund. Finally, for good measure, he questioned whether $8 million earmarked for Korea in Section 302 of the MAP bill was not wasted.

Ohly found little sympathy for his pointed remarks. Both Rusk and Butterworth attacked his question about Korea, and Rusk, according to the meeting's record, took "quite a slug at the Ohly point by recalling the way in which the Defense Department [where Ohly had recently worked] got out of Korea." On the question of the other uses for the 303 fund, Ohly received no enlightenment when "Rusk and others pointed out that the emergencies for which it was set up cannot be anticipated." A consensus emerged from the meeting, with Ohly excepted, that the $75 million could be used for a variety of emergencies, including Indonesia. It adjourned with an agreement that Rusk, Ohly, and Butterworth would work out new language on the 303 fund's use.[41]

The Military Blitz

With the State Department's desired language for NSC–48 more or less agreed upon (there would be one subsequent draft incorporating general language about prompt programming of 303 funds) by early December, the Pentagon suddenly cast the paper's future in doubt. The department received indications in mid-December that the long-rumored JCS change of heart about the importance of Formosa was imminent. The catalyst had been the creation of the 303 fund.

By October, the Joint Chiefs had begun to have second thoughts about the importance of Formosa. While they still opposed occupations, they considered the island worth assisting in the form of military advisors and material. The JCS declined to press the matter, however, because a 19 October CIA estimate predicted that all aid short of direct American military intervention would be futile and because there were no funds available for an aid program.[42] Instead, the military leaders maintained their formal August position until December, when word leaked from the Pentagon that they were about to have a change of heart. Butterworth had picked up hints of the change by late October and Rusk, who was in charge of liaison with the military as well as the NSC, reported to Acheson the possible JCS reversal on 9 December.[43]

While the uniform service chiefs agonized over Formosa, Louis Johnson and Wellington Koo lobbied the White House and the State Department for military aid to the island. Johnson, anticipating the JCS reversal (which he directly encouraged), sent President Truman a memorandum on 15 December with an attachment giving General MacArthur's views on Formosa as conveyed to Under Secretary of the Army Tracy Voorhees. Johnson noted that Formosa was one question soon to be dealt with during an NSC review of Asian policy. "Generally speaking, the staffs agree that efforts should be continued and perhaps increased to deny Formosa to the Communists. The nature and extent of such efforts are now being considered in some detail for the purpose of defining them more accurately. They include political and economic aid, and also military advice and assistance short of overt military action."

The attached summary of MacArthur's views revealed that the general wanted the island defended, but did not think it was necessary to commit American troops. All it would take to hold Formosa would be "merely by a declaration under the Potsdam Agreement that the U.S. would treat any attempt to invade Formosa as an act of war. . . . If necessary a large part of the $75,000,000 recently appropriated to be used in connection with Chinese matters should be employed for the protection of Formosa."[44]

The Chinese ambassador performed his role by submitting a request on 23 December for technical, military, and economic aid for Formosa supervised by up to seventy American military, political, and economic experts. This request, which the embassy must have realized would not soften the hearts of Dean Acheson or Walt Butterworth, would nonetheless kill a possible argument that Formosa did not need aid because the Nationalists did not request it.[45]

The NSC–48 project appeared to be falling apart; Formosa policy was in doubt and other aspects of Asian policy were being withdrawn from consideration. At the last minute, the military also wanted to omit discussion of policy toward Japan. Furthermore, the National Security Resources Board wanted to postpone discussion of trade with Communist China. FE took the occasion of the confusion to attempt to cancel the paper. Butterworth explained to Rusk in a 20 December memorandum that NSC–48 was "almost valueless." Existing papers on Korea, Japan, Formosa, trade with Communist China, and Southeast Asia were, in the main, satisfactory to the State Department. All the present paper—in this case, a 15 December draft—did was to suggest the creation of a Pacific Pact and call for a dangerous program of domestic propaganda.[46] The implication of the NSC's approval of the current version would mean the reversal of previously approved department positions on trade with Communist China and Formosa policy.

Butterworth concluded with a foreign service officer's traditional view on the conduct of foreign policy. The solution to the policy conflict would "lie in having the highest level of the NSC agree on the respective roles of the various agencies." While the "needs and desires" of each agency would be taken into account, the council would recognize "that the Defense Department will have the responsibility for recommendations regarding military policy and that responsibility for foreign policy in the political and economic fields lies with the State Department."[47]

Despite Butterworth's protest, the project went forward when the NSC staff presented their final draft, designated NSC–48/1, to Executive Secretary Souers on 23 December. This paper incorporated most of the State Department's revisions but also accommodated the divergent views of the military on Formosa policy.[48] On the same day, the Joint Chiefs of Staff, as predicted, produced a memorandum that proposed a "modest, well directed, and closely supervised program of military aid to the anti-Communist government in Taiwan" along with stepped-up political, economic, and psychological support. To gather specific details for this program, they recommended that General MacArthur send a survey mission to the island to judge just what was needed.[49] The JCS memorandum reached the NSC in time to be incorporated in the less important analysis section of NSC–48/1 and appeared after a long passage quoting the CIA October estimate holding that anything less than military occupation of the island would be futile. NSC–48/1's conclusions thus contained a split recommendation: the Pentagon calling for an aggressive policy of denying Formosa by "military advice and assistance." The State Department proposed denying Formosa only "through diplomatic and economic means."[50]

The Bureau of Far Eastern Affairs took a predictably cold view of the Joint Chiefs' of Staff revised position. Among other things, Butterworth wrote to Acheson on 28 December, it paralleled "with extraordinary fidelity" Ambassador Koo's request for assistance. He suggested that the Chinese note represented one more Nationalist attempt to involve the United States in the civil war and, specifically, "to capitalize on our military as open pleaders for increased aid." Butterworth argued that the provision of military advisors violated past experience from General Joseph Stilwell to General Barr. He was willing to allow former military officers to advise the Formosa regime, but the Chinese government had expressed no interest in having them. Further military aid would only encourage the Nationalists futilely to carry the war to the mainland and, in the process, aggravate the British, who opposed any further American aid to Formosa on the ground that it might ultimately be used against them in Hong Kong. FE was only willing to continue ECA aid "not appreciably in excess" of $30 million over the next eight months if Congress again extended the China Aid Act authorization.[51]

Policy Climax

The climax of the State and Defense Departments' confrontation was scheduled for an NSC meeting on 29 December when the council was to review NSC–48/1. The Formosa issue, however, was resolved in substance a week earlier. On the 20th, both Acheson and Johnson lobbied the president for their respective positions. Two days later, Truman told Johnson at lunch that he would not argue the Formosa question with him but that his decision was against sending an aid survey mission to the island. Later in the week the defense secretary went on vacation to Florida and deliberately missed the NSC meeting.[52]

In light of this presidential decision, a 29 December State Department-JCS meeting on the question of sending aid to Formosa proved to be anticlimactic. It revealed, however, why the Pentagon had proposed military aid to Formosa. Acheson called the meeting, as he explained to the Joint Chiefs of Staff, to express puzzlement over their assessment of the strategic importance of Formosa. In the past, he noted, the military had not thought Formosa to be of such significant strategic importance to warrant the use of American military force.

JCS Chairman Omar Bradley reviewed the military's position, recalling that in February the president had overruled their proposal for basing minor naval units on the island. Their opinion about the wisdom of sending military aid and advisors had changed in October but, since there were no funds for military aid, they did not press the matter. The 23 December recommendation, Bradley explained, "was based on the existence of funds under Section 303 of the Military Assistance Act." He pointed out that the money could be spent on aid the Chinese needed. A survey team should now proceed to the island "since money was available to meet those needs." General Lawton Collins supported Bradley, stressing the value of Formosa in diverting the Communists from expansion into Southeast Asia, while Admiral Forrest Sherman said that the political situation had improved with the appointment of the progressive K. C. Wu as the island's governor. Collins also noted that the CIA would soon revise its gloomy October forecast and maintain that, with a comparatively small expenditure of funds, the island could hold out longer than it otherwise would.

Acheson responded by describing the general problem of checking communism in Asia. Since the Communists now controlled China, it was likely that they would attempt to subvert China's neighbors to the south. It was important that the United States do its utmost to strengthen non-Communist countries in the region. Moreover, there was the prospect that the Chinese Communists themselves might turn against Moscow as the Soviets proceeded to detach China's northern tier of provinces. "This situation . . . is our one important asset in China and it would have to be for a very important strategic purpose that we would take an action which would substitute ourselves for the Soviets as the imperialist menace to China." It was against this backdrop that the State Department viewed Formosa, an island likely to go the way of the mainland. To commit American prestige to its survival would "excite and bring upon ourselves the united Chinese hatred of foreigners," which belonged to the Soviet Union. Throughout Asia, "we would be represented as the supporters of this discredited, decayed Kuomintang Government. If at this price we acquire an island essential to the defense of the United States then it might be worth the price but there does not appear to be demonstrated a claim that the loss of Formosa really breaches our defense."

The vanquished Joint Chiefs of Staff concluded with Bradley reiterating that they presented "a purely military point of view which reflected the fact that Congress had appropriated money to support these people who were resisting Communism and that he recognized that political considerations might override their view."[53]

In the afternoon NSC meeting, Acheson won formal approval for the State Department's position when the council endorsed a set of revised conclusions based largely on NSC–48/1. NSC–48/2, the paper carrying the council's views, emerged with slightly harsher language than the State Department had originally wanted but with no significant policy alteration. The State Department's Formosa paragraph, a reissue of the 3 March paper NSC–37/5, triumphed over the Pentagon's effort to set a more aggressive policy to save the island. The paragraph following it, which had been in NSC–48/1 and apparently uncontested, disallowed overt military action to save the island only "so long as the present disparity between our military and our global obligations exist." Since the "disparity" was destined to continue indefinitely, this formulation met little resistance. On mainland China policy, nothing changed and the report even contained explicit sanctions for existing trade policy with Communist China.[54]

The State Department had thus won the latest round of competition with the military on China policy by keeping the ambiguous policies adopted nine months earlier largely intact. The flexibility that allowed the department to pursue a Titoist policy in China had been largely reaffirmed. The old Formosa policy had also been preserved.

While NSC–48/2 endorsed the old package of China policies, the document also pointed to a new direction in American Far Eastern policy. The council added to NSC–48/1 a new paragraph calling for "development of sufficient military power in selected non-Communist nations of Asia to maintain internal security and to prevent further encroachment by Communism." It also added a new paragraph to the previous draft that dealt with the 303 fund, using language drafted by the JCS: "The sum of $75,000,000 for assistance to the general area of China, which was made available under Section 303 of the Mutual Defense Assistance Act of 1949, should be programmed as a matter of urgency." President Truman, in a rare appearance, attended this council meeting and approved the NSC document as redrafted on 30 December. His only reservation concerned the 303 fund. "A program will be all right," he told Souers, "but whether we implement it depends on circumstances." His reservations proved short-lived.[55]

11

Containment of Communist China

As the new year began, the Pentagon found itself beaten back after its long drive to reverse China policy had failed. It had not, however, given up. The ambiguities of the previous year's China policies had not, after all, yielded to a consistent policy of encouraging Chinese Titoism. The saving of Formosa continued to be national policy even if no significant action could be taken to achieve that end. The Defense Department, furthermore, soon found that the political discussion that occurred after NSC–48/2's adoption played into its hands. On Sunday, 1 January 1950, James Reston reported the essence of the document's conclusions on the front page of the *New York Times*.[1]* For the next several weeks, the Formosa question would be debated in Congress and in the press with an intensity surpassing the China debates of 1949. In the course of the controversy, the White House and State Department found themselves in increasingly isolated opposition to the military, the lounder voices in Congress, the China lobby, and public opinion.

Formosa Weeks

Senator William Knowland fired the first shot on Monday morning, 2 January, when he released a letter from former President Herbert Hoover

*The source of this leak appears to have been the president.

urging continued American support for Formosa and opposition to the Communists. On the same day Senate Republican Policy Committee Chairman Robert Taft and Knowland also called for renewed Formosa support.[2]

On Tuesday, Knowland received a valuable weapon in his attack. On 23 December 1949, the State Department's public affairs office had issued a confidential memorandum to department representatives abroad and to other government agencies stating that Formosa's fall was "widely anticipated" and dispelling the "false impression" that the island was strategically important. The document, which was a low-level background paper, leaked from General MacArthur's headquarters in Tokyo. When Knowland learned of its existence from a United Press dispatch, he expressed amazement in a Senate floor speech and demanded the document in a phone call to Under Secretary of State James Webb. When Webb did not oblige, the senator wrote Acheson demanding the memorandum.[3] On the same day, Republican Senator H. Alexander Smith of New Jersey, who had recently returned from a Far Eastern trip, called for an "aggressive" Asian policy and expressed hope that "we will find a formula for occupying Formosa."[4] The only dissenting Senate Republican voice was that of Henry Cabot Lodge, Jr., who said he had "grave doubts" about undertaking military action in Formosa.[5]

After visiting Capitol Hill on Wednesday, Chen Chih-mai, minister-counselor to the Nationalist embassy and chief envoy to the China bloc, informed Ambassador Koo that the Republicans appeared "prepared to launch an all-out fight on the issue." The future of the Republican Party, and the 1950 election, said one Republican leader, "depend on this issue."[6]

Dean Acheson, it appears, reached a similar conclusion and on Wednesday laid plans for an instant counterattack. He discussed Formosa policy with the president in the early afternoon and later went to the Capitol where he arranged with Chairman Tom Connally to summon the Senate Foreign Relations Committee in the following week to hear a review of Asian policy. He also attempted to consult Senator Arthur Vandenberg, who could not be reached, but did see John Kee, chairman of the House Foreign Affairs Committee. To Kee, Acheson explained the background of the Formosa question and the current situation: the island currently had enough war material to defend itself if it had the will. But if the island fell, the consequence would not be great. "He said," an aide wrote later, "that there seems to be some magic that flows from the use of the term 'island' which seems to immediately give everyone the jitters, whereas, if Formosa had happened to be a peninsula we would probably have heard nothing more about it."[7] The next morning, 5 January, Acheson saw Congressman Charles Eaton of New Jersey, the ranking Republican on the House Foreign Affairs Committee. Long a supporter of the administration's foreign policy, Eaton had made a surprising statement the previous day calling for American military action to hold Formosa.[8]

Acheson devoted the rest of the day to the public relations aspect of China policy. At 10:30 A.M. he arranged for the president to issue a State Department-drafted statement clarifying American Formosa policy. In an effort to rebut the Republican contention that the island technically belonged to Japan, the statement reviewed American wartime and postwar policy toward the island, recalling that in 1943 the Allies stated at Cairo that Formosa would be returned to China and that the United States signed a document reaffirming this pledge at the 1945 Potsdam Conference. "The United States," the draft stated, "had no desire to obtain special rights or privileges or to establish military bases on Formosa or to detach Formosa from China." In conclusion, it asserted that the United States would not furnish military aid or advice to Formosan forces. The only American assistance that would continue would be "the present ECA program of economic assistance."

Shortly before President Truman read the statement, NSC Executive Secretary Admiral Sidney Souers called Acheson to inform him that, on Truman's instruction, he had read the draft over the phone to Defense Secretary Louis Johnson and Joint Chiefs of Staff Chairman Omar Bradley. At Bradley's request, Souers amended the statement by inserting "at this time" after the disclaimer about not wishing to establish military bases and by deleting the phrase forswearing a desire "to detach Formosa from China." The State Department's deleted phrase, in effect, would have repealed NSC–37/5, which the NSC and Truman had reendorsed less than a week before. Bradley, Souers explained, thought it possible that the Chinese might "march south" and that the United States might then wish to detach Formosa from the mainland. Acheson told Souers that the deletion was all right but that he would have preferred to leave the phrase in. When the secretary saw Truman two hours later, the president explained that Bradley had wanted the phrase "at this time" added in the event of a possible future war. The statement as finally issued read: "The United States has no desire to obtain special rights or privileges or to establish military bases on Formosa at this time."[9]

Although the statement had been weakened in favor of the military's position, the secretary of state was determined to make the most of it. Five minutes after talking to Souers, Acheson received in his office Senators Knowland and Smith who had come to discuss Formosa. Acheson opened by saying that all continental China was lost to the Communists and that Britain and most British Commonwealth countries would soon recognize the new regime. After reviewing the problems of Southeast Asia, he focused on "the Formosan question." The secretary admitted to the senators that there was a legal case to be made that the island was not part of China until the Allies signed a Japanese Peace Treaty, something both men had argued adamantly, but Acheson said that he preferred to deal with the reality that Formosa has historically been a part of China. If the United States wished to uphold the legal argument, then the American people would have to be prepared to hazard a war to save it. There was no meeting of the minds. The meeting ended with "courteous but restrained goodbyes . . . offered by those present."[10]

After a 12:30 meeting with the president, the secretary held a press conference devoted to interpreting the statement Truman had issued in the morning. Asked why the White House revised the policy statement at the last minute to add "at this time," Acheson said that the phrase did not qualify the policy in the least: "It is a recognition of the fact that, in the unlikely and unhappy event that our forces might be attacked in the Far East," the United States could take action it deemed necessary for its security.[11]

Like the definitive policy statements of the previous year, the current effort provided only lightning rods for China bloc attacks. On the day of the announcement, Knowland began a five-hour debate in the Senate by pointing his finger at the "small group of willful men in the Far Eastern Division of the State Department who had the backing of their superiors." To buttress his argument he inserted an excerpt from a recent Joseph Alsop magazine article alleging that during the Second World War in China, "the American representatives there actively favored the Chinese Communists." In the midst of the colloquy, an ominous new voice joined in the chorus. Senator Joseph McCarthy, a junior Republican from Wisconsin, asked Knowland if he could "shed some light" on the arrest of Foreign Service Officer John Service, who the Senator charged as saying that "the only hope of Asia was communism" and who was arrested by the FBI on charges of espionage. He was not tried, he was not convicted, but was brought home, promoted, and put in charge of personnel and placement in the State Department." Knowland offered no specific answer. McCarthy spoke no more in this debate but would be heard from again soon.

Other Republicans joined in the attack, but the debate was not one-sided. Wayne Morse, a maverick Oregon Republican, warned that American military intervention in Formosa might lead to a new world war. Democrats Scott Lucas, Tom Connally, Brien McMahon, and Hubert Humphrey rallied to the administration's defense. What did the China bloc propose, asked Connally? "Do they want to send in an army with guns in their hands? Do they want to send the Navy, with flags unfurled, to protect Formosa in a civil war?" "Do they want us to go to war over China, or do they not?" asked McMahon.[12]

On Friday, Acheson told a cabinet meeting that he thought reception of the Formosa statement had been favorable.[13] Gallup Poll results, however, were ambiguous. Of the sample interviewed during the week of 8 January, 25 percent supported American aid to the island, ranging from financial and military assistance to armed intervention. Twenty-one percent supported a wait and see policy.[14] Acheson was aware that popular and congressional opinion were hanging in the balance and was determined to follow through with his public-relations offensive, something he had failed to do in the previous summer. Apart from general political considerations, the stakes on Capitol Hill remained high. There lay before the second session of the 80th Congress bills either funding or refunding the Marshall Plan, MAP, the Korean Aid program, aid to Palestinian refugees, Point IV, and assistance to Yugoslavia. All of this legislation required bipartisan support in both Houses and was subject to China bloc disruption. To gain support, the State Department planned a heavy agenda of "consultation" with congressional committees, to begin in the second week of January, and to hold conversations, on an individual basis, with the approximately 130 members of Congress who had recently returned from trips abroad.[15]

On Tuesday, 10 January, Acheson launched the counterattack in a closed session of the Senate Foreign Relations Committee. After Acheson skirted the Formosa question in his prepared and lengthy "review of the world situation," Senator Vandenberg finally brought him around to China policy with questions about the island's legal status. Once again, the secretary adamantly rejected the legalist argument and redirected discussion to a review of the "crescent" of countries where the "real center of our interests lie." The "arc" ran from Japan around China through Southeast Asia to India. Senator Smith brought him back to

Formosa again by asking a series of questions that Knowland had fed him (Knowland was in the room as a committee guest without the privilege of speaking). The first inquired if John Service or John Davies had a hand in preparing the 23 December Formosa memorandum; the insinuation was that the paper was the product of a "pink" cell within the department. Acheson said he did not know who in the department had written the document but he took responsibility for it. There had been much "nonsense" talked about the document, he said. After further grilling, the meeting, which had begun at 10:30 in the morning, broke at 3:55 in the afternoon with Acheson planning to return in a few days for more questioning.[16]

During the next day, as Acheson delivered the same presentation to the House Foreign Affairs Committee, the Senate China bloc once again excoriated the "left-wing group" in the State Department for defying "the general policy in China laid down by Congress." One recent recruit to the China bloc, Ohio's Republican Senator Robert Taft, told his colleagues that while he was "very doubtful" that aid could now save the mainland, he had not the "slightest doubt" that "the proper kind of sincere aid" to China after the war could have saved the country from communism.[17]

On Thursday, Acheson defended the administration's Asian policy in public remarks before the National Press Club. He opened by gently ridiculing Robert Taft. Referring to the senator's speech without mentioning his name, Acheson said that the word "sincere" raised interesting questions: "Was the aid given with tongue in cheek? Was it insincere?" In any case, he was intrigued by the senator's ability to "move from the area of no doubt to the area of possible doubt." After scoring this point, Acheson forswore dogmatism and gave a brilliant review of postwar developments in Asia and American policy. As in his recent secret congressional testimony, the thrust of this public speech was to point American attention away from China toward two geographic lines of American interests. One was the Pacific perimeter that the United States was committed to defend by military force. The other was a softer line of containment that ran through Southeast and South Asia. In those countries, the "direct responsibility lies with the people concerned"; the United States "could do no more than help." For Korea, Acheson acknowledged "responsibility." By what he said and did not say, he was trying to place the relatively trivial problem of Formosa in the broader context of Asian policy and outside the American-backed containment line.[18]

The speech and the congressional testimony were eloquent efforts at redirecting public and congressional attention away from China and Formosa that failed. China's friends would not drop the subject and the debate continued, feeding on new issues, which seemed to arise daily.[19] One was the 6 January British de facto recognition of Peking, an action that excited China bloc comment in both houses of Congress. Another was the question of whether or not the Pentagon had been thoroughly consulted over the decision to "write off" Formosa and whether the defense secretary and Joint Chiefs of Staff would testify before the Foreign Relations Committee (they finally did in a closed session on 26 January).[20]

As had happened so often in the previous year, the Chinese Communists also fueled the debate by unfriendly actions in China. In a move announced some days in advance, Communist authorities "requisitioned" a significant portion of the American consulate general office in Peking, claiming that the United States had taken it under unequal treaties. When they announced their intention to seize the property, Consul General Clubb, on the highest American authority, informed the Communists that their confiscation would compel the United States to withdraw all official personnel from China. The warning went unheeded and on Saturday, 14 January, Acheson announced that he was pulling all American diplomats out of China.[21]

The China bloc took the Communist action as another occasion to criticize the State Department's bankrupt policy. Knowland connected the Chinese move with Truman's 5 January statement. "Appeasement is but surrender on the installment plan," he charged, and called for the resignation of "the men responsible." The debate continued into a third week with the Democratic senators regrouping and counterattacking on Tuesday.[22] This latest round came to a shocking finale on Thursday, 19 January, when House Republicans defeated the Korean aid bill by a margin of 192 to 191. This unexpected action sobered both the administration and the China bloc.

Aid for Korea and Formosa

The *New York Times* accurately described the vote on Korean aid as the "first major setback for the administration at the hands of Congress on a matter involving foreign affairs since the war's end."[23] The aid bill had been defeated by the same overlapping combination of forces in the

House that had opposed Korean aid in the summer—economizers, Republican partisans, isolationists, and some members of the China bloc. The vote boded ill not only for Asian policy, but indicated that the broad bipartisan coalition that had long supported United States foreign policy was, after many false predictions of demise, finally crumbling.

The administration reacted quickly. In private, Acheson told his cabinet colleagues that the vote resulted from a "sad performance" by the House leadership and had "terrified" the nations of Europe and elsewhere who were concerned that the United States was pulling out.[24] In public he expressed "concern and dismay" and concentrated on ways to obtain the $60 million the House had voted down.[25] Support for his effort came from the Senate China bloc. Senator Smith said he was "shocked and disturbed." Knowland, who had voted for Korean aid in the summer, also expressed concern and took the occasion to draw a political lesson for Acheson. The vote "might be a signal light as to what might happen in other foreign policy areas" if the needs of China were ignored.[26] In private, Arthur Vandenberg told Acheson that the vote was "doubly shocking" since the case for Korean aid was superb and the House Republicans were acting stupidly. Like Acheson, he was "concerned about repairing the damage."[27]

There were several existing and potential legislative vehicles available for salvaging Korean aid. The legislation the House killed was a House bill (H.R. 5330) that the Foreign Affairs Committee had reported in June 1949. Its key provision was an authorization of $150 million for economic assistance through 30 June 1950. When the bill stalled in the Rules Committee, Congress passed two interim appropriations in October totaling $60 million. However, when the full House killed H.R. 5330 on 19 January, the House Foreign Affairs Committee also had in its files the Senate Korean aid bill (S. 2319), which had passed the Senate and which also authorized $150 million for use through 30 June. After the House voted to kill its own Korean aid bill, Acheson, Truman, and the House leadership agreed that the Foreign Affairs Committee should now report the Senate bill and allow the House to vote again on Korean aid.[28]

Korean legislation, however, could not, for political reasons, be considered separately from the China question. China aid was becoming an issue again because the latest version of the China Aid Act required that the program terminate on 15 February 1950. In the interim, since its passage in the previous spring, the size of the aid fund had grown from approximately $54 million to over $100 million due to "deobligation" of money slated for Communist-conquered areas of China. New authorizing legislation, though, would be needed to make the money available. Senators Smith and Knowland thus introduced a bill on 12 January amending the old China Aid Act to extend the money's use through 30 June 1950.[29]

After the Korean vote, several schemes for saving Korean aid emerged and some were tied to the China aid question. Senator Smith first recommended that the ECA draw from the MAP 303 fund to get by the immediate period in Korea. The ECA administrator thought that the Smith-Knowland China aid bill might be expanded to allow the China aid fund to support Korea, an idea Smith and Knowland told him they favored.[30] Acheson explained his preferred approach on 24 January before yet another Foreign Relations Committee executive session. While he favored the Smith-Knowland bill extending the China aid legislation, he preferred broadening the fund's area of coverage to include "the general area of China" and to make the money available through June 1951. He explained that the ECA only needed $28 million of the $103 million total residual China aid fund to undertake a program for Formosa through fiscal 1951; the Nationalists themselves were only asking for $55 million for the same period. Whatever the need proved to be, it might be desirable to have the unused balance available for use in the Philippines, Indonesia, Siam, Indochina, and perhaps for advanced funding of the Point IV technical assistance program. For Korean aid, Acheson said he wanted the House to pass S.2319, the original Senate Korean aid bill.

Senator Vandenberg was content to allow the expansion of the China aid bill to cover Southeast Asia: as was Senator Smith, who was for helping "the little people of the Far East" and who trusted the State Department to reserve whatever was necessary for Formosa. Knowland was less obliging. Speaking before the committee as a witness in Acheson's presence, he said he was willing to expand his bill to accommodate Korea but opposed opening it to include aid to "areas which have not had ample congressional hearings."[31] Acheson pressed the case for his version at several points, but the discussion was comparatively harmonious. The administration and the China bloc appeared to be working out their differences once again.[32]

In the following week, both the House and Senate committees acted on their respective Asian aid bills. The House committee, after an Acheson appearance, reported a completely rewritten S.2319. Titled the "Far Eastern Economic Assistance Act of 1950," one section of the bill authorized extension of the China Aid Act through 30 June 1950, but without expanding the allowable area for the money's use to the general area of China. Another section authorized $60 million for Korea through the same date.[33] The House Rules Committee quickly cleared the aid bill for debate. The reason for its smooth sailing, explained one Republican congressman, was that "the Korean hook was now baited with a very succulent piece of legislation which many of us had desired."[34] On 9 February, the House passed its bill by a vote of 240 to 134. Most Republicans who had previously opposed Korean aid supported the legislation.

The Senate Foreign Relations Committee, which did not need to act on Korea, reported the Smith-Knowland amendment as originally written and with the administration's blessings.[35] The day after the House passed the legislation, the Senate concurred in the House amendment to the original Senate Korean aid bill (now a completely rewritten instrument) without debate and sent the measure to the White House where President Truman signed it four days later.[36]

Both sides could again claim victory. The China bloc succeeded in extending China aid and blocked the State Department's soft-peddled amendment, which would have expanded the area where the money could be spent and extended its use through 30 June 1951. The administration, however, had not suffered a defeat, only a delay. It got almost all the Korean aid it had requested (the aid total was reduced from $60 to $50 million in the subsequent appropriations bill) and kept the China aid fund alive long enough to return immediately to Congress to request again the fund's extension into fiscal 1951 and its broadening to include Southeast Asia. The administration also made it clear, even before S.2319's passage, that the ECA intended only to spend $10 million on Formosa through fiscal 1951, a policy consistent with Truman's 5 January policy statement. Thus the China bloc had not changed the administration's policy and, in the wake of the initial Korean aid defeat, even quieted itself down after three weeks of frenzied criticism. However, this relative calm (criticism continued in more subdued tones) lasted only briefly. Senator Joseph McCarthy shattered it permanently in a 9 February speech in Wheeling, West Virginia.

McCarthy and the Bipartisan Counteroffensive

McCarthy's speech, given before the Ohio County Women's Republican Club, charged that the secretary of state was harboring 205 (or 57— there is uncertainty about the exact number) Communists in the State

Department. He repeated the charge at various stops during a speech-making tour throughout the West and Midwest and capped his trip with a telegram to President Truman suggesting that he order Acheson to give the White House a list of the department's disloyal employees. The news of McCarthy's charges became national when it appeared in major Sunday newspapers on 12 February.

The State Department and the Senate Democrats were quick to take up the challenge. While they were not pleased with the attack, the administration supporters saw in it an opportunity to knock over a self-erected Republican straw man and discredit the long-hinted assertion that Communists had infiltrated the State Department. McCarthy appeared to be a weak, wild-swinging opponent who had carried the innuendos of McCarran, Jenner, and the China lobby to their logical conclusion. Two days after McCarthy repeated his charges on the Senate floor, the Senate passed a Democrat-sponsored resolution calling for a Foreign Relations Committee probe. Conducted by a subcommittee, the investigation got under way on 8 March. Shortly before it began, Acheson assured Truman that "arrangements were well in hand for dealing with the McCarthy charges" before the subcommittee.[37]

Acheson was wrong. The hearings, which ran off and on for four months, allowed McCarthy to dominate the headlines with a proliferation of charges of disloyalty. His most frequent targets were men associated with wartime and postwar Asian policy. With the notable exception of Maine's Republican Senator Margaret Chase Smith, McCarthy's party colleagues either rallied to his support or remained mute. The Democrats' counteroffensive, especially in the subcommittee, was ineffectual. Yet, despite the Democrats' ultimate failure to quash McCarthy, it was not clear in the spring of 1950, in the midst of the charges and counter-charges about spies in the State Department, that the senator was destined to become an "ism" that would dominate American politics for the next four years. He was a threat of the first order to the administration's foreign policy and tenure in office, but he was not something to which the State Department under Dean Acheson was willing to surrender.

Acheson, with Truman's full support, fought back in two ways. One was to establish a special inner-department staff to assist the Senate investigation and generally to put the lie to McCarthy's charges. Another response was to intensify his effort to obtain bipartisan support for the department's general foreign policy.[38] The catalyst for the renewed bipartisan offensive was the terminally ill Arthur Vandenberg, who was largely confined to his hotel room. In late March, Vandenberg wrote a letter to Paul Hoffman, which soon appeared in the *New York Times,* celebrating the success of the Marshall Plan and calling for a nonpartisan review of American foreign policy. When Truman read it, he sent the Michigan senator a warm letter thanking him for his sentiments. Acheson, after returning from a speaking tour of California, telephoned Vandenberg to ask his advice on how to renew bipartisan consultation. The secretary asked particularly about what mechanism might be used to achieve this goal and for the name of a prominent Republican who could serve as a consultant to the department on Asian policy. Unable to meet with Acheson in person, Vandenberg answered the secretary in a 29 March confidential letter recommending that the department consult regularly with the four ranking Republicans of the House and Senate Foreign Affairs Committees and suggesting several names as prospective advisors.[39]

Two days before Vandenberg wrote his letter, Acheson took another step to deflect Republican criticism by reshuffling the department's top Asian policy makers. The secretary removed Butterworth from his job as FE chief, making him a special advisor on Japanese affairs, selected Dean Rusk to replace Butterworth (a "demotion" from his post as deputy under secretary that Rusk had requested), and appointed ex-senator John Sherman Cooper, an internationalist Republican from Kentucky, as a high-level department consultant.[40]

The Cooper appointment proved to be mildly controversial because it suggested that the administration had passed over John Foster Dulles. The press noted the inference and Vandenberg immediately brought it to Acheson's attention in another letter written on 31 March. "The Cooper appointment is excellent and I approve it—although I should have preferred *Dulles* in this particular role." The senator expressed awareness of "political considerations" blocking his candidate's appointment but suggested that the situation called for "impressively broadminded 'give and take.' "[41] The chief "consideration" was President Truman's anger over Dulles's attacks on the "Fair Deal" during the New York senator's special fall election campaign. By 4 April, however, the president told Acheson that it would be all right to hire Dulles, who had lost the election, as long as he was not given the prestigious post of ambassador at large.[42] Following Truman's green light and two days of Acheson-Dulles negotiations (Dulles was worried that his title would not be sufficiently prestigious) the department announced that the Republican statesman would be brought in as a "top advisor."[43] Acheson soon placed

Dulles in charge of negotiating a peace treaty with Japan.

With this latest bipartisan offensive attracting headlines (frequently running in columns next to latest McCarthy stories), Acheson and Truman attempted to convert Styles Bridges to bipartisanship. Bridges was a formidable target to woo in that he was a strong McCarthy supporter and was currently leading a campaign to have Acheson fired. The senator, however, was also an old Senate colleague and friend of Harry Truman. On 26 March, the president wrote him a personal note to explain the damage he was doing to the United States by "joining the 'wolfhounds' in the attack on Dean Acheson." Truman appealed to Bridges—as an "old-time personal friend and Senate colleague"—to reconsider his views and expressed a willingness to discuss matters with him personally.[44]

Bridges responded in a letter to Truman three days later stating that he had arranged to meet Acheson and would like to talk to the president as well.[45] With Bridges possibly willing to reconcile his differences with the administration, Truman, in an impulsive statement at a Key West press conference on 30 March, placed the prospective rapprochement in jeopardy by charging that Senators Bridges, Wherry, and McCarthy were saboteurs of American foreign policy and assets to the Kremlin.[46] It was not a statement calculated to win favor with Bridges, but the senator went ahead with his planned appointment with Acheson. On 5 April, Acheson wrote Truman that he was having Bridges to his house at the end of the week to discuss the senator's personal grievances against him. Acheson did not know what they were but hoped "that a good talk, eased with some bourbon, may result in eliminating what I am sure are misunderstandings."[47]

After a successful Bridges-Acheson meeting, Truman invited the two men to see him at the White House on 18 April. The meeting occurred at an opportune moment; Cold War tensions were high as a result of the recent loss of an American Navy patrol plane near Russia and it was an appropriate time for Americans to close ranks. According to Acheson, the discussion was "very friendly and satisfactory" and there was no discussion of "the McCarthy business." Bridges told reporters afterwards that he welcomed this "very evident gesture on their part to establish a closer relationship with the Republican minority in the Senate." The next day the Senate Republican Policy Committee endorsed Bridges's affirmative statement.[48]

The results of the bipartisan offensive were mixed. In the short term

—the spring of 1950—the effort attenuated the impact of McCarthy's charges against the State Department and preserved bipartisan cooperation on important legislation relating to Europe and Asia. It also relieved some pressure on the State Department's policy of writing off Formosa and pursuing a passive policy of encouraging Chinese Titoism. The Gallup Poll, however, would soon hint at the administration's long-term prospects for gaining bipartisan and popular support for its foreign policy. In early May, Gallup asked a sample population if it had heard about the "bipartisan foreign policy." Only 26 percent had a general understanding of the term and 21 percent thought it was a good idea to have one. Three weeks later, Gallup asked if they had heard of McCarthy's charges against the State Department. Eighty-four percent had. Thirty-nine percent thought the charges did more good than harm; 29 percent thought they were harmful; 16 percent had no opinion.[49]

Slippage of the Tito Policy

In the wake of the Formosa debate and the McCarthy attack, Truman, Acheson, and the State Department remained committed to the passive policy of encouraging a Sino-Soviet split. Given the broad objective of allowing the Chinese to remain in the Soviet camp only as briefly as possible, these dominant leaders in the administration tolerated the vacillating Formosa policy only as a political expedient. Acheson explained the balance between the two in remarkably candid testimony before a closed 29 March session of the Senate Foreign Relations Committee. The Communists were currently in control, he said, and there were two things the United States could do. One was to fight them; the other was "to do everything you can to separate them from Moscow." He preferred the second approach. The "Chinese inevitably, we believe, will come into conflict with Moscow, because the very basic objectives of Moscow are hostile to the very basic objectives of China. . . . What we want to say to the Chinese is, watch out! Look what has happened" in areas where the Russians were pursuing their territorial interests at China's expense. Senator Henry Cabot Lodge asked if it was not true "that the sooner we disconnect ourselves from [Nationalist] China the better?" "There are many reasons that it is not upon us," Acheson replied, "including the attitude of a large number of people in the United States and the Congress. . . . We have it [Chiang Kai-shek] very definitely on our backs."[50]

The trade-off between what the administration thought to be a wise policy and political prudence constituted a China policy in the winter and spring of 1950 that skirted the shoals of commitment to either Titoist policy toward the mainland or a pro-Nationalist policy toward Formosa. The United States continued to recognize the Nationalist regime as China's government and supported Chiang's claim to a United Nations seat. It granted the island limited economic assistance and allowed it to draw from the residue of the $125 million fund for small-scale military assistance. The State Department was unwilling, however, to use the veto to back the Nationalists' claim to the UN seat or to grant further military aid. When Chiang's American-made airplanes and bombs attacked mainland cities, the department issued strong protests.[51]

Policy toward the Communists continued on hold. Its most active ingredient was propaganda in a variety of forms that called attention to Soviet imperialism at China's expense.[52] The State Department appeared to be waiting for a succession of events to occur before normalizing relations. These included Formosa's fall, the development of a less heated domestic American political climate, and evidence that Peking was becoming disenchanted with the Russians and willing to deal correctly with the United States. Unfortunately for Acheson, only Formosa's turnover to the Communists appeared to be even close to occurring. All other signs were discouraging. While there were fleeting hints suggesting that elements within the Chinese Communist Party still wanted to deal with the West, these groups were obviously not ascendant; and most contacts Americans in China had with Communist officials and all public propaganda continued to be hostile. The new regime consistently praised Russia and attacked the United States for supporting Chiang's Formosa regime and failing to recognize China's new rulers.[53] One manifestation of this hostility had been the confiscation of the American consular property in Peking. Another was the growing Soviet presence in China and the consummation of a Sino-Soviet treaty that became known in the West on 14 February.[54] The agreement granted China restoration of all rights in Manchuria by 1953, the revocation of the "unequal" 1945 Sino-Soviet treaty, and grant of a $300 million credit to the Chinese over five years (a gesture diminished by the subsequent devaluation of the Russian ruble).[55] While the treaty did not come as a surprise in Washington and did not immediately dissuade Acheson from his long-term quest for a Sino-Soviet split, it did nothing to reinforce the department's prediction that China and Russia would eventually part company.

Along with the China bloc-Chinese Communist push and pull away from rapprochement with Peking, the State Department continued to be challanged by both the Pentagon's support for a strong pro-Formosa policy and doubts among the department's own top officers. The military renewed its offensive against the Chinese Tito policy on the day the Sino-Soviet treaty was made public. On 14 February, Secretary Johnson wrote Acheson requesting guidance about further military aid to the Formosan regime. In light of the president's 5 January statement, he inquired if the military could complete transactions under authority of the $125 military aid grant in the 1948 China Aid Act and continue to dispose of naval equipment authorized in a 1946 act allowing transfer of lesser American naval equipment to the Chinese.[56] The Pentagon apparently felt confident of an affirmative reply. Reviewing the letter the next day, an officer in the Army's Plans and Operations Division observed that "in view of the political interest in the subject a negative reply is considered unlikely at this juncture."[57]

After a delay of two months, Acheson responded to Johnson's query. The department allowed the Pentagon to fulfill "orders in the process of procurement and delivery" but discontinued procurement or transfer of American military material to the Chinese government.[58] Three weeks later, Johnson wrote back interpreting these guidelines to mean allowance to deliver goods in the pipeline to China only as of 14 April under the 1948 act and as of 5 February under the 1946 legislation.[59] After the passage of another three weeks, Acheson wrote Johnson on 1 June explaining that it was permissible to exhaust all 1948 military aid funds, even if procurement began 14 April; no reference was made to allowing cash sales.[60] The three-and-a-half-month exchange of letters had produced yet one more compromise in a compromising policy. The State Department had backed off slightly from its policy of granting no more military aid to the Nationalists.

Rusk Takes FE

The source of the softening appears to have been Dean Rusk, who took over control of FE on March 28.* Before Rusk assumed his new post as assistant secretary, Acheson and his subordinates in FE were in a mood to break relations with Formosa. One important stimulus to their thinking

*Full documentation for the department's decision making for 1950 is not yet available. This account is drawn largely from the few documents printed and described in footnotes in *FR*, 1950, VI (Washington, D.C.: GPO, 1976).

was the Nationalist bombing of Chinese cities and American-owned facilities therein, especially the raid on the Shang-hai Power Company on 9 and 10 February.[63] In mid-February Philip Sprouse complained to FE director Livingston Merchant about an unsatisfactory Nationalist reply to an American protest over the bombing and expressing indignation about the weak American response. Not only was American property being damaged with American-made bombs and airplanes, but the Nationalists were doing violence to the tattered remains of the American position on the mainland. They owed their existence to the United States and would probably fall if American support were withdrawn. "It seems incredible, therefore, that we permit the Chinese Government brazenly to do the damage to our position in China that it is doing." The United States "cannot drift between the two courses, as we seem to be doing at present."[62]

Merchant took a less excited view of the ambiguous China policy but held the same position. After reading Sprouse's memorandum setting forth his exasperation, he forwarded it to Dean Rusk, still deputy under secretary, with a cover note stating that in the two-year effort at disengagement from the civil war "we must expect some apparent confusion in our actions for some little time to come." It would be out of the question to follow either the Formosa or mainland policy to its extremity. It was necessary, however, "that we should be clear in our minds in which direction we are moving in order to give a consistent emphasis in our daily actions to the policy which is fundamental." That policy, he gathered, was "complete freedom of movement and disassociation in the Chinese mind with the Kuomintang as rapidly as events at home and abroad permit."[63]

Dean Acheson, who was spending much of his days at the front line fighting the China bloc, was even less ready to temporize. In the early evening of 17 February he telephoned Merchant's office with a pointed question. An aide, who took the call in Merchant's absence, noted that the secretary "referred to the note which the Chinese had given to us 'telling us to go to hell with our protest of the Shanghai bombing.'" Acheson "wanted to ask if this note gave us a chance to get out of Formosa and withdraw aid from the Nationalists." The aide said that FE was actively reviewing the question and would soon furnish an answer. Acheson replied, "Fine, fine, I just wanted to be sure that you are thinking about it."[64]

The secretary of state's strong negative feelings about the Nationalists failed to translate into policy. Instead of breaking with Formosa, he appointed Dean Rusk to be his chief Asian policy advisor. As Acheson might well have predicted, Rusk began to reverse existing policy in an effort to save Formosa. One of Rusk's first moves was to demonstrate to Acheson that the situation on the island was improving; he did this by sending him a revised CIA appraisal of Formosa's survival potential on 17 April. The agency continued to predict the island's fall by the year's end but noted that "the possibility of a somewhat longer survival of the Nationalist regime . . . should not be excluded."[65]

Nine days later, on 26 April, Rusk forwarded reports from the American military attachés in Hong Kong and Taipei that stated that extensive Soviet aid to China made a successful Nationalist defense of Formosa doubtful and warned that China would exert full pressure on Southeast Asia after conquering the island. The Hong Kong attaché reported the high morale of the Nationalist troops on Hainan and Chushan Islands. The Taipei attaché wanted a $10 million Formosa aid program. Rusk also forwarded a dissenting cable from the senior State Department official on Taipei but did not highlight its contents.* He passed these cables along, he explained, to apprise the secretary of the stepped-up Soviet military support for a possible invasion which "may prompt further strong recommendations, official and otherwise, for countervailing aid to the Nationalist Government."[66]

As the spring progressed, Rusk continued his effort to reverse policy with increased vigor and with support from important allies in the military. The Pentagon's civilian and military high command continued to favor aiding Formosa and, although they rarely spoke out in public, they made their views forcefully known in private. One close aide to Johnson, Assistant Defense Secretary Paul Griffith, expressed his and Johnson's support for Formosa aid to Ambassador Koo and suggested that public opinion might force Acheson to leave office.[67] In Japan, General MacArthur gave John Foster Dulles a long memorandum on the importance of saving Formosa; Dulles, who himself had recently written a long brief for Formosa aid, quoted its contents in a 22 June telegram to Washington.[68]

With Dean Rusk representing the State Department, the military was

---

*This representative, *Chargé d'affaires* Robert Strong, wrote Sprouse on 20 April expressing his concern "that the representations of other agencies of the U.S. Government are lining up solidly behind this regime, are emphasizing the minor improvements and overlooking the major failures, and are not considering the Mainland and its potentialities." *FR*, 1950, VI, p. 334.

DRAWING THE LINE

now in a stronger position to chip away at the prohibitions against aiding
the Nationalists. In a 25 May meeting with Defense Department officials
from the Office of Military Assistance, Rusk agreed to seek a change in
the State Department policy. As one military official wrote later, Rusk was
willing: (1) to determine whether the State Department's provision on
aiding Formosa as expressed in the 14 April Acheson letter to Johnson
could be broadened; (2) "to take steps within the Department of State to
authorize and facilitate the granting of export licenses to the . . . [Nation-
alists] for military equipment purchased in the United States"; and (3) "to
request Presidential release of . . . 303 funds" for "covert action in
support of resistance on Formosa."[69]

Within five days Rusk honored his agreement by calling a meeting of
Jessup, Paul Nitze, the new Policy Planning Staff director, Merchant,
Sprouse, and Fisher Howe, a departmental intelligence officer. In a mem-
orandum to his superior, Howe wrote that Rusk was

> still working toward raising the question of Formosa, basing his think-
> ing generally along the lines that world opinion and US opinion are
> generally unhappy at lack of a forthright action on our part in the Far
> East; that Formosa presents a plausible place to "draw the line" and
> is, in itself, important politically if not strategically, for what it repre-
> sents in continued Communist expansion. . . . I believe that the
> representation at this meeting, plus Dulles, constituted the only ones
> who are aware of this move on Rusk's part.

During the meeting the participants "generally agreed" that Rusk should
propose to Acheson that the United States pressure Chiang into requesting a UN trusteeship for Formosa that would allow the American Navy
to interpose itself in the situation by saving the island from the Communists and for the United Nations.[70]

There is no evidence that Acheson agreed to Rusk's proposal if, indeed, Rusk made it. It is clear, however, that the secretary adopted half
of the plan by the end of the month. On 24 June, Washington learned
of the North Korean attack on the South. The next day, Truman summoned his senior foreign policy advisors to an evening meeting at Blair
House. Before dinner General Omar Bradley read MacArthur's long
memorandum emphasizing the importance of denying Formosa to the
Communists. After dinner, the president called on Acheson to open
discussion. Reviewing the Korean situation and the UN role in the con-

flict, the secretary suggested, according to Philip Jessup's notes, "that the President should order the Seventh Fleet to proceed to Formosa and prevent an attack on Formosa from the Mainland."[71] President Truman announced the decision two days later.[72] The beleaguered policy of encouraging Chinese Titoism was now shelved.

12

Containment in Southeast Asia

The Truman administration's concern about Southeast Asia and the world in general intensified in 1950. A benchmark in its alarmed perception was the national security bureaucracy's adoption of NSC–68 as national policy in the spring. The paper's authors and supporters, which included the senior ranks of the State and Defense Departments, held an unambiguous view of the Soviet Union's purpose in the world. It was "the complete subversion or forcible destruction of the machinery of government and structure of society in the countries of the non-Soviet world and their replacement by an apparatus and structure subservient to and controlled from the Kremlin. To that end Soviet efforts are now directed toward the domination of the Eurasian land mass."[1] It was not a new view, but NSC–68 articulated it with precision and laid out its ramifications in great detail. After a lengthy analysis, the paper called for a rapid buildup of "Free World" strength. The paper was a general analytical document and did not focus on regional problems, but it was in harmony with the heightened concern with which the Truman administration viewed developments in Southeast Asia.

Throughout 1949, the State Department and other government agencies had written dark assessments of conditions in Southeast Asia and even darker predictions about the consequences of the region's fall to

Communist control. In 1950, the assessments of individual countries continued, with justification, to be a mixture of optimism and gloom. The prospects for a non-Communist, postcolonial government looked brighter in Indonesia than they had in the previous year. Thailand continued to be relatively stable and was leaning more decisively toward the West. Burma remained chaotic. The Philippines' economy was still deteriorating as a result of inflation, corruption, and mismanagement, and the government was being challenged by Communist guerillas. Communist guerillas were battling the British in Malaya and the French-Bao Dai position in Indochina looked doubtful.[2]

The administration's private papers and public pronouncements describing the region's importance to America and the West stressed themes heard in the previous year. Europe was still considered of prime importance, but, because of its economic resources and because it served as a market for Western goods, Southeast Asia was vital to the West's economy. Because of its critical location, the region was a "vital segment in the line of containment." Because of the psychological blow its fall to communism would have on the rest of the "Free World," it was crucial that Southeast Asia remain non-Communist for global propaganda reasons, especially in light of the recent Communist conquest of mainland China. And, finally, the debit on the Western side caused by the subcontinent's loss would show up as a plus on the Soviet ledger; resources, markets, strategic advantage, and psychological victory would all go to Russia. As a result of these great stakes, it was in the vital American interest to compete with Russia in Southeast Asia by encouraging the success of non-Communist political elements in every country of the region.[3]

While the Truman administration's assessment of the American interests in Southeast Asia had not changed, its enthusiasm for acting to protect them had changed dramatically since the drafting of PPS-51 in early 1949. The change can be measured in the increased number of documents circulated within the State and Defense Departments on the subject, in the number of private and public statements officials made on aspects of Southeast Asia policy, and in the refinement in thoughts expressed. A series of events carried over from the old year that helped compel the administration to act: the Communist victory in China; the fall and winter policy reassessment; and the authorization and appropriation of money to finance an active policy. These events combined in the new year with the political necessity of appearing to be active in combating communism in Asia and the departure of a few key State Department officials, who leaned marginally against an active policy, from important positions of responsibility and their replacement with officers eager to move aggressively to defend American interests in Southeast Asia.

Extension of the 303 Formula

As with its China policy, the State Department pursued Southeast Asian policy in 1950 mindful of events both in Congress and Asia. After the compromise with the China bloc over the terms for extending the China Aid Act authorization in February, the administration returned to Congress the next month to obtain what it had wanted before. Under the latest extension, approximately $100 million remained authorized for aid to non-Communist areas of China. The State Department continued to want this aid freed for use throughout Asia and again pressed Congress to apply the "general area of China" formula to economic aid. The China bloc, by early March, was prepared to allow some of the money to be spent outside of China, although not all. Since the latest legislation extended the aid fund's life only through 30 June 1950, it was necessary for both sides to review the question once again.

The suggestion to expand the area of the fund's use once again came from Dean Acheson. The occasion was a 7 March public hearing on the administration's bill extending Marshall Plan legislation through fiscal 1951. Tom Connally asked the secretary if he had any suggestions about Formosa aid. Acheson said that he had suggested the "general area" formula in recent testimony before the committee but that some members thought "that we should come up with a more or less detailed program for the whole southeastern Asia area" and the department was not yet prepared to set forth such a program. "I made the suggestion once and I hesitate somewhat to make it again."[4]

Within three days, the department had cast aside hesitation and produced an amendment to the ECA bill proposing a "China Area Aid Act of 1950." It extended the authorized period for the fund's use through 30 June 1951 to "any place in the general area of China which the President deems to be not under Communist control, in such manner and on such terms and conditions as the President may determine." The amendment's purpose, once again, was to obtain economic aid funds for use in Southeast Asia.[5]

The Senate Foreign Relations Committee adopted an altered version of the State Department draft amendment on 21 March. H. Alexander Smith offered the amendment with two substantive changes. One defined the region covered as being "in China and in the general area of China." The other provided that "not less than $50,000,000 of such funds shall be available only for such assistance in areas in China (including Formosa and Hainan)." Senator Millard Tydings suggested that Smith's language would be improved if a qualification were added allowing the $50 million to be spent in China "so long as the President deemed it practicable." Smith agreed. The State Department representative at the meeting said he would prefer that the amount set aside be $30 million instead of $50 million, since that was close to the sum ECA budgeted for Formosa in the next fiscal year, but he did not protest strongly. The committee adopted by voice vote the State Department amendment as amended by Smith and improved by Tydings. It extended the China aid fund's life through 30 June 1951, allowed approximately $50 million for use in the "general area of China," and reserved $50 million for non-Communist areas of China if deemed "practicable" by the president. As with the original "general area of China" fund in the MAP bill, the executive made no attempt to justify an aid program for Southeast Asia and was not challenged to do so. The committee also adopted an amendment authorizing $100 million for economic assistance to Korea for the same period without any significant discussion.[6]

Ten days later the House passed a slightly different version of the same omnibus economic assistance bill, which was largely a European aid measure, and by 19 May the Senate and House adopted a conference report that reserved $40 million for "China (including Formosa)," $40 million for the "general area," $6 million for educating Chinese students in the United States, and $8 million for famine relief in China. The Formosa aid was to be used only if the president deemed it practicable. On 5 June, Congress passed the foreign aid legislation and the president signed it into law. Along with European, Chinese, and Korean aid, another title authorized $35 million for a "Point IV" technical assistance program for "economically underdeveloped countries" (the appropriation for this program was ultimately cut to $27 million). Even before the omnibus bills enactment, policy planners in the executive branch could, by early spring, count on approximately half of the remaining China aid fund being available for use in Southeast Asia.[7]

While Congress was busy voting economic assistance for Southeast Asia, the State Department was at work determining how the money

might be spent. In anticipation of some funds being available, Walt Butterworth recommended in January that a mission be sent to the region
to determine what aid might be granted.[8] The State Department quickly
assembled a small group of experts headed by R. Allen Griffin, the retired
deputy chief of the ECA China mission and Republican editor of the
Monterey Peninsula Herald. Under Secretary of State James Webb gave
Griffin his instructions on 1 March. The mission's purposes were to select
country projects that could be financed with 303 funds "which would
have immediate political significance" and which would "lay the ground-
work for the anticipated Point IV program in the Southeast Asia countries."[9] Although Webb did not mention the prospects, the mission members also assumed that between $50 and $100 million would soon be
available from congressional extension and broadening of the China
aid.[10]

The Griffin mission, composed of eleven men, visited Indochina, Sin-
gapore, Burma, Thailand, and Indonesia between 6 March and 22 April.
While its findings helped shape the future American economic aid program to the region, its cables to the department recommending aid
programs only buttressed existing views. Their well-publicized mission's
immediate function was to demonstrate active American interest in constructive opposition to communism in Asia. The targets of the public-
relations aspects of their mission lived in both Asia and the United States.

Military Aid Authorized

After adoption of NSC–48/2, executive branch papers on programming 303 funds proliferated. Louis Johnson, whose Defense Department
theoretically had equal say with the State Department on the money's use,
quickly pressed his "military point of view" on Dean Acheson. On 1
February, Johnson sent the State Department a Joint Chiefs of Staff
memorandum on military assistance calling for "a program of overt assistance and covert operations in the general area of China [to] be initiated as early as possible." The chiefs tentatively recommended reserving
$15 million for Indochina, $5 million for Indonesia, $10 million for
Thailand. As a contingency reserve they suggested that the balance be
reserved for the Malayan states ($5 million), Burma ($10 million), and
covert operations in China including Taiwan and Tibet ($30 million). In
his cover note to Acheson, Johnson observed that "from this [that is, the
military's] planning there will presumably be developed a joint recom-

mendation which you and I may make to the President on the programs called for in NSC 48/2."[11]

With Secretary Johnson's gratuitous assertion of Pentagon dominance brushed aside, the two departments programmed the 303 funds in relative harmony. By 9 January Acheson, with Johnson's support, had already requested that Truman grant approval of $5 million of the 303 fund for the police equipment for the Indonesian constabulary. The president promptly authorized the aid.[12] On 15 February, at the Pentagon's request, Truman authorized another $6,524,721 for use to improve airfields in Japan.[13] On 9 March, with Johnson's approval, Acheson requested that Truman set aside "in principle" $10 million for Thailand and $15 million for Indochina military aid.[14] (This recommendation was preceded in the State Department by further consideration in the legal office of whether—given statements in the Senate about the fund being unavailable in colonial areas—the money could be spent in Indochina; the question was resolved in favor of granting aid.)[15] Truman approved this request on 10 March.[16]

With the principle of aid to Indochina and Thailand established, the two departments prepared another request asking for actual allocation of the money. Along with military aid, the State Department also sought Pentagon sanction for use of another $5 million to begin funding an Indochina economic assistance program. The Defense Department gave its grudging approval but, in its formal reply, noted that the 303 fund was really for military aid and that such use was "not so intended when the Department of Defense originated the idea of this fund and supported it."[17] Acheson soon forwarded to the president requests for authorization of the Indochina economic aid and the Thai and Indochinese military assistance already agreed to in principle. On 1 May, the president, on advice of the budget director, authorized $10 million for military aid to Indochina, $3 million for Thailand and $750,000 for a medical program in Indochina. The rest of the requested money, he assured Acheson and Johnson, would be granted when plans for the monies' use were more sharply formulated.[18] By late June, after more formal requests and grants of approval, Truman had signed off on an additional $3.5 million for Burma, $2,930,000 for propaganda projects in Southeast Asia, a total of $21 million in military aid for Indochina (with the State Department preparing to press for at least $10 million more) and $6.5 million for covert military aid for purposes not revealed in available records.[19]

While the executive branch programmed 303 funds for FY 1950 (1 July

1950 to 30 June 1951), it requested that Congress grant another $75 million in unvouchered funds for the "general area of China." The request went to the hill with a presidential message on 1 June asking for a second omnibus MAP authorization bill. "The value of having these [general area of China] funds available," the message read in part, "has been amply demonstrated. Programs of assistance to countries in this area, such as Indochina, are now under way."[20]

Although Congress never considered the ramifications of the Indochina aid program the administration was in the process of implementing, the request for more 303 funds did not come as a surprise and its purpose was not obscure. The State Department and the news media had kept it well informed about the progress of American Southeast Asia policy and, in particular, about plans to render economic and military assistance. Much of Acheson's executive testimony to the Senate Foreign Relations Committee on 10 January was devoted to emphasizing the importance of holding the line of containment in the "crescent" of countries running from Japan to India. His 12 January Press Club speech, as well as others in the spring, informed the American public of this intention. The secretary and the department appeared particularly eager to discuss the active American Southeast Asia policy to demonstrate that they were, in fact, doing something positive to stop the spread of Asian Communism. They consistently stressed the importance of holding the line in Indochina.

Muffled Doubts

American Indochina policy took a short and predictable journey from the "wait and see" policy of the previous year to Charlton Ogburn's "scrap heap" in the early months of 1950. On 2 February, Acheson informed President Truman that France had, "in effect," established Vietnam, Laos, and Cambodia as "independent states within the French Union" as a result of the French Assembly's ratification of the 8 March 1949 accord five days earlier. As a result of this action, the secretary of state recommended that the United States extend diplomatic recognition to the "three legally constituted governments." Truman approved the move on the next day with the endorsement of his cabinet.[21] On 7 February, the State Department announced that recognition had been accorded.[22] A month later, the president approved the "principle" of granting military assistance to French Union forces in Indochina.

While the administration moved closer to Bao Dai, the State Department was disconcerted by an overture Ho Chi Minh's government made to Marshall Tito requesting Yugoslav recognition of his regime. To an institution convinced of Ho's close tie to Moscow, this did not quite compute. Tito granted the recognition in late February. The department was at first irritated with Tito's move but came to view it with favor; it subtracted nothing from Bao Dai and injected "Titoism" into Southeast Asia. The whole issue, however, was thrown into doubt when Ho's radio denounced Tito as a "spy for American imperialism" in the following month. The question was slightly clarified only after *New York Times* reporter C. L. Sulzberger interviewed a Viet Minh official in Thailand who assured him that the Democratic Republic of Vietnam desired friendly relations with both Moscow and Belgrade.[23] Meanwhile, the Indochina war ground on and the French showed no sign of winning.[24]

As Ho attempted to deal with the Russian-Yugoslav split and as the United States moved closer to Bao Dai and the French, some senior policy makers within the State Department continued to express doubts about the wisdom of backing Bao Dai. While the doubts were ultimately muffled by positive thinking or replacement of the doubters, a number of senior department officials indulged in intellectual double-entry bookkeeping in what they told the public, Congress, the president, and themselves.

Misgivings about the experiment persisted into the new year because Bao Dai showed no sign of capturing popular sympathy, because Ho Chi Minh's forces continued to prosper, and because the French were not backing their own puppet with much conviction. A *New York Times* dispatch from Paris in mid-April summarized the private French assessment of the problem. The "blunt fact" was that Bao Dai had "not been able to provide the desired political stabilization or to alter the military picture." Non-Communist Vietnamese were reluctant "to rally to the standards of Bao Dai" and French officials conceded that the Viet Minh "still [had] the initiative."[25] The rulers of neighboring Asian states also perceived his weakness and refused to recognize the Vietnamese government after the ratification of the 8 March accord and after British and American diplomatic recognition.[26]

One of the earliest and strongest doubters within the State Department was consultant Raymond Fosdick. "My belief," he wrote Philip Jessup on 4 November 1949, "is that the Bao Dai regime is doomed." The "independence" granted Vietnam was "shabby business" and "a mockery of all the professions we have made in the Indochinese case." Ho Chi Minh was an "unpleasant" alternative, but "there may be unpredictable and unseen factors in this situation which in the end will be more favorable to us than now seems probable."[27] Jessup sent the note to Butterworth with a cautious supporting comment agreeing "that we have got to be very careful not to be tied to the French and Bao Dai in a debacle."[28] Butterworth replied on 17 November with a memorandum to Fosdick drafted in the Office of Philippines and Southeast Asian Affairs (PSA, a successor to SEA): "Because the odds are heavily against a horse entered in a given race, is no reason to withdraw that horse from a given race although I agree that there is likewise no reason in these circumstances to back that horse heavily."[29] Fosdick, however, had given up the fight a day before when he apparently approved, with Everett Case, a policy paper on Indochina endorsing existing policy.[30]

Philip Jessup was another muffled doubter. While on a worldwide journey as ambassador at large, he sent the department a cable from Saigon in late January stating that, although Bao Dai appeared sincere and somewhat cognizant of his difficulties, he was not a man of "great force or great strength" and his "actual and potential authority" was "somewhat dubious." Yet, since the decision had already been made to back him, Jessup urged the department to move as quickly as possible with recognition. When he returned to Washington, Jessup chose not to burden either his colleagues or Congress with doubts about developments in Indochina.[31] At a Foreign Relations Committee executive briefing after his return, he was upbeat in his description of the Indochina situation. He found that "very considerable numbers of the Vietnamese nationalists are beginning to rally to Bao Dai now that the French have ratified the 8 March accord." In Vietnam "the thing is moving and . . . the nationalist spread is toward Bao Dai and away from Ho Chi Minh."[32]

Walton Butterworth also revealed reservations about Bao Dai after attending, with Jessup, a February meeting of American chiefs of mission in Bangkok. Following the conference, he sent his deputy, Livingston Merchant, a telegram questioning the sincerity of French professions about fully supporting their puppet. "We should realize ECA and military aid from US, just as recognition by US, do not constitute the 'missing components.' " Missing was further French action that "would place Vietnam in category of independent state." He recommended that Indochina be granted no aid until France gave public assurance that the colony would be made independent.[33] Shortly after his return to Washington, Acheson removed Butterworth from his job as FE chief as a result of long-existing political pressure from Congress.

Charlton Ogburn, who was transferred from PSA to FE to serve as a "policy information" officer, blew hot and cold over Indochina policy. One foil for his thought was the enthusiastic new American chief of mission in Saigon, Consul General Edmund Gullion. On 18 March, Gullion sent the department a cable urging that 303 military aid be sent to Vietnam as rapidly as possible. During his brief tenure, Gullion had expressed opposition to applying heavy pressure on France to back Bao Dai, reported that Ho Chi Minh was controlled by "the bosses," and stated, in confused language, that the "missing component" in Indochina was more American military assistance. Gullion, in his own words, was a "special pleader" for the French. After receiving the cable recommending prompt aid, Butterworth asked Ogburn to read it and comment. Ogburn responded three days later with a memorandum stating that he regretted that the Saigon consulate general lacked an able chief of mission. Since there was no worthwhile political reporting from Vietnam, there was no way of knowing what was happening in Indochina. It was his "hunch," however, that "unless the French are prepared to police Vietnam indefinitely or are enabled by the magnitude of our assistance" to kill over a hundred thousand Vietnamese—and perhaps not even then —Ho Chi Minh's party would take over "a couple of years hence."[34]

Another Ogburn memorandum that conveyed a scathing criticism of American policy was an exceptionally vivid recapitulation of an hour-and-a-half conversation with *Newsweek* reporter Harold Isaacs in mid-April. Isaacs, who had spent the postwar years covering Southeast Asia, characterized the ex-emperor, in Ogburn's words, as "a figure deserving of the ridicule and contempt with which he is generally regarded by the Vietnamese." Any "supposition that he could succeed or that a French army in Indochina could possibly be an asset to us could be entertained only by one totally ignorant of Asian realities." Ogburn erected the department's standard policy defense: Popular support would shift from Ho to Bao Dai as France granted the non-Communist leader autonomy and as Ho's "Communist iron-hand" became increasingly evident to the native population. He asked if Isaacs had not received reports of Ho's decreasing popularity, of Bao Dai's increasing support, and of the Viet Minh's "growing loss of initiative." Isaacs was unaware of such reports. If they existed, they could have come only from the French or from our Consul General in Saigon, in either of which case they were palpably lies and totally at variance with the reports of every American correspondent who had visited the area, to all of whom it was abundantly evident that all the Vietnamese who counted were on the side of the resistance and that Bao Dai's regime was a fraud.

Ogburn asked for a "constructive suggestion." Isaacs advised that the United States should try to "claw" its "way back up the precipice over which we have thrown ourselves, by which he means wash our hands of Bao Dai." While he realized this might mean a Communist victory, "we could not, he contended, expect not to have to pay for five years of irresponsibility." The United States could

> recognize that between the "Democratic Republic of Vietnam" and-
> /or the Soviet Union and Communist China, irreconcilable diver-
> gences of interest exist which are bound to have their effect, and in
> the meantime, while writing off Indochina, we would exert ourselves
> to strengthen Thailand and Burma economically and politically.

Ogburn suggested that recent developments like Soviet recognition confirmed that Ho was "aligned completely" with Russia. Isaacs "threw up his hands and asked what we expected the results of our conduct to be." In what he admitted was not a strong defense, Ogburn observed that it would be difficult to justify "before the American people and the Congress the course of abandoning an anti-Communist force which is at grips with a Communist force" and noted that the policy had almost universal support in the press. Isaacs recalled that the

> policy of supporting the Chinese Nationalists had once also had the
> sympathy of the press, and that he hoped we could derive some
> consolation from that memory since we are going to go through the
> same process all over again. . . . If the American Congress was deter-
> mined to make a military issue of every conflict between non-Commu-
> nist and Communist elements and arm the former up to the level of
> their needs, the Congressmen should be bluntly informed that they
> had better stop thinking in terms of piddling sums of $30 million and
> start making appropriations to put America on a war footing.

In conveying the six-page memorandum to his superior, Ogburn explained that he had covered the conversation fully since Isaacs "expressed as completely, and certainly as aggressively, the opposition view on Indochina as I have yet heard set forth."[35] He circulated it in FE, PSA, and the Policy Planning Staff, but to no apparent constructive purpose.

The highest-level skeptic was Dean Acheson, who had been impressed with Nehru's views about Ho and Bao Dai when the Indian prime minister visited Washington in October. Yet, while he was aware of the shortcomings of the French-sponsored regime, Acheson was even more impressed by the specter of communism moving south from China into Southeast Asia.[36] The result was that he too began to accentuate the positive about Bao Dai. His effort at positive thought was reflected in testimony before the Senate Foreign Relations Committee. While in October 1949 he had described the Bao Dai experiment as being "fairly fragile," he found that the situation had changed for the better by 10 January. "Indochina has improved a great deal in the past year," he told the senators. France had "turned over the administration of Viet Nam to Bao Dai and his people" and even Ho was sobered by the Chinese Communist victory. "There is some cause of optimism here, but not great optimism. It is better than it was and the French are moving."[37] While his affirmative view was supported by few facts, Acheson expressed a hope that the State Department intended to make real by positive action.

As 1950 progressed and doubts about the pro-Bao Dai policy became unfashionable, the State Department began to back away from its effort to pressure France into granting Bao Dai the "missing component" (real independence) that the Far Eastern Bureau had identified as necessary to make the experiment work. For awhile it pressed a list of proposals on the French regarding what they should do to support their puppet more fully. While the list was never directly tied to possible military and economic assistance for Indochina—something the French formally requested on 16 February—the question of American aid and firmer French support for Bao Dai had been implicitly linked since 1948. Included in this list of suggestions were recommendations that French authorities in Saigon yield the colonial governor's palace to Bao Dai, that control of Vietnamese affairs within the French government be transferred from the Overseas Territory Ministry (a colonial office) to the Foreign Ministry, and that Paris make a public statement that the 8 March accord ratification was only a first step in an "evolutionary" process leading to full Vietnamese independence.[38] At the insistence of FE, the department had recommended these steps to the French in various forums over the objection of EUR, the American embassy in Paris, and the consulate general in Saigon. The French, however, refused to give in, and, after Butterworth's retirement in late March, the State Department apparently quit pressing its reformist views with vigor.

With the pressure on them diminishing, the French began dabbling in blackmail in an effort to extract large amounts of aid from the United States. Before his government formally requested assistance, French Foreign Ministry official Maurice Couve de Murville hinted to Charles Bohlen in a 6 February conversation in Paris that France might find it difficult to hold on alone in Indochina.[39] After the French formally requested aid, another official bluntly warned an officer in EUR that unless Britain and the United States helped share the Indochina burden, France would be obligated to "abandon Indochina to Moscow" ("painful though that might be").[40] Two days later, on 22 February, another Foreign Ministry official made the same point to the American ambassador in Paris.[41]

It is not clear how aware Dean Acheson was of the French threat to withdraw. Whatever his perception, he was not deterred from signing the 9 March note to President Truman requesting $15 million from the 303 fund for Indochina military aid. In an accompanying memorandum justifying the request, the department made the questionable assertion that "many other anti-Communist nations of the world" would soon recognize the Indochina governments and that, since China and Russia had recently recognized the Ho government, "the issue becomes more clearly defined as an anti-communist versus communist effort." The president was informed that the aid was urgently needed and that "the French are irrevocably committed in Indochina."[42]

The memorandum to Truman and the department's affirmative statements to Congress reflected not a purposeful effort at dissembling, but an affirmative decision to back the Bao Dai experiment despite the risks. Discussion of policy had reached a point where it was time for all concerned to put the best face on the situation, back it vigorously, and hope that the forced optimism would prove accurate. The military establishment was already on board; American diplomats in EUR, Paris, and Vietnam had long been pleading the French case; and in FE/PSA, the old doubters were gone or quieted and a new team factored out most of the remaining uncertainty about the wisdom of offering France and its puppet unqualified support.

303 Fund Dispersement and Renewal

In response to the French request for military assistance, the State Department presented an aide-memoire to the French embassy on 28

April stating that "The interested departments and agencies of this Government are agreed in principle that the United States shall furnish military assistance to the armed forces of the Associated States and to the French forces in Indochina."[43] This was not news to the French. On 10 November 1949, Acheson, in effect, had invited a French request for aid. After conferring with Foreign Minister Schuman in Paris, the secretary reported to Truman that he had assured the French foreign minister that they "were on [the] right track with Bao Dai (although perhaps not moving as fast as desirable) and we wanted to be as helpful as possible. I said we would consider sympathetically any specific proposals [the] French cared to make although basically we felt that primary task was French."[44] A month earlier, Louis Johnson had made an even more explicit offer of money from the 303 fund to French military leaders.[45]

After Truman's 1 May approval of specific allocations of military and economic aid from the 303 fund for Indochina, Acheson's way was clear to offer the aid in a foreign ministers meeting in Paris a week later. During a long conversation on the morning of 8 May, French Foreign Minister Schuman indicated to the secretary his gratitude for the "possible" American willingness to grant France military and economic aid in Indochina. The two things he would like most immediately were fighter planes and naval vessels.

Acheson thanked Schuman for his "wise and progressive statements." In assessing the current situation he said (as an aide summarized the conversation in his name) that they were entering a "critical period which must be measured in weeks, not months. First enthusiasm for Bao Dai is subsiding and things are at dead stall but they must not be allowed to slip back." Then, without requiring any change in French policy, Acheson said that the aid question could be worked out "satisfactorily." "In realm of figures, I could say on confidential basis that about $20,000,000 are available for [the] remaining six weeks of fiscal year [1950] but no estimate possible for fiscal 1951 until appropriations made by Congress." After the meeting Acheson publicly announced the decision to grant the aid.[46] The decision, long hinted in the press, was the headline story in the following day's New York Times.[47]

Shortly after he returned from Europe, Acheson appeared before a public session of a combined Senate Foreign Relations and Armed Services Committees. As part of his prepared statement in support of renewed funding for MAP, he explained the benefit of the previous year's 303 fund. More of the same, he said, was needed.[48] In appearances before

executive sessions of both the House and Senate committees, Dean Rusk
also defended the request and reviewed Southeast Asian policy. Both he
and Defense Department witnesses gave a general breakdown of how the
existing 303 fund was in the process of being programmed. The area of
highest priority, they stressed, was the strategically critical Indochina.
Unlike earlier statements by Acheson, Jessup, and Butterworth, Rusk did
not gloss over the hazards of backing Bao Dai, at least to the House
Foreign Affairs Committee. On 20 June, he admitted:

> I would be unfair with the committee if I indicated there was any
> snowball here rolling strongly in Bao Dai's favor. We still have a hard,
> up-hill job in Indochina; part of it turning on Bao Dai's own energy;
> part of it turning on the French willingness to give Bao Dai the
> position which he can use to go out and get the non-Communist
> national support; part of it due to strict military factors under which
> they can extend their forces over the expanse of Indochina.[49]

His testimony before the Senate committee twelve days earlier was
slightly more optimistic. There had been progress when Bao Dai first
came in; this was followed by some backsliding, and "for awhile there has
been sort of a balance. . . . Now we feel a little bit more of an increase
in the movement toward Bao Dai." Other discussion, however, was off the
printed record and its content is unknown. On the record he was dog-
matic in his assertion that Ho Chi Minh was an agent of the "Politburo."
At one point, when asked if France wanted to turn the problem over to
the United States, Rusk assured the senators that the French "have not
at any point told us that if we did not help them they would pull out."[50]

No member of Congress appears to have questioned the wisdom of the
Indochina or general Southeast Asia policy that was well reported in the
papers and described to them during the MAP hearing. The only challenge to the renewal of the 303 fund questioned whether or not the $75
million should once again be unvouchered. At the insistence of Senators
Smith and Knowland, the Foreign Relations Committee and, ultimately,
both Houses, adopted a three-tiered system for reporting how the money
would ultimately be spent. The use of $40 million would have to be
reported in the public record; $35 million could be reported only to the
Senate Foreign Relations and Armed Services Committees and the
House Foreign Affairs Committee; $7.5 million of the $35 million could,
if the executive desired, be completely unvouchered.[51]

On 21 June, the Senate committee reported the MAP bill to the floor.

Four days later the North Koreans attacked the South. Three days after the attack, on the advice of Dean Acheson, Truman ordered an "acceleration in the furnishing of military assistance to the forces of France and the Associated States of Indochina and the dispatch of a military mission to provide close working relations with those forces."[52] On 30 June, the Senate unanimously passed the MAP bill, including the committees' $75 million provision. After the House passage of the unamended Senate bill, the president signed the legislation into law on 26 July.[53]

The first direct and intentional American military assistance sent to anti-Viet Minh forces in Indochina was transferred to the French in Saigon on 29 June. The aid consisted of eight C–47 cargo planes that had been on their way to Vietnam on a priority before the outbreak of the Korean War. Later there would be much more.[54]

13

Conclusion

The American containment policy in Southeast Asia arose from the ashes of its failed policy in China. Through 1949, civilian, military, and congressional policy makers had debated over what stands to take toward the emerging communist regime in Peking. By early 1950, hopes for better relations in the forseeable future collapsed, to the chagrin of some and the delight of others. In the aftermath of this debacle, Washington's several rival power centers threw their energy into doing something all could agree upon—checking the further spread of communism in Southeast Asia. In a few brief months this policy transformed an area that most American barely knew into one deemed so vital that its defense justified a major effort to keep it from falling into the Soviet orbit. The rapid discovery of Southeast Asia should be understood as a byproduct of both strategic assessments and bitter internal debate: both within the executive branch and between the executive branch and Congress. The foundation laid in 1949 and 1950 supported the effort of the American containment policy in the region for the next quarter century.

The Rube Goldberg policy-making process that led to the alienating of Communist China and the embrace of Southeast Asia was unique in its detail but not in its general dimensions. It was replete with political infighting, bureaucratic backstabbing, confused lines of authority, and undercutting and lack of follow-through on decisions reached at the highest level. The process reflected the determination of bureaucrats, diplomats, and politicians to pursue their own version of American interests, the special pleading of lobbyists and committed citizens, congressional horse trading, character assassination in pursuit of personal goals and policy objectives, and an underlying bewilderment among the better informed about what to do to protect American interests in East Asia.

During the first eighteen months of the Truman administration, China policy existed on a continuum. At one end dangled a carrot holding out the prospect for normal relations with Peking if it behaved according to the norms of the international community. This approach assumed that, with luck, the Communist leadership might eventually go the way of Marshall Tito. The stick poised at the other end threatened to isolate the Communists, continue to back the Nationalists and other resistance forces, and, generally, make life difficult for the new regime in the hope that it would eventually fall. The State Department, with the significant exception of Dean Rusk, finally settled on a Titoist policy by the end of 1949, and, for a while, Dean Acheson persuaded the president to go along. In contrast, the military establishment championed a punitive approach. Before the Korean War, it succeeded in obtaining a China policy that fell between the two extremes.

The military's ultimate success in June 1950 depended upon the important support of other forces. The congressional China bloc, with its power to embarrass and obstruct the administration, and with its influence on the size and uses of foreign aid funds, shared a significant amount of credit. The China lobby, in its varied dimensions, made an important contribution by feeding its political allies with information and innuendo. More distantly, the Chinese on both sides of the civil war worked in ironic tandem to exacerbate tensions between Washington and Peking and to play into the hands of the activists. Finally, the activists were playing with a politically stacked deck. By 1949, the American public was becoming accustomed to its government taking direct action in coping with national security threats. When North Korea invaded the South, administration officials who had championed the tattered Titoist policy for the previous eighteen months kicked it over in an evening, without much apparent regret and with full public support.

The State Department meanwhile, had begun to focus American attention elsewhere. Ever since the administration had suggested an omnibus European military assistance program in 1947, some officials considered how military aid might promote American interests in Southeast Asia. As prospects for MAP grew in the following months, a few policy planners in the department began studying the situation in the region in greater detail and with increasing alarm. By 1949, the plans of aid budgeters, the calculations of regional planners, and the political necessity for diverting attention from China militated for a more activist approach in the region.

Specifically, the State Department sought to bury the China question and lead Congressional and public attention toward the "great crescent" of nations that formed an arc from Japan to India. In the process of doing so, through publication of the White Paper and the assembly of the "wise men," the department succeeded in stimulating Congress to direct foreign aid money, initially proposed for non-Communist warlords in China's interior, into an unvouchered fund available for use in all of Asia. The consequence of the fund's creation was threefold: it stimulated the executive branch to plan a more activist policy in Southeast Asia; briefly spawned another pitch battle over China policy; and ultimately funded the first American military assistance to non-Communist forces in Vietnam.

Three decades later, the monolithic view of Asian communism lay shattered. Even though Washington had lost a war in Indochina, the Far East was not lost to Soviet influence. Titoism reigned in China as Soviet and Chinese armies faced each other along the Sino-Soviet border; a Soviet-backed Communist Vietnam had invaded and occupied a Chinese-backed Communist Cambodia; China, which had fought a brief war with its former Vietnamese ally, actively courted non-Communist countries in Southwest and Southeast Asia; and more countries in Asia than not remained non-Communist and Western-oriented.

Today it is arguable that the intervening hostility between China and the United States was in part avoidable. With hindsight, one can imagine an American policy that encouraged the emergence of Chinese Titoism while not promoting the spread of communism in other areas of East Asia. The core of this policy might have been what one contemporary observer described as "judicious leaving alone," a policy of allowing China to work out its internal problems without further American interference. The policy would not have meant embracing the Communists or abetting their victory, only accepting what most observers of the day regarded as inevitable. Washington could have recognized the new regime after receiving assurances that American diplomats would not be mistreated. Certainly, economic and cultural ties might have been preserved. Simultaneously, the United States could have made clear its opposition to Chinese efforts to export its revolution to surrounding countries and been prepared to translate that opposition into deeds.

How the Chinese Communists would have responded had the United States consistently followed such a policy can only be guessed at. The answer lies in the internal dynamics of the Chinese Communist Party as composed in the late 1940s. There was, apparently, a debate within the party, along the lines outlined in the Chou demarché, that ended in mid-1949 in triumph for the side arguing for close ties with Moscow. The influence of the "liberal" wing of the party had declined; Soviet advisors were arriving in increasing numbers; Manchuria was under the control of a Chinese Stalinist; the Russian's insistence on special treaty rights in Manchuria threatened to detach it and other areas of the country from Peking's control. Not surprisingly, perhaps, Mao and the party's dominant wing thought it was time to align with Stalin.

It does not follow, however, that a benign American policy would not eventually have had a constructive impact. Decisions reached in the summer of 1949 that favored Moscow were not irreversible, nor even destined to hold for the next decade. While the United States could not have reversed this trend in the short term, a longer-range policy could have been followed that would not have accentuated the lean toward the Soviet Union but kept the way open—and discreetly encouraged—a tilt the other way.

The Truman administration might have also followed a more benign policy toward Communists in Vietnam, but with uncertain results. Had it done so, the short-term outcome would probably have been Vietnamese Communist domination of the former French colonial empire and a wave of shock to non-Communists throughout Southeast Asia. At that point the West could have regrouped around Thailand—as SEA chief Charles Reed once urged—and hoped that Ho Chi Minh's talk about neutralism was genuine. Also, at that point several unpredictable variables would have come into play to determine subsequent events in the region: the durability of the "militant solidarity" between a Communist Vietnam and China in the absence of pressure from the West; the ability of the non-Communist nations in the region, especially Thailand, to rebound from the psychological blow of Ho's triumph; the willingness of the United States to sustain non-Communist regimes in the region; and the willingness of the Soviet Union and China to furnish the military hardware necessary to sustain Vietnamese dominance in Indochina.

Thirty years later, faced with its uneasy dominance of all Indochina, Hanoi found that many of these variables did not work in its favor. Perhaps the relevant question is whether under Ho Chi Minh, and without the experience of two war behind them, the Vietnamese might have proved more accommodating to the West. However, since mendacity was a cornerstone in Ho's career and that of his party, one cannot take his words of reassurance given to foreign journalists and diplomats at face value. The answer to what might have been in Vietnam thus remains unclear.

What ever else might have been, it is clear that the American political environment of 1949 and 1950 did not encourage a flexible policy toward either China or Vietnam. The political environment of those years was created in part by the impact of an unambiguous Soviet challenge in Europe over the preceding three years, in part by the appearance (the reality was somewhat different) of a direct Soviet challenge in Asia, and by the interaction of these events with domestic American politics. The result was a popular American view that held Communist ideology to be a tool of an international Communist conspiracy. It was not a view that allowed for distinctions between Communist leaders who varied only in the degree of their hostility toward the United States; the phenomenon of Titoism, which was still new in 1949 and 1950, had little impact on popular perception of a monolithic Communist bloc. Although the public was made aware of occasional Chinese Communist expressions of interest in the West, it was unaware of the Chou demarché and other behind-the-scenes signs of Chinese Titoism. It would likely have been unimpressed even had it been more fully informed. Ho Chi Minh's comments about seeking better ties with the West were occasionally reported but had no apparent effect on popular perception.

The popular perception of a ubiquitous Soviet threat—the Russians were also believed to be boring from within—lent itself to a low order of domestic political exploitation. Following a time-honored tradition, the Republicans, as the opposition party, attacked a policy that was not yielding prompt, fruitful results. As part of that tradition, they attacked the policy makers, but with a sustained vehemence unusual in modern American politics. The Republicans, and their Democrat associates, not only charged that the policy makers were wrong, but that they were treasonous as well.

The China bloc's attack revealed several strengths and weaknesses in both itself and its administration defenders. Its most notable aspect was its informal, but important, association with the other friends of China: the China lobby, the Nationalist government, and Nationalist sympathizers in various levels of the executive branch. While the whole effort against the administration lacked central coordination, the common goal allowed the various elements to work in tandem, and sometimes in conspiracy, to reverse administration policy and destroy its policy makers.

Also notable was the pitiful effort the congressional Democrats made to defend themselves and the administration. Most senior party members recognized the partisan character of the China bloc's attack and devised numerous schemes to defend the administration's policy, but their efforts failed to quell the drumbeat of criticism. The administration and the majority leadership, with the support of key Republicans, did demonstrate considerable skill in either blocking enactment of China legislation hostile to administration policy or in shaping it to support administration policy in Southeast Asia. While their public-relations campaign was feeble, their legislative accomplishments were impressive.

The China bloc's attack also revealed the confusion within the Truman administration in both policy and the question of how to deal with Congress. Not until the Korean War did the administration speak with one voice on China policy. Before that, Dean Acheson would, from time to time, attempt to assert his views, both publicly and privately, but he frequently found his instruction undercut by the Pentagon or ignored within his own department; furthermore, his own follow-through was weak.

Until the early fall of 1949, Acheson was unsure of what to do about China, and the uncertainty was reflected throughout the State Department. Only once in this crucial period, in early January 1950, did President Truman make a significant public statement on China policy; he did so in support of the State Department's position and was promptly undercut by his own Defense Department as well as by some officials in the State Department who thought something forceful should be done to save Taiwan. The result of the confusion was a contradictory China policy and a weak defense in the face of a strong congressional attack.

By mid-1949, the administration began to pursue consistently one key strategy in its defense; its answer to charges of a weak China policy became a strong Southeast Asian policy. As conceived in late June, the policy was a combination of dramatic public statements by senior administration officials about the need for dramatic moves in the subcontinent, coupled with substantive action in Southeast Asia. Like its more direct efforts to defend its China policy, the administration's efforts to dramatize its new Southeast Asian policy were not successful in deflecting China bloc criticism.

The administration was, however, successful in obtaining money from Congress to fund the policy and in launching it in the spring of 1950 without opposition, cursory examination, or serious comment by either congressional friends or foes. While Congress largely ignored the question of policy in areas of Asia outside of China, it predictably would have been hostile to any effort to accommodate Ho Chi Minh. Apart from playing this negative role, which discouraged examination of alternatives, Congress showed little interest in questioning the Southeast Asian policy that the administration began to implement in 1950. However, it did not hesitate to fund the program and did so, more or less unwittingly, in the fall of 1949. Only a decade and a half later did Congress begin to question seriously the containment policy it had played a fundamental role in creating.

Abbreviations
and Acronyms

CA	Division (after 3 October 1949: Office) of Chinese Affairs, Department of State
DRV	Democratic Republic of Vietnam
ECA	Economic Cooperation Administration
EUR	Office (after 3 October 1949: Bureau) of European Affairs, Department of State
FACC	Foreign Assistance Correlation Committee, an interagency committee created in December 1948
FE	Office (after 3 October 1949: Bureau) of Far Eastern Affairs, Department of State.
JCS	Joint Chiefs of Staff
NEA	Office (after 3 October 1949: Bureau) of Near East and South Asian Affairs, Department of State
NSC	National Security Council
PSA	Office of Philippine and Southeast Asian Affairs, Department of State (successor to SEA)
SANACC	State-Army-Navy-Air Force Coordinating Committee (successor to SWNCC)
SEA	Division of Southeast Asian Affairs, Department of State
SWNCC	State-War-Navy Coordinating Committee
WE	Division (after 3 October 1949: Office) of Western European Affairs, Department of State

Bibliography

BOOKS AND ARTICLES

Acheson, Dean. *Present at the Creation.* New York: W. W. Norton, 1969.

Allen, Louis. *The End of the War in Asia.* London: Hart-Davis, MacGibbon, 1976.

Allen, Robert S. and Shannon, William V. *The Truman Merry-Go-Round.* New York: Vanguard Press, 1950.

Allison, John M. *Ambassador from the Prairie, or Allison Wonderland.* Boston: Houghton Mifflin, 1973.

Almond, Gabriel Abraham. *The American People and Foreign Policy.* New York: Frederick A. Praeger, 1960.

Anderson, Patrick. *The Presidents' Men.* New York: Doubleday, 1968.

Bachrack, Stanley D. *The Committee of One Million: "China Lobby" Politics, 1953–1971.* New York: Columbia University Press, 1976.

Bain, Chester Arthur. *Vietnam: The Roots of Conflict.* Englewood Cliffs, N.J.: Prentice-Hall, 1967.

Barnett, A. Doak. *China and the Major Powers in East Asia.* Washington, D.C.: The Brookings Institute, 1977.

———. *China on the Eve of the Communist Takeover.* New York: Frederick A. Praeger, 1963.

Barrett, David D. *Dixie Mission: The United States Army Observer Group in Yenan, 1944.* Berkeley: Center for Chinese Studies, 1970.

Bator, Victor. *Vietnam, A Diplomatic Tragedy: The Origins of United States Involvement.* Dobbs Ferry, N.Y.: Oceana, 1965.

Boardman, Robert. *Britain and the People's Republic of China, 1949–1974.* New York: Barneys & Noble, 1976.

Bodard, Lucien. *The Quicksand War: Prelude to Vietnam.* Boston: Little, Brown & Co., 1967.

Bodde, Derk. *Peking Diary: A Year of Revolution, 1948–1950.* New York: Abelard-Schuman, 1950.

Bohlen, Charles E. *Witness to History, 1929–1969.* New York: W. W. Norton, 1973.

Boorman, Harold L., and Howard, Richard C., eds. *Biographical Dictionary of Republican China.* 4 vols. New York: Columbia University Press, 1968.

Borg, Dorothy. "Economic Cooperation Administration and American Policy in China." *Far Eastern Survey,* 24 August 1949.

Borklund, C. W. *Men of the Pentagon from Forrestal to McNamara.* New York: Frederick A. Praeger, 1966.

Brown, William Adam, Jr., and Opie, Redvers. *American Foreign Assistance.* Washington, D.C.: The Brookings Institute, 1953.

Bueler, William M. *U.S. China Policy and the Problem of Taiwan,* Boulder, Colo.: Colorado Associated University Press, 1971.

Buhite, Russell D. *Patrick J. Hurley and American Foreign Policy.* Ithaca: Cornell University Press, 1973.

Bullitt, William. "The Saddest War." *Life,* 29 December 1947, pp. 64–69.

Cady, John F. *The United States and Burma.* Cambridge: Harvard University Press, 1976.

Cameron, Allan W., ed. *Viet Nam Crisis: A Documentary History,* 2 vols. Ithaca, N.Y.: Cornell University Press, 1970.

Carrol, Holbert N. *The House of Representatives and Foreign Affairs.* Pittsburg: University of Pittsburg Press, 1958.

Chassin, Lionel Max. *The Communist Conquest of China: A History of the Civil War, 1945–1949.* Cambridge: Harvard University Press, 1965.

Cline, Ray S. *Secrets, Spies, and Scholars: Blueprint of the Essential CIA.* Washington, D.C.: Acropolis Books, 1977.

Clubb, O. Edmund. *China and Russia: The Great Game.* New York: Columbia University Press, 1971.

———. *The Witness and I.* New York: Columbia University Press, 1974.

Cochran, Bert. *Harry Truman and the Crisis Presidency.* New York: Funk & Wagnall, 1973.

Cohen, Warren I. *America's Response to China.* New York: John Wiley & Sons, 1971.

Colbert, Evelyn. *Southeast Asia in International Politics, 1941–1956.* Ithaca, N.Y.: Cornell University Press, 1977.

Cole, Allen B. ed. *Conflict in Indo-China and International Repercussions: A Documentary History, 1945–1955.* Ithaca, N.Y.: Cornell University Press, 1956.

Connally, Tom. *My Name is Tom Connally.* New York: Thomas Y. Crowell, 1954.

Cooper, Chester L. *The Lost Crusade.* New York: Dodd, Meade, & Co., 1970.

Crozier, Brian. *The Man Who Lost China.* New York: Charles Scribner's Sons, 1976.

Devillers, Philippe. *Histoire du Viet-Nam de 1940 à 1952.* Paris: Editions du Sevil, 1952.

———. "Vietnamese Nationalism and French Policies." In *Asian Nationalism and the West,* edited by William S. Holland. New York: Macmillan Co., 1953.

Divine, Robert A. *Foreign Policy and U.S. Presidential Elections, 1940–1948.* New York: New Viewpoints, 1974.

Dulles, Foster R. *American Policy Toward Communist China.* New York: Thomas Y. Crowell, 1972.

Etzold, Thomas H., ed. *Aspects of Sino-American Relations Since 1784.* New York: New Viewpoints, 1978.

Fairbank, John K., and others. *Next Step in Asia.* Cambridge: Harvard University Press, 1949.

Fall, Bernard. *The Two Viet-Nams: A Political and Military Analysis.* 2d rev. ed. New York: Frederick A. Praeger, 1967.

———. "U.S. Policies in Indochina, 1940–1960," In *Last Reflections on a War.* New York: Doubleday, 1967.

BIBLIOGRAPHY

Feis, Herbert. *From Trust to Terror: The Onset of the Cold War, 1945–1950.* New York: W. W. Norton, 1970.

———. *The China Tangle.* Princeton: Princeton University Press, 1953.

Fenn, Charles. *Ho Chi Minh: A Biographical Introduction.* New York: Charles Scribner's Sons. 1973.

Fetzer, James A. "Congress and China, 1941–1950." Ph.D. dissertation, Michigan State University, 1970.

Fifield, Russell H. *Americans in Southeast Asia: The Roots of Commitment.* New York: Thomas Y. Crowell, 1973.

Fitzgerald, C. P. *The Birth of Communist China.* Baltimore: Penguin Books, 1964.

Fontaine, Andre. *History of the Cold War, Vol. 1: From the October Revolution to the Korean War, 1917–1950.* New York: Random House, 1968.

Fosdick, Raymond B. "Asia's Challenge to Us—Ideas, Not Guns." *The New York Times Magazine,* 12 February 1950.

Freeland, Richard M. *The Truman Doctrine and the Origins of McCarthyism: Foreign Policy, Domestic Politics, and Internal Security, 1946–1948.* New York: Alfred Knopf, 1972.

Fried, Richard M. *Men Against McCarthy.* New York: Columbia University Press, 1976.

Frye, William. "The National Military Establishment." *American Political Science Review* 43, no. 3 (June 1949) pp. 543–45.

Gallup, George H. *The Gallup Poll: Public Opinion 1935–1971,* 2 vols. New York: Random House, 1972.

Gimbel, John. *The Origins of the Marshall Plan,* Stanford: Stanford University Press, 1976.

Gittings, John. *The World and China, 1922–1972.* London: Eyere Methuen, 1974.

Goulden, Joseph, *The Best Years: 1945–1950.* New York: Antheneum, 1976.

Halberstam, David. *The Best and the Brightest.* New York: Random House, 1972.

Hammer, Ellen J. *The Struggle for Indochina.* Stanford: Stanford University Press, 1954.

Harper, Alan D. *The Politics of Loyalty: The White House and the Communist Issue, 1946–1952.* Westport, Conn.: Greenwood Publishing Corp., 1969.

Hayes, Samuel P., ed. *The Beginning of American Aid to Southeast Asia: The Griffin Mission of 1950.* Lexington, Mass.: Lexington Books, Health, 1971.

Haynes, Richard F. *The Awesome Power: Harry S. Truman as Commander in Chief.* Baton Rouge: Louisiana State University Press, 1973.

Herring, George C. "The Truman Administration and the Restoration of French Sovereignty in Indochina." *Diplomatic History,* Spring 1977, pp. 97–117.

Hooper, Edwin B., and others. *The United States Navy and the Vietnam Conflict, Vol. 1: The Setting of the Stage to 1959.* Washington, D.C.: Naval History Division, 1976.

Horton, Philip, "The China Lobby—Part II." *The Reporter,* 22 April 1952, p. 11.

Hsu Kai-yu. *Chou En-lai.* New York: Doubleday, 1968.

Hudson, G. F., and others, *The Sino-Soviet Dispute.* New York: Frederick A. Praeger, 1961.

Huyen, N. Khoc. *Vision Accomplished? The Enigma of Ho Chi Minh.* New York: Macmillan Co., 1971.

Iriye, Akira. *Across the Pacific: An Inner History of American-East Asian Relations.* New York: Harcourt, Brace & World, 1967.

———. *The Cold War in Asia: A Historical Introduction.* Englewood Cliffs, N.J.: Prentice-Hall, 1974.

Irving, Ronald E. M. *The First Indochina War: French and American Policy 1945–1954.* London: Groom Helm, 1975.

Isaacs, Harold R. *Images of Asia* (formerly titled *Scratches on Our Minds*), New York: Harper & Row, 1958, 1972.

Jessup, Philip C. *The Birth of Nations.* New York: Columbia University Press, 1974.

Johnson, Robert H. "The National Security Council: The Relevance of Its Past to Its Future," *Orbis* 13, no. 3, Fall 1969, pp. 709–35.

Kahn, E. J., Jr. *The China Hands: America's Foreign Service Officers and What Befell Them.* New York: Viking Press, 1972, 1975.

Kalb, Marvin, and Abelo, Elie. *Roots of Involvement: The U.S. in Asia, 1784–1971.* New York: W. W. Norton, 1971.

Keeley, Joseph. *The China Lobby Man: The Story of Alfred Kohlberg.* New Rochelle, N.Y.: Arlington House, 1969.

Kennan, George F. *Memoirs: 1925–1950.* Boston: Little, Brown & Co., 1967.

Khrushchev, Nikita S. *Khrushchev Remembers: The Last Testament.* Edited by Strobe Talbott. Boston: Little, Brown & Co., 1974.

Klein, Donald W., and Clark, Anne B. *Biographic Dictionary of Chinese Communism, 1921–1965, Vols. 1 and 2.* Cambridge: Harvard University Press, 1971.

Koen, Ross Y. *The China Lobby in American Politics.* New York: Macmillan Co., 1960.

Koo, Madame Wellington, with Taves, Isabella. *No Feast Lasts Forever.* New York: Quadrangle, 1975.

Korb, Lawrence J. *The Joint Chiefs of Staff: The First Twenty-Five Years.* Bloomington, Ind.: Indiana University Press, 1976.

Krock, Arthur. *Memoirs: Sixty Years on the Firing Line.* New York: Funk & Wagnall, 1968.

Lacouture, Jean. *Ho Chi Minh: A Political Biography.* New York: Vintage Books, 1968.

Lancaster, Donald. *The Emancipation of French Indochina.* London: Oxford for the Royal Institute of International Affairs, 1961.

Leary, William M., Jr., "Aircraft and Anti-Communists: CAT in Action, 1949–1952," *China Quarterly*, no. 52, 1972, pp. 654–69.

———. "Portrait of a Cold Warrior: Whiting Willover and Civil Air Transport." *Modern Asian Studies*, no. 5, 1971, pp. 373–88.

Lilienthal, David E., *The Journals of David E. Lilienthal, Vol. 2, The Atomic Energy Years, 1945–1950.* New York: Harper & Row, 1964.

Liu, F. F. *A Military History of Modern China, 1924–1949,* Princeton: Princeton University Press, 1956.

Liu Shao-ch'i. *Collected Works of Liu Shao-ch'i, 1945–1957.* Hong Kong: Union Research Institute, 1969.

Mao Tse-tung. *Selected Works, Vol. 5, 1945–1949.* New York: International Publishers, n. d.

McAlister, John T., Jr., and Mus, Paul. *The Vietnamese and Their Revolution.* New York: Harper & Row, 1970.

McAlister, John T., Jr. *Viet Nam: The Origins of Revolution.* New York: Alfred A. Knopf, 1969.

McLane, Charles B. *Soviet Strategies in Southeast Asia, An Exploration of Eastern Policy Under Lenin and Stalin.* Princeton: Princeton University Press, 1966.

McLellan, David S. *Dean Acheson: The State Department Years.* New York: Dodd, Mead, & Co., 1976.

McVey, Ruth T. *The Calcutta Conference and the Southeast Asian Uprisings.* Ithaca, N.Y.: Cornell University Press, 1958.

Melby, John F. *The Mandate of Heaven: Record of a Civil War, China 1945–1949.* Toronto: University of Toronto Press, 1968.

Miller, Merle. *Plain Speaking: An Oral Biography of Harry S. Truman.* Berkeley: Berkeley Publishing Co., 1973.

Millis, Walter, ed. *The Forrestal Diaries.* New York: Viking Press, 1951.

Nagai, Yonosuke, and Iriye Akira, eds. *The Origins of the Cold War in Asia.* New York: Columbia University Press, 1977.

BIBLIOGRAPHY

Paddock, Paul. *China Diary: Crisis Diplomacy in Dairen.* Ames, Iowa: Iowa State University Press, 1977.

Panikkar, K. M. *In Two Chinas: Memoirs of a Diplomat.* London: George Allen and Unwin, 1955.

Patterson, James T. *Mr. Republican: A Biography of Robert A. Taft.* Boston: Houghton Mifflin, 1972.

Phillips, Cabell. *The Truman Presidency: The History of a Triumphant Succession.* New York: Macmillan Co., 1966.

Rankin, Karl L. *China Assignment.* Seattle: University of Washington Press, 1964.

Ronning, Chester. *A Memoir of China in Revolution: From the Boxer Rebellion to the People's Republic.* New York: Pantheon Books, 1974.

Rose, Lisle A. *Roots of Tragedy: The United States and the Struggle for Asia, 1945–1953.* Westport, Conn.: Greenwood Publishing Corp., 1976.

Rostow, W. W. *The Great Transition: Tasks of the First and Second Post-War Generations.* Cambridge: Leeds University Press, 1967.

Sainteng, Jean. *Ho Chi Minh and His Vietnam.* Chicago: Cowles, 1970.

Schurman, Franz. *The Logic of World Power: An Inquiry Into the Origins, Currents, and Contradictions of World Politics.* New York: Pantheon Books, 1974.

Service, John S. *The Amerasia Papers: Some Problems in the History of U.S.-China Relations.* Berkeley: Center for Chinese Studies Research Monograph no. 7, 1971.

Schaller, Michael. *The U.S. Crusade in China, 1938–1945.* New York: Columbia University Press, 1979.

Simmons, Robert S. *The Strained Alliance.* New York: Macmillan Co., 1975.

Smith, Gaddis. *Dean Acheson.* New York: Cooper Square Publications, 1972.

Souers, Sidney W. "Policy Formulation and the National Security Council." *The American Political Science Review* 43, no. 3, June 1949, pp. 534–543.

Stanton, Edwin F. *Brief Authority: Excursions of a Common Man in an Uncommon World.* New York: Harper & Row, 1956.

Stuart, John L. *Fifty Years in China: The Memoirs of John Leighton Stuart, Missionary and Ambassador.* New York: Random House, 1954.

Sulzberger, C. L. *Long Row of Candles: Memoirs and Diaries, 1934–1954,* New York: Macmillan Co., 1969.

Theoharis, Athan. *Seeds of Repression: Harry S. Truman and the Origins of McCarthyism.* Chicago: Quadrangle Books, 1971.

Thornton, Richard C. *China: The Struggle for Power, 1917–1972.* Bloomington: Indiana University Press, 1973.

Topping, Seymour. *Journey Between Two Chinas.* New York: Harper & Row, 1972.

Tozer, Warren W. "Last Bridge to China: The Shanghai Power Company, the Truman Administration, and the Chinese Communists." *Diplomatic History* 1, Winter 1977.

Truman, Harry S. *1946–1952, Years of Trial and Hope: Memoirs by Harry S. Truman, Vol. 2.* New York: Signet Books, 1965, 1956.

Truman, Margaret. *Harry S. Truman.* New York: William Morrow & Co., 1973.

Tsou, Tang. *America's Failure in China, 1941–1950.* Chicago: The University of Chicago Press, 1963.

Tuchman, Barbara. "If Mao Had Come to Washington." *Foreign Affairs,* October 1972.

Vandenberg, Arthur S. *The Private Papers of Senator Vandenberg.* Boston: Houghton Mifflin, 1952.

Wertenbaker, Charles. "The China Lobby," *The Reporter,* 15 April, 1952.

Westwood, Andrew F. *Foreign Aid in a Foreign Policy Framework.* Washington, D.C.: The Brookings Institute, 1966.

Wolf, Charles, Jr. *Foreign Aid: Theory and Practice in Southern Aisa.* Princeton: Princeton University Press, 1960.
Yergin, Daniel. *Shattered Peace: The Origins of the Cold War and The National Security State.* Boston: Houghton Mifflin, 1977.

CONTEMPORARY PERIODICALS

Magazines:	**Newspapers**
Life	*New York Times*
Newsweek	*Oakland Tribune*
Speeches of the Day	*Times of London*
The Reporter	*Washington Post*
Time	

DOCUMENTS

Executive Branch:

U.S., Department of Defense, *United States-Vietnam Relations, 1945–1967.* (Printed by U.S., Congress, House, Committee on Armed Services, Committee Print, Washington, D.C.: GPO, 1971).
U.S., Department of State, *Bulletin,* 1948–1950.
U.S., Department of State, *Foreign Relations of the United States,* Volumes for 1948–1950 (Washington, D.C.: GPO, 1973–78).
U.S., Department of State, *Foreign Service List,* 1 January, 1 April, 1 July, 1 October 1949, 1 January, 1 April, 1 July 1950 (Washington, D.C.: GPO, 1948–50).
U.S., Department of State, *Register of the Department of State,* 1 April, 1949, 1 April 1950 (Washington, D.C.: GPO, 1949–50).
U.S., Department of State, *United States Relations with China: With Special Reference to the Period 1944–1949* (Washington, D.C.: GPO, 1949).
U.S., President, *Public Papers of the President of the United States, Harry S. Truman, 1949* (Washington, D.C.: GPO, 1964).

Congress, General:

U.S., Congress, *Congressional Directory,* 81st Cong., 1st and 2d sess., 1949–50 (Washington, D.C.: GPO, 1949–50).
U.S., Congress, *Congressional Record,* 80th Cong., 2d sess., 1949, 81st Cong., 1st and 2d sess., 1949–50.

Congress, Senate:

U.S., Congress, Senate, Committee on Appropriations, *Hearings on H.R. 6427, An Act Making Supplemental Appropriations for the Fiscal Year Ending June 30, 1950, and for Other Purposes,* 81st Cong., 1st sess., 12 October 1949.
U.S., Congress, Senate, Subcommittee of the Committee on Appropriations, *Hearings on Departments of State, Justice, and Commerce Appropriation Bill for 1950,* 81st Cong., 1st sess., 1949.
U.S., Congress, Senate, Committee on Appropriations, *Foreign Aid Appropriations for 1951,* 81st Cong., 2d sess., 1950 (Washington, D.C.: GPO, 1950).

U.S., Congress, Senate, Committee on Appropriations, *Departments of State, Justice, Commerce, and the Judiciary Appropriations for 1951, Hearings,* pt. 1, 81st Cong., 2d sess., 1950 (Washington, D.C.: GPO, 1950).

U.S., Congress, Senate, Committees on Armed Services and Foreign Relations, "Military Situation in the Far East," Hearings before the Committee on Armed Services and the Committee on Foreign Relations, 82–1 Summer 1951 to conduct an inquiry into the military situation in the Far East and the facts surrounding the relief of General of the Army Douglas MacArthur from his assignment in that area, pts 1–5, 82d Cong., 1951, 1st sess.

U.S., Congress, Senate, Committee on Foreign Relations, *Executive Sessions of the Senate Foreign Relations Committee* (Historical Series), vol. 1, 80th Cong., 1st and 2d sess., 1947–48 (Washington, D.C.: GPO, 1976).

U.S., Congress, Senate, Committee on Foreign Relations, *Foreign Relief Assistance Act of 1948, Hearings held in Executive Session on United States Assistance to Certain Countries* (Historical Series), 80th Cong., 2d sess., 1949 (Washington, D.C.: GPO, 1973).

U.S., Congress, Senate, Committee on Foreign Relations, *Legislative History of Committee on Foreign Relations,* 81st Cong., 1st and 2d sess., 1949–50 (Washington, D.C.: GPO, 1950).

U.S., Congress, Senate, Committee on Foreign Relations, *Economic Assistance to China and Korea: 1949–1950, Hearings held in Executive Session on S.1063, S.2319, and S.2845* (Historical Series), 81st Cong., 1st and 2d sess., 1949–50 (Washington, D.C.: GPO, 1974).

U.S., Congress, Senate, Committee on Foreign Relations, *Reviews of the World Situation: 1949–1950, Hearings held in Executive Session on the World Situation,* 81st Cong., 1st and 2d sess., (Washington, D.C.: GPO, 1974).

U.S., Congress, Senate, Committee on Foreign Relations, *Executive Sessions of the Senate Foreign Relations Committee* (Historical Series), Vol. 2, 81st Cong., 1st and 2d sess., 1949–50 (Washington, D.C.: GPO, 1976).

U.S., Congress, Senate, Committee on Foreign Relations, *State Department Employee Loyalty Investigations, Hearings before a Subcommittee pursuant to S.Res. 231,* pts 1, 2, and 3, 81st Cong., 2d sess., 1950 (Washington, D.C.: GPO, 1950).

U.S., Congress, Senate, Committee on Foreign Relations, *Extension of European Recovery, 1950, Hearings on S.3101,* 81st Cong., 2d sess., 1950 (Washington, D.C.: GPO, 1950).

U.S., Congress, Senate, Committee on Foreign Relations, *Nomination of Philip C. Jessup, Hearing before a Subcommittee on the Nomination of Philip C. Jessup,* 82d Cong., 1st sess., 1950 (Washington, D.C.: GPO, 1951).

U.S., Congress, Senate, Committee on Foreign Relations, *The United States and Vietnam: 1944–1947,* Staff Study no. 2 by Robert M. Blum (Washington, D.C.: GPO, 1972).

U.S., Congress, Senate, Committee on Foreign Relations, *The United States and Communist China in 1949 and 1950: The Question of Rapprochment and Recognition,* Staff Study by Robert M. Blum, (Washington, D.C.: GPO, 1973).

U.S., Congress, Senate, Committee on Foreign Relations, *Hearings on the Causes, Origins and Lessons of the Vietnam War,* 92d Cong., 2d sess., 1972 (Washington, D.C.: GPO, 1973).

U.S., Congress, Senate, Committees on Foreign Relations and Armed Services, *Military Assistance Program, Joint Hearings on S.2388,* (Washington, D.C.: GPO, 1949).

U.S., Congress, Senate, Committees on Foreign Relations and Armed Services, *Military Assistance Program: 1949, Joint Hearings held in Executive Session on S.2388* (Historical Series), 81st Cong., 1st sess., 1949 (Washington, D.C.: GPO, 1974).

U.S., Congress, Senate, Committees on Foreign Relations and Armed Services, *Mutual Defense Assistance Program, 1950, Hearings on the Mutual Defense Assistance Program, 1950,* 81st Cong., 2d sess., 1950 (Washington, D.C.: GPO, 1950).

U.S., Congress, Senate, Committee on Government Operations, Subcommittee on National

Policy Machinery, *Organizing for National Security,* vol. 2 (Washington, D.C.: GPO, 1961).

U.S., Congress, Senate, Select Committee to Study Government Operations with Respect to Intelligence Activities, *Supplementary Detailed Staff Report on Foreign and Military Intelligence, Book IV, Final Report,* 94th Cong., 2d sess., 1975 (Washington, D.C.: GPO, 1976).

Congress, House:

U.S., Congress, House, Committee on Appropriations, *Department of State Appropriations for 1951, Hearings before a Subcommittee,* pt. 1, 81st Cong., 2d sess., 1950 (Washington, D.C.: GPO, 1950).

U.S., Congress, House, Subcommittee of the Committee on Appropriations, *Hearings on Second Supplemental Appropriation Bill for 1950,* 81st Cong., 1st sess., 1949 11 October 1949.

U.S., Congress, House, Committee on Foreign Affairs, *Korean Aid, Hearings on H.R.5330* (Washington, D.C.: GPO, 1949).

U.S., Congress, House, Committee on Foreign Affairs, *To Amend the Economic Cooperation Act of 1948, As Amended, Hearings on H.R. 7378,* pt. 1, 81st Cong., 2d sess., 1950 (Washington, D.C.: GPO, 1950).

U.S., Congress, House, Committee on International Relations, *Selected Executive Session Hearings of the Committee, 1943–1950,* Vol. 1–8 (Washington, GPO, 1976).

PUBLIC RECORDS

Records of the Senate Committee on Foreign Relations, Record Group 46, National Archives.

Records of the Bureau of the Budget, Record Group 51, National Archives.

Records of the Department of State, Record Group 59,
National Archives including:
Decimal File
Lot Files:
Records of the Office of Chinese Affairs, 1944–50;
Current Foreign Relations, 1946–50;
White House Daily Summary, 1946–50;
Daily Summary, 1945–51;
Secretary's Weekly Summary, 1947–49;
Daily Staff Summary, 1945–51;
Records of the Executive Secretariat, 1949–52;
Verbatim Reports of the Secretary's Press Conference, 1949–70;
Records of the Philippines and Southeast Asia Division, 1944–52;
Records of the Policy Planning Staff, 1947–55.

Records of the Joint Chiefs of Staff, Record Group 218, National Archives.

Records of the Economic Cooperation Administration, Record Group 286, National Archives.

Records of the Army Staff, Plans and Operations, Record Group 319, National Archives.

Records of the Office of the Secretary of Defense, Record Group 330, National Archives.

Records of the State-Army-Navy-Air Force Coordinating Committee, Record Group 353, National Archives.

Records of the Central Intelligence Agency (through Freedom of Information Act).

Records of the National Security Council (through Freedom of Information Act).

Senate Republican Minority Conference Committee Minutes, Capitol Building, Washington, D.C.

BIBLIOGRAPHY

MANUSCRIPT COLLECTIONS

Dean G. Acheson Papers, Truman Library.
Joseph and Stewart Alsop Papers, Library of Congress.
W. Walton Butterworth Papers, George C. Marshall Research Foundation, Lexington, Virginia.
Claire M. Chennault Papers, Library of Congress (microfilm).
Clark M. Clifford Papers, Truman Library.
Matthew J. Connally Papers, Truman Library.
Tom Connally Papers, Library of Congress.
John Foster Dulles Papers, Princeton University.
Raymond B. Fosdick Papers, Princeton University.
Philip E. Gallagher Papers, Office of Military History, Department of the Army, Washington, D.C.
Theodore Francis Green Papers, Library of Congress.
Paul H. Hoffman Papers, Truman Library.
Philip C. Jessup Papers, Library of Congress.
Louis A. Johnson Papers, University of Virginia.
George F. Kennan Papers, Princeton University.
H. Wellington Koo Papers, Columbia University.
H. Alexander Smith Papers, Princeton University.
J. Leighton Stuart Papers, Washington, D.C.
Robert A. Taft Papers, Library of Congress.
Harry S. Truman Papers, Truman Library.
Arthur H. Vandenberg Papers, University of Michigan.
James E. Webb Papers, Truman Library.

ORAL HISTORIES

W. Walton Butterworth, Truman Library.
O. Edmund Clubb, Truman Library.
Matthew J. Connally, Truman Library.
Jack McFall, Truman Library.

Walter H. Judd, Truman Library.
H. Wellington Koo, Columbia University.
Francis Russell, Truman Library.
Philip E. Sprouse, Truman Library.

INTERVIEWS

David D. Barrett, 1971.
Lucius D. Battle, 1977.
W. Walton Butterworth, 1972.
Harland Cleveland, 1979.
O. Edmund Clubb, 1973.
H. Fulton Freeman, 1971.
Philip Fugh, 1977.
Ernest A. Gross, 1975.
Philip Jessup, 1972.

Kenneth P. Landon, 1971.
Carl Marcy, 1978.
Abbot Low Moffat, 1971.
Charlton Ogburn, 1972.
Dean Rusk, 1977, 1978.
John S. Service, 1971, 1972.
Philip E. Sprouse, 1971, 1972, 1973.
John Carter Vincent, 1971.
Frank White, 1971.

Notes

Chapter 1. CHINA ROOTS

1. For generally reliable accounts of American involvement in China during the Second World War and early postwar years, see Michael Schaller, *The U.S. Crusade in China, 1938–1945* (New York: Columbia University Press, 1979); Herbert Feis, *The China Tangle* (Princeton: Princeton University Press, 1953); Tang Tsou, *America's Failure in China, 1941–1950* (Chicago: University of Chicago Press, 1963); for a briefer account, see Warren I. Cohen, *America's Response to China* (New York: John Wiley & Sons, 1971).

2. For published accounts of the "Dixie Mission," see John S. Service, *The Amerasia Papers: Some Problems in the History of U.S.-China Relations* (Berkeley: Center for Chinese Studies, 1971); Col. David D. Barrett, *Dixie Mission: The United States Army Observer Group in Yenan, 1944* (Berkeley: Center for Chinese Studies, 1970); Schaller, *U.S. Crusade;* and Barbara Tuchman, "If Mao Had Come to Washington," *Foreign Affairs,* October 1972. OSS documents for the mission are open to researchers at the Modern Military Branch of the National Archives. State Department reports from the mission are available from a variety of sources. The author is grateful to John Service, the late David Barrett, and Raymond Ludden for sharing with him their experiences on the Dixie Mission.

3. For standard military accounts of the Chinese civil war, see F. F. Liu, *A Military History of Modern China, 1924–1949* (Princeton: Princeton University Press, 1956); Lionel Max Chassin, *The Communist Conquest of China: A History of the Civil War, 1945–1949* (Cambridge: Harvard University Press, 1965); and U.S., Department of State, *United States Relations with China* (Washington, D.C.: GPO, 1949).

4. This summary of events is drawn from the secondary works cited above as well as from documents in U.S., Department of State, *Foreign Relations of the United States* (hereafter cited as *FR*), 1948, VII (Washington, D.C.: GPO, 1973), and *FR,* 1949, VIII (Washington, D.C.: GPO, 1978).

5. NSC–37/1, 19 January 1949, *FR*, 1949, IX (Washington, D.C.: GPO, 1974), p. 272.

6. Ibid., p. 172; memo, Lovett to president, 14 January 1949, *ibid.*, p. 266. The American consul in Taipei described the Taiwanese as "volatile and immature" in a cable summarized in "Top Secret Daily Staff Summary," 27 October 1948, Records of the Department of State, Record Group 59, National Archives (hereafter cited as RG . . . NA).

7. Airgram, Stuart to secretary, 4 August 1948, *FR*, 1948, VII, pp. 399–400.

8. Telegram, Stuart to secretary, 21 November 1948, ibid., pp. 593–97. For the text of Liu's speech, see *Collected Works of Liu Shao-Ch'i, 1945–1957* (Hong Kong: Union Research Institute, 1969), pp. 123–51.

9. Airgram, Stuart to secretary, 6 December 1948, and airgram, 9 December 1948, *FR*, 1948, VII, pp. 631–32, 637. For the text of Mao's speech, see Mao Tse-tung, *Selected Works, Vol. 5, 1945–1949* (New York: International Publishers, n. d.), pp. 283–86. According to Okabe Tatsumi, the two articles by Mao and Liu appeared in the *People's Daily* on 7 November 1948. "The Cold War and China," *The Origins of the Cold War in Asia*, ed. Yonosuke Nagai and Akira Iriye (New York: Columbia University Press, 1977), p. 241.

10. Telegram, Cabot to secretary, 18 November 1948, *FR*, 1948, VII, p. 837. The Mukden story is continued in *FR*, 1949, VIII, pp. 933–1051.

11. The conditions under which American diplomats operated in China after the takeover are described in the last chapter of *FR*, 1949, VIII. For a vivid description of the conditions in Dairen, see Paul Paddock, *China Diary: Crisis Diplomacy in Dairen* (Ames, Iowa: Iowa State University Press, 1977). For firsthand accounts of conditions in Peking, see O. Edmund Clubb, *The Witness and I* (New York: Columbia University Press, 1974); for conditions in Nanking, see John Leighton Stuart, *Fifty Years in China* (New York: Random House, 1954); Chester Ronning, *A Memoir of China in Revolution* (New York: Pantheon Books, 1974); and K. M. Panikkar, *In Two Chinas* (London: George Allen & Unwin, 1955).

12. For details of the Sino-Soviet negotiations relating to Sinkiang, see *FR*, 1949, IX, pp. 1037–63. For a general description of the border conflict see O. Edmund Clubb, *China and Russia: The Great Game* (New York: Columbia University Press, 1971). On the postwar strain in Soviet-Chinese Communist relations, see the Tatsumi essay in Nagai and Iriye, *Origins of the Cold War,* and John Gittings, *The World and China, 1922–1972* (London: Eyere Methuen, 1974).

13. Telegram, Kohler to secretary, 21 January 1949, *FR*, 1949, VIII, pp. 70–71; see also telegram, Kohler to secretary, 17 January 1949, 893.00/1–1749, RG 59, NA.

14. Telegram, Kohler to secretary, 3 February 1949, *FR*, 1949, VIII, p. 105.

15. Memo, Davies to Kennan, 25 January 1949, 893.00/1–2549, RG 59, NA.

16. Memo, Butterworth to Webb, 25 February 1949, *FR*, 1949, IX, p. 1047. This memo was based on a more lengthy analysis of the Sino-Soviet relationship by W. W. Stuart, 17 February 1949, 761.93/2–2549, RG 59, NA.

17. For accounts of the Truman White House during this period, see Cabell Phillips, *The Truman Presidencey: The History of a Triumphant Succession* (New York: Macmillan Co., 1966), and Richard F. Haynes, *The Awesome Power: Harry S. Truman as Commander in Chief* (Baton Rouge: Louisiana State University Press, 1973). For further insight into the Truman White House, see Robert S. Allen and William V. Shannon, *The Truman Merry-Go-Round* (New York: Vanguard Press, 1950); Patrick Anderson, *The President's Men* (New York: Doubleday, 1968); and David E. Lilienthal, *The Journals of David E. Lilienthal: Vol. 2, The Atomic Energy Years, 1945–1950* (New York: Harper & Row, 1964). On Truman's popularity, see Dr. George H. Gallup, *The Gallup Poll, Public Opinion 1935–1971: Vol. 2, 1949–1958* (New York: Random House, 1972).

18. On Acheson, see Dean G. Acheson, *Present at the Creation* (New York: W. W. Norton, 1969) and David S. McLellan, *Dean Acheson, The State Department Years* (New York: Dodd,

Mead & Co., 1976). The author is also grateful to Lucius D. Battle, a foreign service officer and Dean Acheson's personal aide throughout most of the secretary's tenure, for discussing Acheson's relationship with the White House and his advisors.

19. See Butterworth's "Draft" Oral History, taken in 1972, at the Truman Library. The present author also interviewed Butterworth in that same year.

20. The author interviewed Sprouse in 1971, 1972, and by phone in 1973. See also the letter from Sprouse to the author, printed in *Diplomatic History*, March 1978. The Sprouse Oral History at the Truman Library gives the flavor of the man but is short on specifics about China policy. See also E. J. Kahn, Jr., *The China Hands: America's Foreign Service Officers and What Befell Them* (New York: Viking Press, 1972).

21. The author interviewed Rusk in 1977. The best work on Dean Rusk will be the forthcoming biography by Professor Warren Cohen of Michigan State University, *David Dean Rusk* (Totowa, N.J.: Rowman & Littlefield, forthcoming).

22. The author interviewed Jessup in 1972. For a description of Jessup's background and experiences in the State Department, see Philip C. Jessup, *The Birth of Nations* (New York: Columbia University Press, 1974).

23. George F. Kennan, *Memoirs, 1925–1950* (Boston: Little, Brown & Co., 1967) is surprisingly silent on his involvement in China policy but does reveal his problems with Acheson.

24. Phillips, *The Truman Presidency*, p. 288.

25. Lilienthal, *Journals, Vol. 2*, pp. 508–9.

26. For background on the operation of the National Security Council, see Sidney Souers, "Policy Formulation and the National Security Council," *The American Political Science Review*, June 1949, pp. 534–35; U.S. Senate, Committee on Government Operations, Subcommittee on National Policy Machinery, *Organizing for National Security, Vol. 2* (Washington, D.C.: GPO, 1961), which contains an essay by James S. Lay, Jr. and Robert H. Johnson, "Organizational History of the National Security Council," pp. 417–30; and Robert H. Johnson, "The National Security Council: The Relevance of Its Past to Its Future," *Orbis*, Fall 1969, pp. 709–15. For documents relating to the National Security Council see the chapters on "National Security Policy" in the first volume of *FR* for the years after 1946. NSC papers are also scattered throughout State Department records at the National Archives and may be found in the Truman Papers at the Truman Library.

27. Philip Horton, "The China Lobby—Part II," *The Reporter*, 29 April 1952, p. 11.

28. Stanley D. Bachrack, *The Committee of One Million: "China Lobby" Politics, 1953–1971* (New York: Columbia University Press, 1976), p. 32.

29. Charles Wertenbaker, "The China Lobby," *The Reporter*, 15 April 1952, pp. 14–15.

30. Letter, Kohlberg to the president, 9 May 1949, "China—1949" folder, Robert A. Taft Papers, Library of Congress; Letter, Loeb to Webb, 7 June 1949, 711.93/6–749, RG 59, NA.

31. For evidence of Biffle's association with the Chinese embassy, see letter, Goodwin to Chen Chi-mai, 21 November 1948, and memo, Ku to the ambassador, 31 January 1949, "Inter-Office Memo" files, V. K. Wellington Koo Papers, Columbia University; letter, Biffle to Clifford, 22 November 1948, "China Folder–2," Clark M. Clifford Papers, Harry S. Truman Library. For Griffith's role, see memo, "PHG" to the secretary of defense, 21 April 1949, JCS 1721/28, CCS 452, China (4–3–45) Sec. 7, Pt. 4, Records of the Joint Chiefs of Staff, RG 218, NA; and Koo's memos of conversations with Griffith, 3 and 7 June 1950, "Notes of Conversation—1950," Koo Papers. For examples of military support for the Nationalists, see also: letter, Wedemeyer to Butterworth, 24 May 1949, 893.00/5–2449, RG 59, NA: testimony of Admiral Badger in U.S. Congress, Senate, Committees on Foreign Relations and Armed Services, *Military Assistance Program: 1949*, 81st Cong, 1st sess. ("His-

torical Series" of hearings held in executive session) (Washington, D.C.: GPO, 1974), pp. 515–50; and a summary of MacArthur's views on Formosa attached to a memo, Louis Johnson to president, 15 December 1949, "Foreign Affairs: Far East" folder, President's Secretary's Files, Truman Papers, Truman Library.

32. For a capsule picture of the operation of the Chinese embassy, see Horton, "China Lobby—Part II" and the relevant portions of Ambassador Koo's remarkable Oral History, Columbia University.

33. For documentation of Madame Chiang's lobbying effort, see *FR*, 1948, VIII, (Washington, D.C.: GPO, 1973), pp. 296–306, and letter, General Marshall to Acheson, 22 August 1949, 711.93/8–2249, RG 59, NA.

34. The role of Chen, Ku, and Goodwin is amply documented in the Koo papers which are, in effect, the working papers of the Chinese Nationalist Embassy. See also the Wertenbaker and Horton articles in *The Reporter*.

35. Memo, Chen to the ambassador, 13 May 1949, "Inter-Office Memo" folder, Koo Papers, Columbia University.

36. Memo, Ku to the ambassador, 8 March 1949, "Inter-Office Memo" folder, Koo Papers.

37. See both the Goodwin letter, 15 November 1948, and letter, Goodwin to Chen, November 15, 1948, "Inter-Office Memo" folder, Koo Papers. Ku details the embassy's activities in a memo to the ambassador, 8 March 1949, ibid.

38. For a history of the Service case, see Service, *The Amerasia Papers*. The department at White House insistence, ultimately fired him as a result of political pressure. He won reinstatement after appealing his case to the Supreme Court.

39. For a speech displaying most of these themes, see Senator William Jenner's floor speech quoted in Chapter 5, p. 77.

40. For evidence of the impact of the counter-China lobby, see a dissertation under preparation by Nancy Bernkopf Tucker, *Pattern in the Dust: Why the United States Did Not Recognize the People's Republic in China in 1949 and 1950*, Columbia University.

41. On the conflicting American views of China, see Harold R. Isaacs, *Images of Asia* (former title *Scratches on our Mind*) (New York: Harper & Row, 1958, 1972), pp. xi–xiv; *Gallup Poll, Vol. 1* pp. 773–74; *Gallup Poll, Vol. 2*, pp. 818, 831–32.

Chapter 2. CHINA POLICY SMORGASBOARD, 3 MARCH 1949

1. PPS–39, 7 September 1948, *FR*, 1948, VIII, pp. 146–55.

2. Memo, Kennan to secretary, 30 November 1948, ibid., p. 225.

3. PPS–39, ibid., pp. 146–55.

4. For the army's views, see NSC–22, 26 July 1948, ibid., pp. 118–22, and the NSC staff report, 2 November 1948, ibid., pp. 185–87; memo, Butterworth to acting secretary, 3 November 1948, ibid., pp. 187–89; memo, Kennan to secretary and under secretary, 24 November 1948, ibid., pp. 211–12; PPS–39/1, 3 November 1949, and PPS–45, 26 November 1948, ibid., pp. 208–11, 214–20.

5. For a legislative history of the China Aid Act of 1948 and the subsequent appropriation act and aid programs, see William Adam Brown, Jr., and Redvers Opie, *American Foreign Assistance* (Washington, D.C., The Brookings Institute, 1953), pp. 333–51.

6. For documents concerning the extension and amendment of the China Aid Act of 1948, see *FR*, 1948, VIII, pp. 668–85, and *FR*, 1949, IX, pp. 599–610.

7. Brown and Opie, *American Foreign Assistance*, pp. 337–38.

8. Telegram, Lapham to ECA administrator, 26 November 1948, *FR*, 1948, VIII, pp. 654–58.

9.   Letter, Cabot to Butterworth, 30 December 1948, *FR,* 1948, VII pp. 707–18. Butterworth received this letter about 10 January 1949.

10.   Letter, Cleveland to Lapham, 2 December 1948, *FR,* 1948, VIII, pp. 658–62.

11.   Ibid., p. 660.

12.   Ibid., pp. 660–61

13.   Incoming telegram, TOREP 2374, 15 December 1948 (press conference transcript), OSR, Labor Information Division, Geographic Subject File, 1948–51, Records of the Economic Cooperation Administration, RG 286, NA.

14.   Memo, Butterworth to acting secretary, 18 December 1948, *FR,* 1948, VIII, pp. 665–66.

15.   Memo for the record, 30 December 1948, ibid., pp. 667–68.

16.   Letter, Cleveland to Lapham, 3 January 1949; memo, Butterworth to acting secretary, 14 January 1949; memo for the record, 14 January 1949, and annex, *FR,* 1949, IX, pp. 610–15.

17.   Minutes, Cabinet meeting, 19 January 1949, "Cabinet Meeting—1949" folder, Matthew J. Connally Papers, Harry S. Truman Library.

18.   PPS–45 26 November 1948, Enclosure 1, "Draft Statement Prepared in the Division of Chinese Affairs for the Secretary of State," and memo, Butterworth to acting secretary, 16 December 1948, *FR,* 1948, VIII, pp. 217, 233–34.

19.   NSC–22/2, 15 December 1948, and enclosure, *FR,* 1948, VIII, pp. 231–32.

20.   Telegram, acting secretary to Stuart, 16 December 1948, ibid., p. 235.

21.   Letter, Lovett to Souers, 28 October 1948, ibid., p. 332. On the withdrawal from Tsingtao, see manuscript of Kenneth W. Coudit, Historical Division, Joint Chiefs of Staff, *The History of the Joint Chiefs of Staff: The Joint Chiefs of Staff and National Policy, Vol. 2, 1947–1949,* pp. 454–62, copy in Modern Military Branch, NA.

22.   NSC–11/2, 14 December 1948, ibid., pp. 339–42.

23.   Minutes of the 30th meeting of the National Security Council, 16 December 1948, NSC files, President's Secretary's files, Truman Papers; telegram, acting secretary to Stuart, 28 December 1948, *FR,* 1948, VIII, p. 344.

24.   This decision indicated in NSC–11/2, ibid., p. 341.

25.   Telegram, Stuart to secretary, 18 December 1948, ibid., pp. 235–36; "Summary of General Barr's Telegram No. 871 OAGA of December 18," ibid., pp. 236–37; The decision to defer a decision on whether or not to continue the aid program is indicated in enclosure to memo, Forrestal to Souers, 2 February 1949 (NSC–22/3), paragraph 2, *FR,* 1949, IX, p. 479. The State Department's perception is stated in telegram, secretary to Stuart, 24 January 1949, ibid., pp. 477–78; telegram, Cabot to secretary, 26 January 1949, and Barr to Maddocks, 26 January 1949, ibid., pp. 478, 481–82.

26.   Memo, Forrestal to Souers, 2 February 1949, (NSC–22/3), ibid., p. 480.

27.   Memo, Butterworth to secretary, 2 February 1949, 893.50 Recovery/2–249, RG 59, NA. Emphasis added.

28.   Minutes of the 33d Meeting of the NSC, 3 February 1949, NSC files, President's Secretary's files, Truman Papers.

29.   Cabinet meeting notes, 4 February 1949, "Cabinet Meetings—1949" folder, Connally Papers; memo by "D.A.," 4 February 1949, 893.50 Recovery/2–449, RG 59, NA.

30.   "Memorandum by the Secretary of State of a conversation with President Truman," 2 February 149, *FR,* 1949, IX, p. 486; Arthur S. Vandenberg, Jr., *The Private Papers of Senator Vandenberg* (Boston: Houghton Mifflin, 1952), pp. 530–31. In a telephone conversation with the author in February 1973, Philip Sprouse disputed the Vandenberg account and stated that "Lovett" (Sprouse confused Lovett with Acheson) went into the meeting prepared to

back continued aid to the Nationalists. It is not clear from Vandenberg's account what position Acheson took.

31. Memo, Butterworth to secretary, 4 February 1949, 893.00/2–449, RG 59, NA.

32. NSC–34/2, 28 February 1949, *FR*, 1949, IX, pp. 491–95.

33. NSC–41, 28 February 1949, ibid., pp. 826–34.

34. Memo, acting secretary to president, 14 January 1949, ibid., p. 266.

35. NSC–37/1, 19 January 1949, ibid., p. 274.

36. NSC–37/4, 18 February 1949, ibid., p. 288–89.

37. NSC–37/3, 10 February 1949, ibid., p. 284–86; telegram, secretary to Krentz, 2 March 1949, ibid., pp. 293–94.

38. NSC–37/5, 1 March 1949, ibid., pp. 290–92.

39. Minutes of the 35th Meeting of the NSC, 3 March 1949, NSC files, President's Secretary's files, Truman Papers; presidential approval of the papers indicated in *FR*, 1949, IX, pp. 499, 834, 296–97.

40. Letter, Butterworth to Krentz, 15 January 1949, "Taiwan" folder, Records of the Office of Chinese Affairs, Lot 56D151, RG 59, NA. Emphasis added.

41. "Statement by the Secretary of State . . .," 3 March 1949, *FR*, 1949, IX, p. 295. With the possible exception of the last three paragraphs, printed on p. 296, Philip Sprouse drafted the statement. Sprouse's memo is in the "Taiwan" folder.

Chapter 3. FIRST CHINA BLOC OFFENSIVE

1. Robert A. Divine, *Foreign Policy and U.S. Presidential Elections, 1940–1948* (New York: New Viewpoints, 1974), p. 270.

2. Draft Oral History, W. Walton Butterworth, 6 July 1971, pp. 47–49, Truman Library. Butterworth recalled "that our computations . . . showed that the Nationalist Government at the time we were formulating the Marshall Plan had enough gold and foreign exchange, had military equipment, so that it needed *no* aid program. The aid program arose out of the fact that Senator Vandenberg let it be known that the chances of getting through the Marshall Plan would be vastly improved if there was a China aid program."

3. U.S., Congress, Senate, Committee on Foreign Relations, *Executive Sessions of the Senate Foreign Relations Committee 1947–48* vol. 1, 80th Cong., 1st and 2d sess., ("Historical Series" of hearings held in executive session) (Washington, D.C.: GPO, 1976), pp. 55–70.

4. Letter, Hale et al. to president, 7 February 1949, 893.00/2–749, RG 59, NA.

5. Memo, MSC to S/S (Marshall S. Carter to the Staff of the Executive Secretariate), 10 February 1949, 893.00/2–1049, and memo, MSC to S/S, 11 February 1949, 893.00/2–1149, ibid.

6. Acheson memo of conversation with president, 14 February 1949, 893.00/2–1549, ibid.

7. "Secretary's Notes for Meeting with Republican Congressmen at the House Ways and Means Committee on the Letter they addressed to the Secretary," Dean Acheson Papers, Truman Library.

8. For Sulzberger's notes on the interview, see C. L. Sulzberger, *Long Row of Candles: Memoirs and Diaries, 1934–1954* (New York: Macmillan Co., 1969), pp. 433–36. His articles appeared in the *New York Times* on 11, 14, 15, 16, and 21 February 1949; memo, Chen to ambassador, 23 February 1949, "Inter-Office Memo" folder, Koo Papers. Chen's confident prediction of what his contacts in Congress would do should not be taken at face value.

9. *Time,* 7 March 1949, p. 25. For other accounts of the meeting, see *New York Times,* 25 February 1949, p. 1; two memos from Chen to ambassador, 25 and 26 February 1949, "Inter-Office Memo" folder, Koo Papers.

10.   Bullitt was critical of the administration's Indochina policy in "The Saddest War," *Life,* 29 December 1947, pp. 64–9, and of China policy in a series of articles in *Life* in 1948. For a critical description of his activity in China, see Stuart to secretary, 17 May 1948, *FR,* 1948, VII, pp. 237–39.

11.   For a summary of the Clark proposal, see memo, Butterworth to secretary, 23 November 1948, *FR,* 1948, VIII, pp. 682–83, and *New York Times,* 21 November 1948. Bullitt recommended aid in testimony before the "Watchdog" Committee as described in *New York Times,* 7 and 8 January 1949, pp. 1–2. On the political background to the Clark mission, see Wertenbaker, "China Lobby—Part I," 15 April 1952, p. 19.

12.   *New York Times,* 29 January 1949, p. 3; letter, McCarran to Acheson, 28 January 1949, 893.50 Recovery/1–2849, RG 59, NA.

13.   See memo to Butterworth, 8 February 1949, and attachments, 893.50 Recovery/1–2849, RG 59, NA.

14.   The bill, S. 1063, is printed in U.S. Congress, Senate, Committee on Foreign Relations, *Economic Assistance to China and Korea: 1949–1950,* 81st Cong., 1st and 2d sess. ("Historical Series" of hearings held in executive session) (Washington, D.C.: GPO, 1974), pp. 232–39.

15.   For memoranda and drafts reflecting this drafting process, see 893.50 Recovery/2–2849, RG 59, NA. The 14 March letter is printed in *FR,* 1949, IX, pp. 607–9, but with the date incorrectly given as 15 March. For the original, see the bill file in Records of the Senate Committee on Foreign Relations, RG 46, NA.

16.   The letter is printed in Foreign Relations Committee, *Economic Assistance,* pp. 1–2.

17.   *Ibid.,* pp. 2, 9.

18.   See *Newsweek,* 21 March 1949, p. 18. Even McCarran realized that the cosigners were not all for his bill. See memo of conversation with Senator McCarran, 31 March 1949, "Notes of Conversation—1949" folder, Koo Papers.

19.   See Senator Green's comment in Foreign Relations Committee, *Economic Assistance,* p. 3.

20.   Memo by Dort, 28 September 1948, *FR,* 1948, VIII, pp. 670–71; memo by Magill and Johnson, 1 December 1948, ibid., pp. 681–82. See the testimony of ECA representatives in Foreign Relations Committee, *Economic Assistance,* passim; memo of conversation, 10 March 1949, *FR,* 1949, IX, pp. 630–32, and "Comments on the Memorandum from Mr. Cleveland to Mr. Hoffman of February 8, 1949, on the subject of Aid to China Policy— Means of Maintaining U.S. Contact with and influence in China," 893.50 Recovery/3–1049, RG 59, NA; the basic State-ECA agreement on the aid program is summarized in memo of conversation, 10 March 1949, *FR,* 1949, IX, pp. 630–32. The breakdown of projected uses of the $56 million is contained in testimony in Foreign Relations Committee, *Economic Assistance,* pp. 91–92, and, in greater detail, in U.S., Congress, House, Committee on International Relations, 1943–50, *United States Policy in the Far East, Vol. 7, Pt. 1* "Historical Series" of hearings held in executive session) (Washington, D.C.: GPO, 1976), pp. 385–89. The Formosa policy statement is from NSC–37/5, *FR,* 1949, IX, p. 292. For documents reflecting the State Department's intended use of the aid, see memo by Butterworth, 29 January 1949, ibid., pp. 601–6, especially last paragraph; memo, Butterworth to secretary, 4 February 1949, 893.00/2–449, RG 59, NA; telegram, Cabot to secretary, 11 March 1949, *FR,* 1949, IX, p. 299; memo, Butterworth to secretary, 15 March 1949, ibid., p. 607; telegram, Stuart to secretary, 23 March 1949, ibid., p. 302; telegram, secretary to Stuart, 24 March 1949, ibid., p. 304; memo, Butterworth to secretary, 15 April 1949, ibid., p. 635; and telegram, secretary to Ludden, 26 April 1949, ibid., p. 638; for the text of this bill, H.R. 3539, see International Relations Committee, *Policy in the Far East, Vol. 7. pt. 1,* p. 469.

21.   Ibid., pp. 343–51.

22. Ibid., pp. 368–69.

23. Ibid., pp. 375–76.

24. Memo, Butterworth to secretary, 15 March 1949, *FR*, 1949, IX, p. 607.

25. International Relations Committee, *Policy in the Far East, Vol. 7, Pt. 1*, pp. 387–89.

26. Ibid., p. 402.

27. Telegram, secretary to Stuart, 24 March 1949, *FR*, 1949, IX, p. 304.

28. For Lapham's views, see memo, Lapham to Hoffman, 9 March 1949, ibid., pp. 626–30, and International Relations Committee, *Policy in the Far East, Vol. 7, Pt. 1*, p. 393.

29. See H.R. 3830 printed in ibid., p. 470.

30. Memo of telephone conversation with Judge Kee by LDB, 1 April 1949, 893.50 Recovery/4–149, RG 59, NA; U.S., Congress, House, *Congressional Record*, 81st Cong., 1st sess, pp. 3823–29.

31. Ibid., pp. 39, 42.

32. Ibid., pp. 99–100, 107.

33. Ibid., pp. 113–114.

34. U.S., Congress, *Congressional Record*, 81st Cong., 1st sess, 1949, pp. 3765, 3769, 3771, 3787.

35. Telegram, secretary to Stuart, 24 March 1949, *FR*, 1949, IX, p. 304.

36. See, for example, James A. Fetzer, *Congress and China, 1941–1950*, (Ph.D. diss., Michigan State University, 1970) pp. 181–82; David S. McLellan, *Dean Acheson, The State Department Years* (New York: Dodd, Mead & Co., 1976), p. 189; and Tang Tsou, *America's Failure in China, 1941–1950* (Chicago: University of Chicago Press, 1963), pp. 500–01.

37. Memo of conversation, 4 April 1949, *FR*, 1949, VII, pt. 2 (Washington, D.C.: GPO, 1977), pp. 1140–41.

Chapter 4. PROSPECTS FOR CHINESE TITOISM

1. For reports of Chinese Communist propaganda, see the documents in file 893.9111/–49, RG 59, NA.

2. *New York Times*, 19 March and 4 April 1949, pp. 4 and 1.

3. Telegram, Kohler to secretary, 19 April 1949, *FR*, 1949, VIII, pp. 249–51; and telegram, Stuart to secretary, 26 April 1949, ibid., pp. 277–78.

4. Dispatch, Cabot to Stuart, 20 April 1949, ibid., pp. 256–57.

5. For a discussion of this problem, see telegrams printed in *FR*, 1949, IX, p. 906.

6. Telegrams, Smyth to secretary, 10 March 1949, Clubb to secretary, 10 March 1949, and Stuart to secretary, 18 March 1949, ibid., pp. 910–11, 934–36, and 916–17; telegrams, secretary to certain diplomatic and consular officers in China, 1 April 1949, and secretary to Cabot, 3 May 1949, ibid., pp. 926–27, 936–38; telegram, Clubb to secretary, 30 April 1949, ibid., pp. 974–76. Clubb's recommendations are also indicated in memo, Magill to Davies, 2 May 1949, "NSC Reports" folder, Lot 56D151, RG 59, NA; telegram, Cabot to secretary, 27 April 1949, *FR*, 1949, IX, pp. 1252–53; telegram, Clark to secretary, 29 April 1949, ibid., pp. 934–36; memo, Magill to Davies, 2 May 1949, "NSC Reports" folder, Lot 56D151, RG 59, NA; Secretary's Daily Meeting, 3 May 1949, RG 59, NA.

7. Telegram, Clubb to secretary, 30 April 1949, *FR*, 1949, IX, pp. 976–77.

8. Memo, Butterworth to under secretary, 26 January 1949, *FR*, 1949, VIII, pp. 664–67, and memo, Butterworth to secretary, 14 April 1949, "Status of Ambassador and Embassy in Nanking" folder, Lot 56D151, RG 59, NA.

9. Airgram, Stuart to secretary, 10 March 1949, *FR*, 1949, VIII, pp. 173–77.

10. Airgram, secretary to Stuart, 6 April 1949, ibid., pp. 230–31.

11.   Telegram, secretary to Stuart, 11 April 1949; memo, Rusk to secretary, 22 April 1949; telegram, secretary to Stuart, 22 April 1949, ibid., pp. 676, 682–83.

12.   See telegrams, ibid., pp. 723–24; *New York Times*, 26 April 1949, p. 1; diary of J. Leighton Stuart, 25 April 1949, Stuart Papers, in possession of Philip Fugh, Washington, D.C.; interview with Philip Fugh, 1977, Washington, D.C.

13.   Telegram, Stuart to secretary, 3 May 1949, *FR*, 1949, IX, pp. 14–15.

14.   Telegram, secretary to certain diplomatic and consular officers, 6 May 1949, ibid., p. 17.

15.   For the department's perception of the foreign response, see par. 5, telegram, secretary to Stuart, 13 May 1949, ibid., pp. 21–23. For a report indicating that the British were independently bargaining with the Communists on terms for recognition that would secure their interests in Southeast Asia and Hong Kong, see telegram no. 294, Acheson to Clubb (sanitized, source deleted), 13 May 1949, 893.00B/5–1349, RG 59, NA. The British were on record as believing that "to refuse to accord any sort of recognition to a government which in fact effectively controls a large portion of territory is not only objectionable on legal grounds but leads to grave practical difficulties." British embassy to the State Department, 19 March 1949, *FR*, 1949, IX, pp. 11–12. Britain reiterated this position as indicated in telegram, Douglas to secretary, 19 May 1949, ibid., pp. 25–26.

16.   Telegram, secretary to Stuart, 13 May 1949, ibid., pp. 21–23.

17.   Telegram, Stuart to secretary, 11 May 1949, *FR*, 1949, VIII, pp. 741–42.

18.   Memo, Butterworth to secretary, 12 May 1949, 893.00B/5–1149, RG 59, NA.

19.   Telegram, Stuart to secretary, 14 May 1949, *FR*, 1949, VIII, pp. 745–47; Stuart Diary, 13 May 1949, Stuart Papers; telegram no. 1050, Stuart to secretary, 17 May 1949, 893.00B/5–1749, RG 59, NA.

20.   Telegram, Cabot to secretary, 31 May 1949, *FR*, 1949, VIII, pp. 355–57.

21.   Telegram, Clubb to secretary, 1 June 1949, ibid., pp. 357–60. For background on Barrett, see David D. Barrett, *Dixie Mission: The United States Army Observer Group in Yenan, 1944* (Berkeley: Center for Chinese Studies, 1970). On Keon, see Lionel M. Chassin, *The Communist Conquest of China: A History of the Civil War, 1945–1949* (Cambridge: Harvard University Press, 1965), pp. 160–64. Clubb mentions the demarché in *The Witness and I* (New York: Columbia University Press, 1974), p. 80.

22.   Telegram, Clubb to secretary, 2 June 1949, *FR*, 1949, VIII, pp. 363–64.

23.   Telegram, Clark to secretary, 6 June 1949, ibid., p. 370.

24.   Stuart Diary, 3 June 1949, Stuart Papers; telegram, Stuart to secretary, 7 June 1949, *FR*, 1949, VIII, pp. 372–73.

25.   Telegram, Cabot to secretary, 6 June 1949, *FR*, 1949, VIII, pp. 370–71; the speech was also quoted in the *New York Times* in a dispatch from Walter Sullivan, 7 June 1949, p. 1. This was significant because Sullivan had cleared it through censors in Shanghai, a fact that gave it the aspect of a trial balloon. Seymour Topping, *Journey Between Two Chinas* (New York: Harper & Row, 1972), pp. 84–85.

26.   Telegram no. 1064, Clubb to secretary, 23 June 1949, 893.00/6–2349, RG 59, NA.

27.   Telegram, Stuart to secretary, 9 June 1949, *FR*, 1949, VIII, pp. 377–78.

28.   Derk Bodde, *Peking Diary: A Year of Revolution* (New York: Henry Schuman, 1950), p. 200, and *New York Times*, 9 June 1949, p. 16.

29.   Telegram, secretary to Clubb, 17 May 1949, *FR*, 1949, VIII, p. 957; and *New York Times*, 31 May 1949, p. 11.

30.   The charge was probably not without foundation. Documents relating to the Mukden consulate general's difficulties are sanitized in the National Archives and in *FR*, 1949, VIII, in a manner consistent with current restrictions on public access to intelligence-related material, especially of CIA origin. See, for example, telegrams, Clubb to secretary, 12

February 1949, secretary to Clubb, 17 May 1949, Stuart to secretary, 21 June 1949, and Wellborn to secretary, 10 December 1949, ibid., pp. 936, 957, 970, and 1044–46. The existence of an intelligence operation in Mukden prior to the Communist takeover has also been confirmed by several retired foreign service officers in conversations with the author. For the Communist charge, see *New York Times*, 19 June 1949, p. 17, and U.S., Department of State, *Bulletin*, 11 July 1949, p. 36.

31. Memo, Butterworth to the acting secretary, 7 June 1949, "China—1949" folder, President's Secretary's Files, Truman Papers.

32. Telegram, acting secretary to Clubb, 14 June 1949, *FR*, 1949, VIII, pp. 384–85.

33. Memo of conversation, Webb and Truman, 16 June 1949, ibid., p. 388.

34. Mao Tse-tung, *Selected Works, Vol. 5, 1945–1949* (New York: International Publishers, A.d.), pp. 405–08; telegram, Clubb to secretary, 20 June 1949, *FR*, 1949, VIII, pp. 392–94.

35. Telegram, Clubb to secretary, 22 June 1949, ibid., pp. 394–95.

36. Telegram, Stuart to secretary, 22 June 1949, ibid., pp. 395–96.

37. Telegram, Clubb to secretary, 22 June 1949, ibid., pp. 394–95.

38. Telegram, Clubb to secretary, 24 June 1949, ibid., pp. 397–98.

39. Telegram no. 1267, Clubb to secretary, 1 August 1949, 893.00B/8–149, RG 59, NA.

40. Telegram, Stuart to secretary, 30 June 1949, *FR*, 1949, VIII, pp. 766–67.

41. Stuart Diary, 23 June 1949, Stuart Papers.

42. Ibid., 28 June 1949; and telegram, Stuart to secretary, 30 June 1949, *FR*, 1949, VIII, pp. 766–67.

43. Ibid.

44. Memo, Davies to Kennan, 30 June 1949, ibid., pp. 768–69.

45. Marginal notes, footnote, ibid.; *New York Times*, 1 July 1949, p. 1; "Secretary of State Dean Acheson Appointment Book," 30 June 1949, Dean Acheson Papers, Truman Library.

46. *Vital Speeches of the Day*, 1 October 1949, p. 749; telegram no. 1443, Stuart to secretary, 6 July 1949, 893.00/7–649, RG 59, NA.

47. Secretary's Appointment Book, 1 July 1949, Acheson Papers; telegram no. 775, secretary to Stuart, 1 July 1949, 123 Stuart, J. Leighton, RG 59, NA. The copy printed in *FR*, 1949, VIII, p. 769, omits "repeat no."

Chapter 5. *RENEWED CHINA BLOC OFFENSIVE*

1. Summary of Daily Meeting with Secretary (hereafter cited as Secretary's Daily Meeting), 8 March 1949, Records of the Executive Secretariat, Lot 58D609, RG 59, NA.

2. *New York Times*, 16 April 1949, p. 3; for evidence of Fulbright's interest in continued aid to China, see Foreign Relations Committee, *Economic Assistance*, p. 185; and letter, Fulbright to Chennault, 29 July 1949, Reel 12, Chennault Papers, Library of Congress (Chennault's original papers are at the Hoover Institute).

3. *New York Times*, 17 April 1949, p. 25.

4. Memo, Butterworth to under secretary, 20 April 1949, 893.50 Recovery/4–2049, RG 59, NA.

5. For Knowland's S. Res. 30, see *Congressional Record*, 81st Cong., 1st sess., 21 and 28 April 1949, pp. 4861–63, 5238–41.

6. "Meeting in the President's Office with Senators Wherry and Bridges on China," memo by Acheson, 28 April 1949, 893.00/4–2849, RG 59, NA.

7. *New York Times*, 29 April 1949, p. 5.

8. Secretary's Daily Meeting, 3 May 1949.

9. Memo, Hall to Peurifoy, 20 April 1949, 893.50 Recovery/4–2049, RG 59, NA.

10. U.S., Congress, Senate, Subcommittee of the Committee on Appropriations, *Hearings on Department of State, Justice, and Commerce Appropriation Bill for 1950*, 81st Cong., 1st sess., pp. 94–108.

11. Ibid., pp. 122–31, and *Washington Post,* 7 May 1949, p. 6.

12. Withholding such information from McCarran could have been a hazardous course for the State Department. In connection with an immigration bill pending before the Senate Judiciary Committee, Chairman McCarran threatened to jail Attorney General Tom Clark for contempt of Congress for failure to respond to a similar request for personnel dossiers. The senator was also not above using the State Department's appropriation bill as a tool to change its foreign policy. Because he opposed the administration's policy toward Spain, McCarran warned Acheson during the 5 May hearing "that until that policy is changed, I am going to examine your appropriations with a fine tooth comb." Appropriation Subcommittee, *Hearings,* p. 94; *Washington Post,* 4 June 1949, p. 6.

13. Secretary's Daily Meeting, 6, 9, 11 May 1949; Cabinet meeting notes, 6 May 1949, Matthew J. Connally Papers, Truman Library; and letter, Clifford to Acheson, 17 May 1949, U.S. Department of State, *FR,* 1949, IX, p. 1367.

14. The ECA and State Department had originally sought $182 million. See memo, Butterworth to Webb, 23 May 1949, 895.50 Recovery/5–2349, RG 59, NA. The Budget Bureau wanted only $125 million as indicated in Secretary's Daily Meeting, 2 May 1949.

15. U.S., Congress, House, Committee on Foreign Affairs, *Hearings on Korean Aid,* 81st Cong., 1st sess., p. 9.

16. International Relations Committee, *Policy in the Far East, Vol. 8, Pt. 2,* p. 32.

17. Ibid., pp. 164, 168.

18. Ibid., p. 185.

19. Foreign Affairs Committee, *Hearings,* p. 27; *New York Times,* 9 June 1949, p. 18.

20. House Report No. 926, reprinted in International Relations Committee, *Policy in the Far East, Vol. 8, Pt. 2,* pp. 382–84.

21. Foreign Relations Committee, *Economic Assistance,* pp. 185–91.

22. Memo by A. B. Moreland, 22 August 1949, 840.20/8–2249, RG 59, NA.

23. "Editorial Note," *FR,* 1949, VII, pt. 2 (Washington, D.C.: GPO, 1976), pp. 1039–40.

24. *Congressional Record,* 81st Cong., 1st sess., 28 April 1949, pp. 5238–40.

25. Ibid., 17 May 1949, p. 6306, and the London *Times,* 5 May 1949, p. 3.

26. *Congressional Record,* 81st Cong., 1st sess., 26 May 1949, pp. 3259–60. This contains H. Con. Res. 6, a sense of Congress resolution Rep. Chester E. Merrow (R-N.H.) submitted calling for a $1 billion aid program.

27. For background on Chennault's lobbying activities, see Charles Wertenbaker, "The China Lobby," *The Reporter,* 15 April 1952 and Horton, "China Lobby—Part II." See also Reel 12, Chennault Papers; Claire L. Chennault, *The Way of a Fighter* (1949); and the 1945 movie "God is My Co-pilot," based on the autobiography of Flying Tiger Col. Robert Lee Scott (Raymond Massey portrays a calm, heroic Chennault).

28. Various versions of the Chennault plan appear in: U.S., Congress, Joint Committee on Economic Cooperation, 81st Cong., 1st sess., 3 May 1949 (typed transcript of executive session hearing), Reel 12, Chennault Papers; *New York Times,* 4 May 1949, p. 1; *FR,* 1949, IX, pp. 520–23; International Relations Committee, *Policy in the Far East, Vol. 8, Pt. 2,* pp. 283–89; "Summary of Present Crisis in Asia," 10 May 1949, 893.00/6–1049, RG 59, NA; "Last Call for China—A Fighting American Says that a Third of its Good Earth and 150,000,000 People Can be Saved," *Life,* 11 July 1949, pp. 36–37; *Washington Post,* 4 May 1949, editorial page.

29. *New York Times,* 4 May 1949, p. 1; letter, Chennault to Snyder, 3 June 1949, Reel 12, Chennault Papers; International Relations Committee, *Policy in the Far East, Vol. 8, Pt.*

2, pp. 283–89; "Summary of Present Crisis in Asia," 10 May 1949, 893.00/6–1049, RG 59, NA.

30. For examples of Chennault's lobbying, see "Radio Broadcast (transcript) from Your Senator's Office (Kefauver)," 31 July 1949; letter, Knowland to Kefauver, Lodge, et al., 6 July 1949; and other documents on Reel 12, Chennault Papers; H. V. Wellington Koo Draft Oral History, I–273, vol. 6, pt. 1, Columbia University; memo, Chen Chih-mai to ambassador, 26 July 1949, "Inter-Office Memo" folder, Koo Papers; and *Washington Post*, 18 July 1949, p. 2. For the estimate of eighty-five senators, see Wertenbaker, "China Lobby," p. 10.

31. *Life*, 11 July 1949, pp. 36–37.

32. Memo, Webb to Butterworth, 10 May 1949, *FR*, 1949, IX, p. 518.

33. Memo of conversation and transcript, 11 May 1949, ibid., pp. 519–23.

34. Handwritten note on memo, Moreland to Butterworth, 27 June 1949, 893.00/6–2749, RG 59, NA.

35. Telegram, Webb to Stuart, 25 May 1949, *FR*, 1949, IX, p. 524.

36. Telegram, Clark to secretary, 6 June 1949, ibid., pp. 526–27; for Stuart's reaction and that of the service attaches, see telegram, Stuart to secretary, 25 May 1949, ibid., pp. 524–25.

37. Memo, Butterworth to Webb, 10 May 1949, ibid., p. 518.

38. Note on Cabinet meeting, 13 May 1949, Connally Papers, Truman Library.

39. For the article and speech, see *Congressional Record*, 81st Cong., 1st sess., 29 June 1949, pp. 8598–601. Documents on Reel 12, Chennault Papers, reveal how closely Chennault and Knowland worked together. In a letter, Chennault to Knowland, 26 July 1949, the general furnished the senator with a "brief summary of the provisions which should be included in any bill authorizing such aid." Knowland proudly acknowledged Chennault's help in his newspaper, *The Oakland Tribune*, 26 July 1949, p. 6D.

40. *New York Times*, 3 May 1949, p. 11; *Congressional Record*, 81st Cong., 1st sess., 17 May 1949, pp. 6306–07.

41. Memos, Ku to ambassador, 3 May 1949 and Chen Chih-mai to ambassador, 13 May 1949, "Inter-Office Memo" folder, Koo Papers.

42. *Congressional Record*, 81st Cong., 1st sess., 12 May 1949, p. 6137.

43. *Washington Post*, 13 May 1949, p. 23; *Congressional Record*, 18 May 1949, pp. 6390–94.

44. Butterworth Draft Oral History, p. 65, Truman Library; author's interview with Butterworth, 1972, Princeton, N.J.; author's interview with Lucas D. Battle, 1977, Washington, D.C.

45. U.S., Congress, Senate, Committee on Foreign Relations, typed hearing transcript, 14 June 1949, pp. 6–8, "Committee on Foreign Relations Minutes and Hearings, June 6–June 30" folder, Records of the Senate Committee on Foreign Relations, RG 46, NA.

46. Foreign Relations Committee, typed hearing transcript, 21 June, pp. 34–35. For the role of the China lobby and embassy, see memo, Chen to ambassador, 26 July 1949, "Inter-Office Memo" file, Koo Papers.

47. *Congressional Record*, 81st Cong., 1st sess., 24 June 1949, pp. 8292–93.

48. Ibid., p. 8294.

49. Ibid., 26 September 1949, p. 13266.

Chapter 6. STATE DEPARTMENT COUNTERATTACK

1. *New York Times*, 22 June 1949, p. 1.

2. Telegram, Bruce to secretary, 20 May 1949; telegram, Foster to secretary, 1 June 1949, *FR*, 1949 IX, pp. 26–27, 32–33. The trend toward recognition would become more pronounced in the fall.

3. For the British attitude see telegram, secretary to Douglas, 29 July 1949, ibid., pp. 867–68; *New York Times*, 2 July 1949, p. 1.

4. For Truman's views, see memo by Merchant, 19 August 1949; memo, McWilliams to Rusk, 22 August 1949; memo of conversation with president, 1 October 1949, *FR*, 1949, IX pp. 1022–24, 1141. For the State Department position in early July, see telegram, secretary to Cabot, 8 July 1949, ibid., p. 1119.

5. Telegram, Cabot to secretary, 1 July 1949, *FR*, 1949, VIII, p. 769.

6. *New York Times*, 2 and 6 July 1949, pp. 4, 1; telegram, McConaughy to secretary, 27 July 1949, *FR*, 1949, VIII, p. 1244.

7. *New York Times*, 30 July 1949, p. 5.

8. Documents relating to Olive, Gould, the consulate occupation, and other problems in Shanghai are printed in *FR*, 1949, VIII, pp. 1155–1294. On Olive see also, U.S., Department of State, *Bulletin*, 2 January 1950, p. 23. The incident was also well covered in the American press.

9. Telegram, Stuart to secretary, 12 July 1949, *FR*, 1949, VIII, p. 424.

10. Telegram, Stuart to secretary, 14 July 1949, ibid., pp. 784–85.

11. Telegram, Acheson to Stuart, 12 July 1949, Stuart to secretary, 18 July 1949, ibid., pp. 781–82, 791; memo of conversation, Koo, president et al., 22 June 1949, *FR*, 1949 IX, pp. 708–10.

12. Telegram, Stuart to secretary, 14 July 1949; telegram secretary to Stuart, 15 July 1949; telegram, secretary to Stuart, 21 July 1949, *FR*, 1949, VIII, pp. 785–88, 803–04. Stuart recounts the difficulties in J. Leighton Stuart, *Fifty Years in China* (New York: Random House, 1954), pp. 255–59.

13. Telegram, Stuart to secretary, 26 July 1949, *FR*, 1949, VIII, pp. 801–02; Stuart Diary, 25 July 1949, Stuart Papers.

14. Interview with Philip Fugh, 1977, Washington, D.C.; Stuart Diary, 30 July 1949.

15. Lionel Max Chassin, *The Communist Conquest of China: A History of the Civil War, 1945–1949* (Cambridge: Harvard University Press, 1965), p. 227.

16. Telegram, Kirk to secretary, 31 July 1949; telegram, McConaughy to secretary, 5 August 1949 and telegram, Jones to secretary, 6 August 1949, *FR*, 1949, IX, pp. 955–57.

17. Interview with Philip Fugh, 1977; Stuart Diary, 20 July 1949, Stuart Papers.

18. Telegram, Stuart to secretary, 13 June 1949; memo by Chen, 22 June 1949 (misdated), annex 2, "Two Talks with Mr. Chou En-lai" and telegram, Stuart to secretary, 13 July 1949, *FR*, 1949, VIII, pp. 756–57, 776–79, 782–83.

19. Telegram, Clubb to secretary, 19 July 1949, ibid., pp. 443–45.

20. Telegram, Cabot to secretary, 7 July 1949, *FR*, 1949, IX, pp. 1261–65.

21. Telegram, Cabot to secretary, 16 July 1949, *FR*, 1949, VIII, pp. 436–40.

22. Ibid.

23. "Vulnerability of a Communist China to External and Internal Pressure" (ORE 72–49), 22 July 1949, draft, pp. 23, 28, CIA. The intelligence organizations of the Army, Navy, and State Department concurred in this estimate. The Air Force filed a dissenting report. Report obtained through FOIA.

24. Memo, Gross to Rusk, 28 June 1949, 893.00/6–2949, RG 59, NA.

25. Letter, Acheson to Connally, 1 July 1949, 893.00/7–149, RG 59, NA.

26. Letter, Clifford to secretary, 17 May 1949, *FR*, 1949, IX, p. 1367.

27. Memo, Kennan to secretary, 28 June 1949, "China—1949" folder, Records of the Policy Planning Staff, Lot 64D563, RG 59, NA. John Davies drafted the memo. The word "dreary" was crossed out.

28. Memo, Rusk to Webb, 4 April 1949, *FR*, 1949, IX, pp. 509–11.

29. Memo of conversation, Koo and Dulles, 18 August 1949, "Notes of conversation, 1949" folder, Koo Papers.

30. For discussion of the White Paper and the consultant group, see the summer months of Secretary's Daily Meeting. Most of the important documents the consultant group generated are bound together in 890.00/11–1849, RG 59, NA. For Acheson's description of the consultants' duties, see his "Press and Radio News Conference," 27 July 1949, President's Appointment File, President's Secretary's Files, Truman Papers.

31. Secretary's Daily Meeting, 6 June 1949.

32. Secretary's Daily Meeting, 22 June 1949.

33. PPS–53, 6 July 1949, *FR*, 1949, IX, pp. 356–59. It is not clear whether or not Kennan conveyed the substance of the memo to Acheson (see ftn. 81) p. 356, ibid., and Secretary's Daily Meeting, 29 June 1949, which reads, in part: "and Mr. Kennan informed him (Acheson) that he had prepared a study on Formosa. The Secretary asked for these papers prior to his meeting with Mr. Hoffman." The Hoffman meeting occurred later in the morning.

34. Memo, Kennan to Webb et al., 8 July 1949, and annex, *FR*, 1949, VII, pt. 2 (Washington, D.C.: GPO, 1976), pp. 1147–51.

35. Blind, Top Secret Memo, 890.00/7–1649, RG 59 NA. Stapled to this is a memo from Charles Yost to Jessup, which refers to "Mr. Rusk's memorandum to the Secretary." The memo's authorship is also indicated on the last page by the words "Rusk July 16, 1949."

36. Memo for the record by "PCJ," 20 July 1949, 890.00/11–1849, RG 59, NA. For Acheson's views on the Chennault Plan, see his 23 June 1949 testimony before the House Foreign Affairs Committee in International Relations Committee, *Policy in the Far East, Vol. 8, Pt. 2*, p. 260.

37. Secretary's Daily Meeting, 18 July 1949.

38. Memo to the secretary, 18 July 1949, and memo of conversation with the president, 18 July 1949, "Memoranda of Conversation with the President's file, Records of the Executive Secretariat, Lot 58D609, RG 59, NA.

39. Philip C. Jessup, *The Birth of Nations* (New York: Columbia University Press, 1974), p. 29.

40. Memo of conversation, Connally et al., 19 July 1949, *FR*, 1949, IX, pp. 1375–76.

41. "Secretary of State Dean Acheson Appointment Book," 22 July 1949, Acheson Papers. This record indicates only that Acheson met with Vandenberg.

42. Memo, Sprouse to Butterworth, 19 July 1949, "UN-Chinese Case Against the Russians" folder, Records of the Chinese Affairs Division, Lot 56D151, RG 59, NA.

43. Memo, Butterworth to secretary, 15 July 1949, *FR*, 1949, IX, pp. 1373–74.

44. Memo, Jessup to secretary, 20 July 1949; letter, Johnson to Acheson and enclosure, JCS to Johnson, 21 July 1949; memo of conversation, Truman and Acheson, 27 July 1949, ibid., pp. 1376–81, 1387.

45. *New York Times*, 24 July 1949, p. 15.

46. Emphasis added. U.S. Department of State, *United States Relations with China, with Special Reference to the Period 1944–1949* (Washington, GPO, 1949), p. xvi.

47. Paper drafted by Davies, 7 July 1949, *FR*, 1949, VII, pt. 2, p. 1148.

48. *Congressional Record*, 81st Cong., 1st sess., 5 August 1959, pp. 10813, 10875.

49. *New York Times*, 6 August 1949, p. 1.

50. *Congressional Record*, 81st Cong., 1st Sess., 8 August 1949, p. 10941.

51. *Congressional Record*, 81st Cong., 1st sess., 19 August 1949, p. 11882.

52. *Washington Post*, 22 August 1949, p. 1.

53. *New York Times*, 6 August 1949, p. 1.

54. Ibid., 7 August 1949, p. 1.

55.   Mao Tse-tung, *Selected Works, Vol. 5, 1945–1949* (New York: International Publishers n.d.), p. 428; *New York Times*, 14 and 16 August 1949, pp. 20, 16.

56.   Documents relating to the closure of selected American missions in China are printed in *FR*, 1949, VIII, pp. 1303–27.

57.   Memo, Butterworth to Rusk, 29 July 1949, "Evacuation" folder, Lot 56D151, RG 59, NA.

58.   For documents relating to evacuation of Americans from China on the *General Gordon*, see *FR*, 1949, IX, pp. 1261–1353.

59.   *New York Times*, 17 August 1949, p. 5.

60.   Secretary's Daily Meeting, 22 June 1949.

61.   Memo, Merchant to Butterworth, 27 July 1949, 711.93/7–2749, RG 59, NA.

62.   Chassin, *Conquest of China*, pp. 225–26; F. F. Liu, *A Military History of Modern China, 1924–1949* (Princeton: Princeton University Press, 1956), p. 269.

63.   Dispatch, Macdonald to secretary, 30 August 1949, *FR*, 1949, IX, pp. 380–81.

64.   Memo, Fisher to Jessup, 10 August 1949, 711.93/8–1049, RG 59, NA.

65.   Memo by Davies, 24 August 1949, *FR*, 1949, IX, pp. 536–40. The Sprouse comment appears in footnote on p. 536. Davies's reservations about the memo are expressed in a cover note to Kennan in the file copy of the memo in "China lobby" folder, Lot 64D563, RG 59, NA; and memo, Davies to Jessup, 29 August 1949, 711.93/8–3049, RG 59, NA.

66.   Memo, Butterworth to Webb, 10 May 1949, *FR*, 1949, IX, p. 518.

67.   Memo, Butterworth to Jessup, 18 August 1949, "American Policy Toward Formosa" folder, Lot 56D151, RG 59, NA; memo, Butterworth to Jessup and Fosdick, 20 August 1949, 711.93/8–2049, ibid.

68.   Telegram, Clark to secretary, 6 June 1949, *FR*, 1949, IX, pp. 526–27; telegram, Clark to secretary, 17 August 1949, *FR*, 1949, VIII, pp. 491–93.

69.   Telegram, McGeary to secretary, 19 August 1949, ibid., p. 498.

70.   U.S. President, *Public Papers of the President of the United States, Harry S. Truman, 1949* (Washington, D.C.: GPO, 1964), p. 421.

71.   Memo, Merchant to Sprouse, 24 August 1949, *FR*, 1949, IX, pp. 870–71.

72.   Memo, Webb to Souers, 24 August 1949, ibid., pp. 540–41.

73.   Telegram, Clark to secretary, 23 August 1949, *FR*, 1949, VIII, pp. 501–02.

74.   Secretary's Daily Meeting, 24 August 1949.

75.   Telegram, secretary to Strong, 25 August 1949, *FR*, 1949, IX, p. 541.

76.   Telegram, Strong to secretary, 6 September 1949, ibid., pp. 546–48.

77.   Telegram, Jones to secretary, 28 August 1949, ibid., pp. 541–44.

78.   *New York Times*, 3 September 1949, p. 5.

79.   Telegram, Strong to secretary, 28 August 1949, *FR*, 1949, VIII, pp. 509–10.

80.   Telegrams, Clark to secretary, 15 and 17 August 1949, ibid., pp. 489, 493–94.

81.   Telegram, Macdonald to secretary, 2 September 1949, ibid., p. 516.

82.   For reports that the Ma's were losing heart or considering falling back to put up guerrilla resistance, see "Joint Weeka 33," 2 September 1949, 893.00(W)/9–249, RG 59, NA; and telegram, McGeary to secretary, 3 September 1949, *FR*, 1949, VIII, p. 518.

83.   Telegram, secretary to Macdonald, 8 September 1949, ibid., p. 523.

84.   Blind memo, n.d., 5 pages, "US Policy Toward Communist China" folder, Records of the Office of Chinese Affairs, Lot 56D151, RG 59, NA.

85.   Lucius Battle, Acheson's aide, recalled such a meeting in a conversation with the author in 1977. He recalled that it occurred on a Friday afternoon with the secretary's senior advisors, that all or most of the participants recommended sending aid to some generals in China, but that on the following Monday, the department learned the generals were giving up the fight. He could not recall the meeting's date or who the generals were. It is

unclear from available records when the department first learned the Ma's had given up. It's strong disenchantment with the prospect of granting further aid to non-Communist forces on the mainland was indicated in the 13 September meeting described in Chapter 9, p. 150.

86. Telegram, Strong to secretary, 9 September 1949, *FR*, 1949, VIII, pp. 523–24.

87. Telegram, Strong to secretary, 15 September 1949 (received 7:10 a.m., 16 September 1949), 893.00/9–1549, RG 59, NA.

88. *New York Times*, 8 October 1949, p. 1.

Chapter 7. SOUTHEAST ASIA POLICY, SPRING–SUMMER 1949

1. U.S., Congress, Senate, Committee on Foreign Relations, *Hearings on the Causes, Origins, and Lessons of the Vietnam War*, 92d Cong., 2d sess., p. 163.

2. On aid to the Philippines, see Brown, and Opie, *American Foreign Assistance*, p. 408.

3. U.S., Congress, Senate, Committee on Foreign Relations, *Hearings on Reviews of the World Situation*, 81st Cong., 1st and 2d sess. ("Historical Series" of hearings held in executive session) (Washington, D.C.: GPO, 1974), pp. 182–83.

4. For the aid cutoff, see Brown and Opie, *American Foreign Assistance*, p. 190. For congressional disapproval of Dutch action in Indonesia, see *Congressional Record*, 80th Cong., 2d sess., pp. 3383–94.

5. The best general source on development in Indochina in this period remains Ellen J. Hammer, *The Struggle for Indochina* (Stanford: Stanford University Press, 1954).

6. Memo, Reed to Butterworth, 29 March 1949, "Indochina 1946–1949, Military Forces Operation" folder, Records of the Office of Philippine and Southeast Asia Affairs, Lot 54D190, RG 59, NA.

7. Memo, Butterworth to Hickerson, 20 April 1948, folder unknown (document copied from loose collection temporarily unboxed and out of their folder), Lot 54D190, RG 59, NA.

8. For the text of the 8 March accord, see Allan W. Cameron, ed., *Vietnam Crisis: A Documentary History, Vol. I: 1940–1956* (Ithaca: Cornell University Press, 1970), pp. 122–128.

9. *Current Biography*, 1949. Mimeographed.

10. PPS-23, Review of Current Trends, 24 February 1948, *FR*, 1948, I, pt. 3 (Washington, D.C.: GPO, 1976) pp. 523–25.

11. For a recent interpretation of American strategy in the early postwar years, see Thomas H. Etzold, "The Far East in American Strategy, 1948–1951," *Aspects of Sino-American Relations Since 1784* ed. Thomas H. Etzold (New York: New Viewpoints, 1978), pp. 102–26.

12. Memo, Reed to Butterworth, 13 August 1948, *FR*, 1948, I, pt. 3, p. 607.

13. Circular Instruction, acting secretary to certain diplomatic posts, 13 October 1948, ibid., pp. 638–44; see also the CIA's OIR Report No. 4778, "Appraisal of Communist Efforts in Southeast Asia: 1948," reproduced by Carrolton Press, Westport, Conn.

14. "Review of the World Situation," 16 December 1948, CIA 12–48, National Security Files, Truman Papers.

15. Charles B. McLane, *Soviet Strategies in Southeast Asia: An Exploration of Eastern Policy under Lenin and Stalin* (Princeton: Princeton University Press, 1966), pp. 352–54; Ruth T. McVey, *The Calcutta Conference and the Southeast Asia Uprisings* (Ithaca: Cornell University, 1958), p. 7; Andre Fontaine, *History of the Cold War From the October Revolution to the Korean War, 1917–1950* (New York: Vintage Books, 1968), pp. 334–35.

16. McLane, *Soviet Strategies*, pp. 355–60; McVey, *The Calcutta Conference, passim*; CIA, "Appraisal of Communist Efforts," pp. 13–16.

17. Memo, Reed to Butterworth, 13 August 1948, *FR*, 1949, I (Washington, D.C.: GPO, 1976), pp. 607–09.

18. "Transcript of Mr. Butterworth's speech at the National Conference on American Foreign Policy," 17 March 1949, pp. 12, 15, Butterworth Papers, George C. Marshall Research Foundation, Lexington, Va.

19. For Butterworth's views on a Marshall Plan for Asia, see memo, Butterworth to Labouisee, 2 March 1949, 893.50 Recovery/2–749, RG 59, NA; on a Pacific Pact, see telegram, secretary to Locket, 23 March 1949, and memo of conversation, Butterworth, Chang, Bond, 8 April 1949, *FR*, 1949, VII, pt. 2, pp. 1126, 1141–42.

20. For the position of Ambassador Bruce on supporting Bao Dai, see telegram, Bruce to secretary, 2 June 1949, *FR*, 1949, VII, pt. 1 (Washington, D.C.: GPO, 1976), pp. 36–38.

21. Memo of conversation, 17 May 1949, ibid., p. 27.

22. Telegram, secretary to Abbott, 10 May 1949, ibid., pp. 23–25.

23. PPS–51, "U. S. Policy Toward Southeast Asia," 29 March 1949, "Reports and Recommendations to the Secretary and Under Secretary of State, Vol. 3, 1949" (bound book), Records of the Policy Planning Staff, Lot 64D563, RG 59, NA. The date on this document is misleading as it was circulated within the department in a slightly different form in April; after revision it apparently retained its original date. For a summary of its contents, see UMD–26 (Summary), 4 April 1949, Under Secretary's Meetings file, Records of the Executive Secretariat, Lot 53D250, RG 59, NA.

24. Ibid.

25. Memo, Reed to Allison, 31 March 1949, "Southeast Asia, 1949—U.S. Policy" folder, Lot 54D190, RG 59, NA.

26. UM S–25, 6 April 1949, and memo for files, 6 April 1949, Lot 53D250, RG 59, NA; memo, Butterworth to Reed, 6 April 1949, 890.00/4–649, RG 59, NA.

27. Secretary's Daily Meeting, 29 June 1949; memo, Kennan to secretary, 19 May 1949, "Reports and Recommendations to the Secretary of State and the Under Secretary of State, Vol. 3, 1949," Lot 64D563, RG 59, NA.

28. Ibid.

29. Memo, Reed to Butterworth, 14 April 1949, 851g.00/4–1449, RG 59, NA.

30. Memo, Reed to Butterworth, 17 May 1949, "Southeast Asia 1949—U.S.Policy" folder, RG 59, NA.

31. Reed's deputy, William S. B. Lacy, states his view in an attachment to ibid., memo, Lacy to Reed, 13 May 1949.

32. Dispatch, Butterworth (for the acting secretary) to Bruce, 6 June 1949 (with enclosure), *FR*, 1949, VII, pt. 1, pp. 38–45.

33. Memo, Ogburn to Reed, O'Sullivan, 28 June 1949, "Indochina: French-Indochina Relations" folder, Lot 54D190, RG 59, NA.

34. Letter, Walner to MacArthur, 14 June 1949; memo, Bruce to secretary, 10 June 1949; memo, Bohlen to secretary, 13 June 1949, 851g.01/6–649; memo, Battle to Bohlen, 11 June 1949, 851g/6–1449, RG 59, NA.

35. Telegram, Bruce to the secretary, 13 June 1949, *FR*, 1949, VII, pt. 1, pp. 45–46.

36. Memo, Ogburn to Reed and O'Sullivan, 28 June 1949, "Indochina: French-Indochinese Relations", and memo by Ogburn, "Courses Open to United States in Indochina Situation" (n.d.), "Indochina 1947–1949—Policy and Information Papers" folder, Lot 54D190, RG 59, NA; U.S., Department of State, *Bulletin*, 18 July 1949, p. 75.

37. Memo, Ogburn to Reed and O'Sullivan, 28 June 1949, "Indochina: French-Indochinese Relations" folder, RG 59, NA.

38. Ibid.; memo by Ogburn, "Courses Open to United States in Indochina Situation" (n.d.), "Indochina 1947–1949—Policy Information Papers" folder, RG 59, NA.

39. For primary documents relating to Ho's wartime and early postwar activity, see Foreign Relations Committee, *Causes;* U.S., Department of Defense, *U.S.-Vietnam Relations,* I.C. (bk. 1) (Washington, D.C.: GPO, 1971), pp. C–66–C–104; and Papers of General Gallagher, Office of the Chief of Military History, Department of the Army, Washington, D.C. The author reviews this subject in U.S., Congress, Senate, Committee on Foreign Relations, "The United States and Vietnam, 1944–1947," 92d Cong., 2d sess. (Committee Print, Staff Study).

40. Memo, Landon to Penfield, 17 February 1948, folder and box unknown, Lot 54D190, RG 59, NA.

41. "SEA Conference—Communist Activities in Southeast Asia" (21–26 June 1948), "SEA Conference, 1948" folder, Lot 54D190, RG 59, NA.

42. Memo, Reed to Butterworth, 13 August 1948, *FR,* 1948, I, pp. 607–609.

43. *Newsweek,* 25 April 1949, p. 44.

44. *New York Times,* 22 May 1949, p. 2.

45. Memo of conversation, Mus, et al., 26 April 1949, 851g.01/4–2649, RG 59, NA.

46. Telegram, Gibson to secretary, 11 May 1949, *FR,* 1949, VII, pt. 1, pp. 25–27.

47. Telegram, secretary to Gibson, 20 May 1949, 851g.01/5–1149, RG 59, NA.

48. Memo of conversation, Isaacs and Reed, 29 June 1949, 851g.01/6–2949, RG 59, NA.

49. Blind memo attached to memo, Reed to Butterworth, 16 May 1949, Lot 54D190, RG 59, NA.

50. Memo by Ogburn, "Courses Open to United States in Indochina" (n.d.), "Indochina 1947–1949—Policy Information Papers" folder, RG 59, NA.

51. Secretary's Daily Meeting, 11 July 1949; draft letter (Rusk) to Bruce, n.d., "Southeast Asia 1949—U.S. Policy" folder, RG 59, NA; letter, Rusk to Lockett, 26 July 1949, *FR,* VII, pt. 2, pp. 1175–76.

Chapter 8. MONEY FOR THE "GENERAL AREA OF CHINA"

1. Letter, Acheson to Patterson, 5 March 1947, *FR,* 1947, III (Washington, D.C.: GPO, 1972) pp. 197–98.

2. Memo, Hilldring to SWNCC Members, 17 March 1947, ibid., pp. 198–99, and SWNCC 360, 21 April 1947, *FR,* 1947, I (Washington, D.C.: GPO, 1973), pp. 725–33.

3. SANACC 360/4, 29 December 1947, Appendix B, Records of State-Army-Navy-Air Force Coordinating Committee, RG 353, NA. Underlined words in source text.

4. See ftn. 3 in *FR,* 1948, I pt. 1 (Washington, D.C.: GPO, 1976), p. 597. The proposed legislation resurfaced briefly a month after the Foreign Assistance Act passed Congress. The secretaries of state and defense submitted a request to the Budget Bureau on 7 May 1948, for approval of military assistance legislation. A week later, this renewed effort was killed when both President Truman and Senator Vandenberg, then chairman of the Senate Foreign Relations Committee, stated at separate news conferences that there were no plans to give military assistance to Europe. Letter, Forrestal to Lovett, 18 May 1948; and letter, Lovett to Forrestal, 21 May 1948, attached to letter, Carl Marcy to Harold Moseley, 25 May 1948, RG 353, NA.

5. NSC–14/1, 1 July 1948, *FR,* 1948, I, pp. 585–88.

6. Department of State Press Release no. 1031, 29 December 1948, copy in possession of author.

7. Memo, Gross to secretary, 26 January 1948, *FR,* 1949, III, (Washington, D.C.: GPO, 1974), pp. 48–50; see also ftn. 2 in *FR,* 1949, I, p. 250; on specific countries the FACC targeted for aid, see MAP D–D/1, 25 May 1949, ibid., pp. 314–20; for the presidential

message transmitting MAP to Congress, see U.S., Congress, House Doc. no. 276, 81st Cong., 1st sess., 25 July 1949; on the secrecy of the aid for Austria, see memo, Williamson to Cong., 25 August 1949, 113/8–1749, Records of the Department of State, RG 59, NA.

8. See SWNCC 630/4 and SNACC 360/11; on the contingency fund, see memo, Sprouse to Allison, 28 January 1949, with attachments, 711.93/1–2849, RG 59, NA; UMD– 20 (Under Secretary's Meeting Document), n. d., Records of the Executive Secretariat, Lot 53D250, RG 59, NA; memo, Gross to Butterworth, 22 March 1949, 893.24/3–2249, RG 59, NA; memo, Alvin Roseman to director, Bureau of the Budget, 7 April 1949, "President's Appointment Folder (1–15 April)," President's Secretary's Files, Truman Papers.

9. See Sections 2 and 13 of S.2341 reprinted in U.S., Congress, Senate, Committees on Foreign Relations and Armed Services, *Military Assistance Program: 1949,* 81st Cong., 1st sess. ("Historical Series" of hearings held in executive session) (Washington D.C.:, GPO, 1974), pp. 633, 646 (hereafter cited as Senate Committees, *MAP-Executive*).

10. Memo, Butterworth to Rusk, 13 June 1949, 890.00TA/6–1349, RG 59, NA; memo, Ogburn to Reed, 1 July 1949, 840.20/7–149, RG 59, NA.

11. Senate Committees, *MAP-Executive,* pp. 5, 19–46; *New York Times,* 3 August 1949, p. 1; memo of telephone conversation between Acheson and Connally, 2 August 1949, 840.20, RG 59, NA.

12. Senate Committees, *MAP-Executive,* pp. 28, 48: *New York Times,* 4 August 1949, p. 1; Secretary's Daily Meeting, 4 August 1949.

13. Senate Committees, *MAP-Executive,* pp. 39, 60; *Congressional Record,* 81st Cong., 1st sess., 4 August 1949, pp. 10737–38; the amendment to S.2388 is in the bill file for the 81st Cong., 1st sess., Records of the Senate Committee on Foreign Relations, RG 46, NA.

14. *Congressional Record,* 81st Cong., 1st sess., 8 August 1949, p. 11014.

15. Memo, Ohly to Lawton, 31 May 1950, MDA 50–II–3. "Funding" folder, Records of the Bureau of the Budget, RG 51, NA.

16. The second draft bill is printed in Senate Committees, *MAP-Executive,* pp. 648– 63.

17. U.S., Congress, Senate, Committees on Foreign Relations and Armed Services, *Hearings on the Military Assistance Program* (public session), 81st Cong., 1st sess., p. 38.

18. U.S., Congress, House, Committee on International Relations, 1943–50, vol. 5, *Military Assistance Program, Pt. 1* ("Historical Series" of hearings held in executive session) (Washington, D.C.: GPO, 1976), pp. 231, 244, 246, 255.

19. Ibid., pp. 347–59.

20. Secretary's Daily Meeting, 17 August 1949; two memos, Gross to Jessup, 17 August 1949, 893.50 Recovery/8–1749, RG 59, NA.

21. Secretary's Daily Meeting, 18 August 1949; memo of conversation with president, "August-September 1949" folder, Acheson Papers.

22. Memo, Gross to secretary, 18 August 1949, 893.24/8–1849, RG 59, NA; *Congressional Record,* 81st Cong., 1st sess., 18 August 1949, pp. 11769–70, 11782–91, 11810–13.

23. Dean Acheson, *Present at the Creation* (New York: W. W. Norton, 1969), p. 312; *New York Times,* 19 August 1949, p. 1; for an analysis of this vote, see James A. Fetzer, "Congress and China, 1941–1950" (Ph.D. diss., Michigan State University, 1970) pp. 203–6.

24. Letter, Knowland to Acheson, 6 August 1949, attached to memo, Gross to Acheson, 8 August 1949, 890.20/8–649, RG 59, NA; letter, Smith to Twitchell, 15 August 1949, "Correspondence re. Far East, 1949" folder, H. Alexander Smith Papers, Princeton University.

25. Senate Committees, *MAP-Executive,* p. 119.

26. *Oakland Tribune,* 8 August 1949, p. 2; *Congressional Record,* 81st Cong., 1st sess., 18 August 1949, pp. 11734–38; Senate Committees, *MAP-Executive,* pp. 179, 185–92; *New York*

Times, 13 August 1949, p. 1; Connally Press Conference Transcript, 12 August 1949, RG 46, NA.

27. Senate Committees, *MAP-Executive,* p. 206.

28. *Congressional Record,* 81st Cong., 1st sess. 19 August 1949, p. 11882; *Washington Post,* 22 August 1949, p. 1; Secretary's Daily Meeting, 22 August 1949.

29. Memo, Gross to secretary, 22 August 1949, 840.20/8–2249, RG 59, NA; memo of telephone conversation with Connally and Johnson, "August–September 1949" folder, Acheson Papers.

30. *New York Times,* 23 August 1949, p. 1; *Washington Post,* 22 August 1949, p. 1; *New York Times,* 25 August 1949, p. 1; *Washington Post,* 25 August 1949, p. 1.

31. *New York Times,* 25 August 1949, p. 15; ibid., 26 August 1949, p. 15; ibid., 27 August 1949, p. 1; Senate Committees, *MAP-Executive,* pp. 369–73.

32. Ibid., pp. 472–76.

33. Secretary's Daily Meeting, 8 September 1949.

34. Memo, Gross to secretary, 8 September 1949, 893.24/8–1849, RG 59, NA.

35. Senate Committees, *MAP-Executive,* pp. 515–50; Connally press conference transcript, 8 September 1949, RG 46, NA.

36. Senate Committees, *MAP-Executive,* pp. 582–97; Connally press conference transcript, 9 September 1949, RG 46, NA.

37. Senate Committees, *MAP-Executive,* pp. 611–28, 684–85.

38. *New York Times,* 13 September 1949, p. 20; Connally press conference transcript, 12 September 1949, RG 46, NA.

39. *Congressional Record,* 81st Cong., 1st sess., 19 September 1949, p. 13022.

40. Ibid., pp. 13023–24.

41. Ibid., 20 September 1949, p. 13051.

42. Ibid., 21 September 1949, p. 13132.

43. International Relations Committee, *Military Assistance Program,* pp. 452–60.

44. For the published records of the appropriation hearings, see U.S., Congress, Senate, Committee on Appropriations, *Hearings on Second Supplemental Appropriation Bill for 1950,* 81st Cong., 1st sess., and U.S., Congress, House, Committee on Appropriations, *Second Supplemental Appropriation Bill for 1950,* 81st Cong., 1st sess.

45. *Newsweek,* 26 September 1949, p. 14.

Chapter 9. DIVIDING THE PIE

1. *Congressional Record,* 81st Cong., 1st sess., 27 September 1949, pp. 13283–84; Minutes, Republican Policy Committee, 21 September 1949, United States Senate; memo, Chen Chih-mai to ambassador, 26 July 1949, "Inter-Office Memo" folder, Koo Papers.

2. The State Department wanted to push the Korean Aid bill through in this session to avoid giving Congress an occasion to review Asian policy in the next session. The Democratic leadership in Congress, backed by the president, supported the supplemental appropriations approach. See comments by Butterworth recorded in minutes, Under Secretary's Meeting, 17 October 1949, Records of the Executive Secretariat, Lot 53D250, Records of the Department of State, RG 59, NA; memo of conversation Acheson, Rayburn, et al., 13 October 1949, Acheson Papers; memo, Humelsine to Acheson (item 1), 17 October 1949, and memo of conversation with president, 17 October 1949, Records of the Executive Secretariat, Lot 58D609, RG 59, NA; and *Congressional Record,* 81st Cong., 1st sess., 19 October 1949, pp. 15089–90.

3. For details of the voyage of the *General Gordon,* see *FR,* 1949 IX pp. 1261–1353.

4. Telegram, Clubb to secretary, 2 October 1949, ibid., p. 93.

5. *New York Times,* 4 October 1949, p. 1.
6. Telegram, Clubb to secretary, 28 September 1949, *FR,* 1949, VIII pp. 537–39.
7. Telegram, Clubb to secretary, 8 October 1949, *FR,* 1949, IX, pp. 112–15.
8. Telegram, Clubb to secretary, 11 October 1949, ibid., pp. 121–22.
9. Telegram, Ambassador Kirk to secretary, 7 October 1949, and telegram, Holmes to secretary, 12 October 1949, ibid., pp. 106–08, 124.
10. See memo of conversation, Graves, Merchant, and Freeman, 11 October 1949, ibid., pp. 120–21; memo by Mr. Gerald Stryker, 2 November 1949, ibid., pp. 154–60.
11. The shifting views of foreign powers on recognition are described in ibid., pp. 93–260.
12. Telegram, Clubb to secretary, 10 October 1949, ibid., pp. 117–18. In a late October Gallup Poll, 20 percent favored recognition, 42 percent opposed. *Gallup Poll, Vol. 2,* p. 868.
13. Telegram, secretary to certain diplomatic and consular offices, 12 October 1949, ibid., pp. 122–23.
14. Annex to memo, Butterworth to secretary, 19 November 1949, ibid., p. 593.
15. "Survival Potential of Residual Non-Communist Regimes in China," ORE 76–49, 19 October 1949, CIA.
16. For a State Department assessment of the Indonesian situation, see memo for file, Under Secretary's Meeting, 2 September 1949; for the CIA view, see "Review of the World Situation," 19 October 1949, President's Secretary's Files, "NSC Meeting No. 47" folder, Truman Library.
17. "Summary of Economic Aspects of U.S. Policy with Respect to South and East Asia," cover memo, UMD–38, 16 May 1949, and memo for file, Under Secretary's Meeting, 25 May 1949.
18. See, for example, memo by Ogburn, "Requirements for the Security of the Countries of Southeast Asia," 20 April 1949, "Collective Security Arrangements and Projects" folder, Records of the Philippine and Southeast Asian Affairs Division, Lot 54D190, RG 59, NA.
19. Memo on Proposed Military Aid Program from USA for China, 15 August 1949, *FR,* 1949, IX, pp. 529–33.
20. Memo of conversation with Senator Knowland, by Koo, 16 August 1949, Koo Papers.
21. See Koo Oral History, Section 8, I, p. 416. Columbia University; and memo of conversation, 21 September 1949, *FR,* 1949, IX, pp. 692–94.
22. Letter, Kan to President, 30 September 1949; memo of conversation, 16 September 1949; and letter, Kan to president, 12 October 1949, ibid., pp. 718–23.
23. Telegram, Strong to secretary, 16 September 1949; telegram, Rankin to secretary, 16 October 1949; telegram, Strong to secretary, 11 October 1949; and telegram, Macdonald to secretary, 10 October 1949, ibid., pp. 548–49, 555, 551, 697–98, and 398–99. See also, telegram, Macdonald to secretary, 2 September 1949, *FR,* 1949, VIII, p. 516.
24. Telegram, Lutkins to secretary, 28 October 1949, ibid., p. 569. Lu's prophecy became self-fulfilling in December when he joined the Communists.
25. Telegram, secretary to Batavia, 19 May 1949; and telegram, acting secretary to Batavia, 8 June 1949, *FR,* 1949, VII, pt. 1, pp. 412–13, 416–17.
26. Memo of conversation, Thai ambassador, Rusk, Reed, 26 July 1949, 840.20/7–2649, RG 59, NA.
27. See memo of conversation, Acheson, Schuman et al., 15 September 1949, *FR,* 1949, V (Washington, D.C.: GPO, 1976), p. 660; memo prepared in American embassy, Paris, 10 November 1949, and telegram, secretary to Paris embassy, 7 December 1949, *FR,* 1949, VII, pt. 2, pp. 95–97, 103.

28. Telegram, Jones to secretary, 3 September 1949, *FR*, 1949, VIII, pp. 519–21.

29. Report by Charles Yost, 16 September 1949, *FR*, 1949, VII, pt. 2, pp. 1204–08.

30. Memo of conversation by the secretary, 13 September 1949, *FR*, 1949, IX, pp. 81–85.

31. Memo, Merchant to Fisher, 29 September 1949, 890.20(MAP)/9–2949, RG 59, NA.

32. Memo, Gross to Butterworth, 21 September 1949, 893.20/9–2149, RG 59, NA.

33. Memo, Wright to Butterworth, 21 September 1949, "Point IV" folder, Lot 54D190, RG 59, NA.

34. These two memos are referred to in memo, Merchant to Fisher, 16 December 1949, 800.20/12–1649, RG 59, NA.

35. Memo, Merchant to Reed, Freeman et al., 29 September 1949, "Southeast Asia 1949—U.S. Policy" folder.

36. Memo, Freeman to Merchant, 3 October 1949, 893.24/10–349, RG 59, NA.

37. Memo, Merchant to Rusk, 14 October 1949, 890.20/10–1449, RG 59, NA.

38. Under Secretary's Meeting, 17 October 1949; memo, Merchant to Sheppard, 19 October 1949, 890.20/10–1949, RG 59, NA.

39. Memo, Butterworth to secretary, 21 October 1949, *FR*, 1949, IX, pp. 568–70.

40. Memo, Butterworth to Webb, 24 October 1949, ibid., pp. 570–74. The identical memo was sent to Acheson through Rusk. See "SEA 1946–1949 Military and Military Aid" folder, Lot 54D190, RG 59, NA. The memo on covert aid is referred to in this memo but remains classified.

41. Memo, Reed to Jessup, 22 August 1949, 851g.00/8–2249 RG 59, NA; see also two memos with same title "Proposed Assistance Projects . . . (Indochina)" folder, 18 October 1949, Lot 54D190, RG 59, NA.

42. Memo, McGhee to secretary, 24 October 1949, 890.20/10–2449, RG 59, NA.

43. Memo for the secretary, 2 September 1949, 711.90/9–249, RG 59, NA. For the inner-departmental memorandum discussing Jessup's draft speech, see 890.00/9–949.

44. Memo of conversation, Dewey, Acheson, Jessup, 21 September 1949, "Memorandum of Conversation" folder, August–September 1949, Acheson Papers.

45. U.S., Congress, Senate, Committee on Foreign Relations, 1949–50, *Reviews of the World Situation* ("Historical Series" of hearings held in executive session) (Washington, D.C.: GPO, 1974), pp. 97–99.

46. Ibid., pp. 97–101.

47. Nonverbatim record of meeting of consultants with the secretary, 26 October 1949, 890.00/10–??49, RG 59, NA.

48. Nonverbatim record of meeting of consultants with the secretary, 27 October 1949, 890.00/10–??49, RG 59, NA.

49. Secretary's Daily Meeting, 28 October 1949; Dean Acheson, *Present at the Creation* (New York: W. W. Norton, 1969), p. 216.

Chapter 10. POLICY SHOWDOWN: NSC–48

1. Memo, Lemnitzer to JCS, 13 September 1949, JCS 1868/107, P&O 091 China, sec. II–A, case 27, Records of the Army Staff, Plans and Operations, RG 319, NA.

2. "A Report by the Joint Strategic Survey Committee on Military Aid to China," 6 October 1949, JCS 1721/37, CCS 45d China, (4–3–45) sec. 7, pt. 5, Records of the Joint Chiefs of Staff, RG 218, NA. For a sanitized version, see *FR*, 1949, IX, pp. 561–67. The report in JCS records is also sanitized, but in different parts. For a brief descriptive reference to the special operations program, see memo, Allen to secretary via Burns, 12 October 1949, CD 6–3–30, Records of the Office of Secretary of Defense, RG 330, NA.

3. This is not evident from the printed hearings of the Senate Appropriation Committee, but the impression may have been conveyed off the record. See U.S., Congress, Senate, Committee on Appropriations, *Executive Session Hearings on H.R. 6427*, 81st Cong., 1st sess., pp. 14–19. Webb discussed the question in Acheson's morning meeting on 13 October. See Secretary's Daily Meeting, 13 October 1949, RG 59, NA. For an early statement by Johnson on the importance of Section 303, see his off the record statement before a group of insurance men, 27 September, 1949, Box 103, Louis A. Johnson Papers, University of Virginia, Charlottesville, Va.

4. Memo of conversation with the president, 13 October 1949, "Memorandum of Conversation" folder, Acheson Papers.

5. Memo, president to secretary of defense, 9 November 1949, "China 1949" folder, Truman Papers; Johnson's offer to the French is discussed in "Top Secret Daily Staff Summary," 21 December 1949, RG 59, NA. The State Department apparently did not learn about Johnson's offer to the French until late December.

6. Memo, Merchant to Parelman, 16 November 1949, 890.24/11–1649, RG 59, NA. Emphasis in text.

7. Memo, Merchant to Sprouse, 1 August 1949, *FR*, 1949, IX, pp. 870–71. Truman's bellicose attitude was also demonstrated in late 1948 and early 1949; see memo, Butterworth to acting secretary, 5 January 1949, ibid., pp. 1210–12, and memo, Butterworth to acting secretary, 2 December 1948, *FR*, 1948, VIII, pp. 336–37; memo, Merchant to secretary, 19 August 1949; memo, McWilliams to Rusk, 22 August 1949; and memo, Butterworth to secretary, 7 September 1949, *FR*, IX, pp. 1022–24, 1027.

8. Memo of conversation with the president, 16 September 1949, ibid., p. 878.

9. Memo of conversation with the president, 1 October 1949, ibid., p. 1141.

10. Memo by the Department of State, 4 November 1949, ibid., pp. 890–96.

11. The Ward incident is covered in *FR*, 1949, VIII (Washington, D.C.: GPO, 1978), pp. 984–1043; in the *New York Times* and other newspapers, magazines, and U.S., Department of State, *Bulletin*.

12. U.S., President, *Public Papers of the President, Harry S. Truman, 1949* (Washington, D.C.: GPO, 1964), pp. 520, 532.

13. Memo of conversation with the president, 31 October 1949, *FR*, 1949, IX, p. 1355.

14. Memo of conversation with the president, "Development of Possible Plan in Connection with Mohammedan and Buddhist Population Along Southern Coast [*sic*] at the U.S.S.R.," 31 October 1949, Memos of Conversation with the President, Records of the Executive Secretariat, Lot 58D609, RG 59, NA. It is not clear whether the unusual geographic and ethnic references originated with Webb or Truman.

15. Memo of conversation with the president, 17 November 1949, *FR*, 1949, VIII, p. 1008; "Memorandum," *FR*, 1949, IX, pp. 582–88.

16. According to a note in "Secretary of State Dean Acheson Appointment Book, March–December 1949," 17 November 1949, Acheson Papers, the discussion in this meeting followed closely a document prepared by the consultants entitled "Outline of Far Eastern and Asian Policy for Review with the President," 16 November 1949, 711.90/11–1649, RG 59, NA. For Acheson's record of the conversation with the president in the early afternoon, see memo of conversation with the president, 17 November 1949, Acheson Papers. Acheson's account of this meeting in *Present at the Creation* (New York, W. W. Norton, 1969), p. 344, is misleading.

17. Memo prepared in CA on China, 7 December 1949, "Ambassador Jessup's Trip" folder, Records of the Office of Chinese Affairs, Lot 56D151, RG 59, NA. The Policy Planning Staff was even more explicit in its endorsement. In a document entitled "Mr. Ward, the Russians and Recognition," 17 November 1949, "Chronological 1949" folder,

Records of the Policy Planning Staff, Lot 64D563, RG 59, NA, the staff noted that "it is in our widest interest to bring about as rapidly as possible a normalization of our relations with the Peking regime." Were it not for the Ward problem, there was "no solid reason why we should not now recognize the Communists."

18. "Summary of Daily Meeting with the Secretary," Secretary's Daily Meeting, 11 July 1949.

19. Memo, Department of State to NSC, 4 August 1949, *FR,* 1949, IX, pp. 369–71; memo, Joint Chiefs of Staff to Secretary of Defense, 17 August 1949, ibid., pp. 376–78.

20. Secretary's Daily Meeting, 31 August 1949.

21. Memo, conversation of Denning, Meade et al., 6 September 1949, *FR,* 1949, IX, pp. 388–90.

22. Telegram, McConanghy to secretary, 6 September 1949, ibid., pp. 382–83.

23. Draft Report by the NSC, 6 October 1949, ibid., pp. 392–97.

24. Minutes of the 47th Meeting of the National Security Council, 20 October 1949, NSC.

25. Letter, Webb to secretary of defense, 20 June 1949, CD 6–3–30, RG 330, NA.

26. Memo, Halaby to secretary of defense, 8 June 1949, and attached draft; memo, Johnson to executive secretary, NSC, 10 June 1949, RG 330, NA. Souers designated this memo NSC–48.

27. Memo, Jessup to Butterworth, 19 July 1949, 711.93/7–1949, RG 59, NA; Marquis Childs, "Washington Calling," *Washington Post,* 28 July 1949, p. 13; Koo Oral History, I–35, Koo Papers.

28. Letter, Webb to Johnson, 12 July 1949, 711.93/7–1249, RG 59, NA.

29. Letter, Johnson to Acheson, 22 July 1949, 893.00/7–2249, RG 59, NA. Emphasis added.; memo, Halaby to Johnson, 19 July 1949, CD 6–30–30, RG 330, NA; U.S., Congress, Senate, Committees on Armed Service and Foreign Relations, *Hearings on Military Situation in the Far East,* 82d Cong., 1st sess., pt. 4, p. 2595.

30. Letters, Johnson to Acheson, 21 July 1949, and 27 July 1949; memo of conversation with the president, 29 July 1949, *FR,* 1949, IX, pp. 1382, 1387, 1390–91. For a report of a "Dutch Uncle" talk the president gave to Acheson and Johnson in which Truman sided with Acheson on China policy, see *Washington Post,* 5 August 1949, p. 2.

31. Memo, Johnson to executive secretary, NSC, 9 September 1949, RG 330, NA.

32. Memo, Kennan to Webb, 14 April 1949, Records of the Under Secretary's Meetings, 15 April 1949; memo of conversation, Souers, Webb et al., 4 May 1949, *FR,* 1949, I, pp. 282–84, 296–98.

33. Memo, Merchant to Allison, 19 October 1949, 890.00/10–1949, RG 59, NA.

34. Memo, Brown to Sprouse, 24 October 1949, "NSC–48" folder, Lot 56D151, RG 59, NA.

35. "Draft for NSC Staff Consideration Only" "The Position of the United States with Respect to Asia," 7 October 1949, NSC Permanent File, National Security Council, Washington, D.C. Released to author through FOI (Freedom of Information) 77–036.

36. Memo, McGhee to Rusk, 4 November 1949, *FR,* 1949, VII, pt. 2, pp. 1208–9.

37. UM D–69, 25 November 1949, and UM D–69/1, 28 November 1949, Records of the Executive Secretariat, Lot 53D250, RG 59, NA. For an earlier State Department draft, see attachment to memo, Allison to Butterworth, Merchant et. al., 1 November 1949, "NSC–48" folder, Lot 56D151, RG 59, NA.

38. Minutes of Special Under Secretary's Meeting on Asia Paper, UM D–69, 1 December 1949, Lot 53D250, RG 59, NA.

39. UM D–69a, 5 December 1949, 53D250, RG 59, NA.

40. Secretary's Daily Meeting, 6 December 1949.

41. Memo for the files and Action Summary, Under Secretary's Meeting, 7 December 1949.

42. The CIA estimate is referred to in memo of conversation, Bradley, Acheson et al., 29 December 1949, *FR,* 1949, IX, pp. 463–67; "Survival Potential of Residual Non-Communist Regimes in China," ORE 76–49, 19 October 1949, CIA.

43. Nonverbatim record of meeting of the consultants with the secretary, 26 October 1949, 890.00/10–??49, RG 59, NA; Secretary's Daily Meeting, 9 December 1949, RG 59, NA; memo, Merchant to Butterworth, 21 December 1949, "American Policy Toward Formosa" folder, Lot 56D151, RG 59, NA.

44. Memo, Johnson to president, 16 December 1949, and memo, Voorhees to Johnson, 14 December 1949, "Formosa" folder, President's Secretary's Files, Truman Papers.

45. Letter, Koo to secretary, 23 December 1949, *FR,* 1949, IX, pp. 457–60. For the same reason Koo presented the department with a request for military aid at the time of the MAP hearing in the summer.

46. NSC–48 "Draft," 15 December 1949, NSC, FOI n-036.

47. Memo, Butterworth to Rusk, 20 December 1949, 711.90/11–249, RG 59, NA.

48. The analysis section of NSC–48/1 is printed in U.S., House, Committee on Armed Services, Committee Print, Department of Defense, *United States-Vietnam Relations, 1945–1967,* bk. 8 (Washington, D.C.: GPO, 1971), pp. 226–64.

49. Memo, JCS to Johnson, 23 December 1949, *FR,* 1949, IX, pp. 460–61.

50. NSC–43/1, Conclusions, NSC Files, Modern Military Branch, NA.

51. Memo, Butterworth to secretary, ibid., pp. 461–63.

52. Johnson mentions the meeting in Senate Committees, *Military Situation in the Far East,* p. 2669; Secretary of State Dean Acheson, Appointment Book, March–December 1949, 20 December 1949 entry, Acheson Papers. The entry notes only that he briefed the president.

53. Memo of conversation, Bradley, Acheson et al., 28 December 1949, *FR,* 1949, IX, pp. 463–67.

54. NSC–48/2, 30 December 1949, *FR,* 1949, VII, pt. 2, pp. 1215–20; Minutes of the 50th Meeting of the NSC, 29 December 1949, NSC files, Modern Military Branch, NA.

55. Memo, Souers to NSC, 30 December 1949, *FR,* 1949, VII, pt. 2, p. 1251; "Memorandum for the Secretary of Defense: Subject: The Position of the United States with Respect to Asia," 29 December 1940. NSC Permanent File, National Security Council. Washington, D.C. Released to author through FOI 77–036.

Chapter 11. CONTAINMENT OF COMMUNIST CHINA

1. *New York Times,* 1 January 1950, p. 1.

2. Ibid., 3 January 1950, p. 1.

3. Ibid., 4 January 1950, p. 1.

4. Ibid., p. 16.

5. Ibid., p. 1.

6. Memo, Chen to Koo, 4 January 1950, "Inter–Office Memo" folder, Koo Papers.

7. *New York Times,* 5 January 1950, p. 1; memo of conversation, Kee, Acheson, McFall, 4 January 1950, Acheson Papers; and "Secretary of State Dean Acheson Appointment Book, January–July 1950," Acheson Papers. On Acheson's inability to reach Vandenberg, see Tom Connally's remarks in *Congressional Record,* 81st Cong., 2d sess., 5 January 1950, p. 103.

8. Memo of conversation with Congressman Eaton, 5 January 1950, Acheson Papers.

9. Secretary of State Dean Acheson, Appointment Book, 5 January 1950 entry, Acheson

Papers; *New York Times*, 6 January 1950, p. 1; U.S., Department of State, *Bulletin*, 16 January 1950, pp. 79–81; memo of conversation, Acheson and Souers meeting with president, 5 January 1950, Acheson Papers. Reporters noted that Truman added "at this time" to his statement; the mimeograph handout apparently did not contain the phrase. *Time*, 16 January 1950, p. 15.

10.   Memo of conversation, Acheson, Knowland, Smith, McFall, 5 January 1950, *FR*, 1950, VI (Washington, D.C.: GPO, 1978), pp. 259–64. The document is a recapitulation of the discussion, not a verbatim transcript.

11.   The president's and Acheson's statements are printed in *Bulletin*, 16 January 1950, pp. 79–81; *New York Times*, 6 January 1950, p. 1.

12.   *Congressional Record*, 81st Cong., 2d sess., 5 January 1950, pp. 79, 80, 86, 101.

13.   Notes on cabinet meeting, 6 January 1950, Connally Papers.

14.   *Gallup Poll, Vol.* 2, p. 887. The results of this poll were not published until 3 February. Another poll published on 11 January, based on interviews conducted in early November, revealed that informed opinion opposed recognition slightly more than two to one, ibid., p. 881.

15.   *New York Times*, 8 January 1950, p. 1.

16.   U.S., Congress, Senate, Committee on Foreign Relations, *Reviews of the World Situation: 1949–1950*, 81st Cong., 1st and 2d sess., ("Historical Series" of hearings held in executive session) (Washington, D.C.: GPO, 1974), pp. 105–71.

17.   *New York Times*, 12 January 1950, p. 1; the quotation is from Taft's statement, *Congressional Record*, 81st Cong., 2d sess., 11 January 1950, p. 298.

18.   The full text of Acheson's speech is printed in Department of State Press Release no. 34, 12 January 1950, W. Walton Butterworth Papers, George C. Marshall Research Foundation, Lexington, Va. The *Bulletin*, 23 January 1950, pp. 111–18, omits the opening comments and concluding question and answers.

19.   *New York Times*, 15 January 1950, p. 1; *Congressional Record*, 81st Cong., 2d sess. 13 January 1950, pp. 388–96.

20.   The military chiefs' testimony is printed in *Reviews of the World Situation*, pp. 239–245.

21.   For documents relating to the consulate general property seizure, see memo by the acting secretary, 10 January 1950, *FR*, 1950, VI, pp. 270–72, and Acheson's 24 January testimony in Foreign Relations Committee, *Economic Assistance*, pp. 201–10. The Communists also seized consular property of the French and Dutch. *New York Times*, 16 January 1950, p. 1.

22.   *New York Times*, 15 January 1950 and 18 January 1950, p. 1.

23.   Ibid., 20 January 1950, p. 1.

24.   Notes of Cabinet Meeting, January 20, 1950, Connally Papers.

25.   *New York Times*, 22 January 1950, p. 1.

26.   Ibid., 21 January 1950, p. 1.

27.   Memo by Acheson, "Substance of Conversation with Senator Vandenberg," 21 January 1950, Acheson Papers.

28.   Ibid; memo of conversation with the president, 23 January 1950, Acheson Papers.

29.   Foreign Relations Committee, *Reviews of the World Situation*, p. 176. The Senate Republican Minority Conference Committee endorsed the Knowland-Smith bill. Senate Republican Minority Conference Committee Minutes, 12 January 1950, Capitol Building, Washington, D.C.; memo, Battle to S/S, 13 January 1950, Acheson Papers. The State Department and ECA had been considering a "general area of China" formula for the China aid fund since the passage of the MAP bill in October. See memo, Wildes to Merchant, 10 October 1949, FEC Working File, 890.00/11–1849, Records of the Department of State, RG 59, NA; memo, Merchant to Butterworth, 14 October 1949, 893.50 Recovery/10–1449,

RG 59, NA; and memo, Robert Yost to Parelman, 22 December 1949, 893.50 Recovery/10–1449, RG 59, NA.

30. Memo, LDB to S/S, 20 January 1950, and memo of conversation, Acheson, Hoffman et al., 23 January 1950, Acheson Papers.

31. Foreign Relations Committee, *Economic Assistance*, pp. 193–227; memo by Acheson, "Substance of conversation with Senator Vandenberg," 21 January 1950, Acheson Papers.

32. The *New York Times*, 25 January 1950, p. 1, quoting informed sources, referred to a "more cooperative air between the administration and the Republicans."

33. House Report 1571, 81st Cong., 2d sess. Acheson's testimony is printed in International Relations Committee, *Policy in the Far East, Vol. 8, Pt. 2*, pp. 404–12: the appendix, pp. 427–43, contains the report.

34. *New York Times*, 8 February 1950, p. 11.

35. Senate Report 1251, 81st Cong., 2d sess.; Foreign Relations Committee, *Economic Assistance*, pp. 229–30.

36. For House action, see ibid., 10 February 1950, p. 1, and *Congressional Record*, 81st Cong., 2d sess., 9 February 1950, pp. 1731–48; for Senate action, see ibid., p. 1763, and *New York Times*, 11 February 1950, p. 1. The only exchange in the debate occurred when Knowland asked Connally if the China provision in S.2319 was not "practically identical" to his own S.2845. Connally agreed.

37. Richard M. Fried, *Men Against McCarthy* (New York: Columbia University Press, 1976), pp. 43–57; memo of conversation with the president, 6 March 1950, Acheson Papers.

38. Acheson's spring bipartisan offensive is detailed in David S. McLellan, *Dean Acheson: The State Department Years* (New York: Dodd, Mead & Co., 1976), pp. 229–38.

39. *New York Times*, 26 March 1950, p. 4; letter, Vandenberg to Acheson, 29 March 1950, Acheson Papers.

40. *New York Times*, 28 March 1950, p. 4.

41. Ibid., 29 March 1950, p. 1; ibid., 2 April 1950, p. E1; letter, Vandenberg to Acheson, 31 March 1950, Acheson Papers.

42. Memo of conversation with president, 4 April 1950, Acheson Papers.

43. See memos of conversation between Acheson and Dulles, 5 April Acheson and Senator Lehman, 4 April and Acheson and Dulles, 6 April 1950, in Acheson Papers.

44. Letter, Truman to Bridges, 26 March 1950, reprinted in Alan D. Harper, *The Politics of Loyalty: The White House and the Communist Issue, 1944–1952* (Westport, Conn.: Greenwood Publishing Corp., 1969), pp. 265–66. For evidence of Republican hostility toward Acheson, see *New York Times*, 26 and 27 March 1950, pp. 1.

45. Letter, Bridges to Truman, 29 March 1950, reprinted in Harper, *Politics of Loyalty*, pp. 269–70.

46. *New York Times*, 31 March 1950, p. 1; ibid., 2 April 1950, p. E1. Acheson hints at his concern over Truman's attack in letter, Acheson to Truman, 5 April 1950, Acheson Papers.

47. Letter, Acheson to Truman, 5 April 1950, Acheson Papers.

48. Memo of conversation with the president and Senator Bridges, 18 April 1950, Acheson Papers; *New York Times*, 19 and 20 April 1950, p. 1 and 6; and Senate Republican Minority Conference Committee Minutes, 19 April 1950, Capitol Building, Washington, D.C.

49. *Gallup Poll, Vol. 2*, pp. 915, 912.

50. Foreign Relations Committee, *Reviews of the World Situation*, pp. 273–75.

51. For a summary of the American position on Chinese representation in the United Nations, see telegram, Acheson to embassy in the United Kingdom, 7 February 1950, *FR*, 1950, II (Washington, D.C.: GPO, 1976), pp. 223–24.

52. For a reference to one covert propaganda effort run on the mainland, see U.S., Congress, Senate, Committee on Foreign Relations, *The United States and Communist China in 1949 and 1950: The Question of Rapprochment and Recognition*, Staff Report by Robert M. Blum (Washington, D.C.: GPO, 1973), p. 6, ftn. 19. For one example of the department's public propaganda efforts, see the "background" data released on China printed in *New York Times*, 26 January 1950, pp. 1 and 2. See also telegram, Acheson to Bruce, 25 January 1950, *FR*, 1950, VI, pp. 294–96.

53. For details of an apparent overture by General Chen Yi, which echoed the previous spring's Chou demarché, see telegrams, McConoughy to secretary, 21 and 26 January 1950, *FR*, 1950, VI, pp. 289–93 and 296–300. The consistent Communist attitude toward the United States appears in an 11 April telegram from Clubb conveyed to the department through the British, printed in ibid., p. 329.

54. For a CIA analysis of this presence in June 1950, see "Reviews of the World Situation, 14 June 1950," NSC Files, Truman Papers.

55. For a summary of the treaty, see editorial note, *FR*, 1950, VI, p. 311.

56. Letter, Johnson to Acheson, 14 February 1950, p. 91 (sec. 21), Records of the Army Staff, Plans and Operations, RG 319, NA.

57. Memo for the record by Lt. Col. Gilchrist, 24 February 1950, 091 China, Case 6(7), RG 319, NA.

58. Letter, Acheson to Johnson, 7 March 1950, *FR*, 1950, IV, pp. 316–17. Acheson's interim reply to the 14 February letter from Johnson is noted in letter, Acheson to Johnson, 14 April 1950, ibid., pp. 325–26.

59. Letter, Johnson to Acheson, 6 May 1950, ibid., p. 339.

60. Letter, Acheson to Johnson, 1 June 1950, ibid., pp. 351–52.

61. *New York Times*, 10 February 1950, p. 12.

62. Memo, Sprouse to Merchant, 16 February 1950, *FR*, 1950, VI, pp. 312–14.

63. Ibid., p. 314, ftn. 6.

64. Ibid., p. 313, ftn. 4.

65. Memo, Rusk to secretary, 17 April 1950, ibid., p. 330.

66. Memo, Rusk to Acheson, 26 April 1950, ibid., pp. 333–35. Since Hainan was then in the process of falling to the Communists—in part, collapsing from within—the Rusk memo was ill-timed.

67. Memo of conversation with Paul Griffith, 3 June 1950, Koo Papers.

68. Telegram, Sebald to Acheson, 22 June 1950, *FR*, 1950, VI, pp. 366–67. The full text of MacArthur's message is printed in *FR*, 1950, VII (Washington, D.C.: GPO, 1976), pp. 161–65. For the Dulles memo, dated 18 May, to which Rusk attached his name, see *FR*, 1950, VI, pp. 349–51 and *FR*, 1950, I (Washington, D.C.: GPO, 1977), pp. 314–16.

69. Memo, Burns to Rusk, 29 May 1950, *FR*, 1950, VI, pp. 346–47.

70. Memo, Howe to Armstrong, 31 May 1950, ibid., pp. 347–79.

71. Memo of conversation by Jessup, 25 June 1950, *FR*, 1950, VII, p. 158.

72. U.S., President, *Public Papers of the President of the United States, Harry S. Truman, 1950* (Washington, D.C.: GPO, 1964), p. 492.

Chapter 12. CONTAINMENT IN SOUTHEAST ASIA

1. NSC-68, 7 April 1950, *FR*, 1950, I (Washington, D.C.: GPO, 1977), p. 238.

2. For a general description of Southeast Asia in early 1950 as perceived by a member of the Griffin Mission, see Samuel P. Hayes, *The Beginnings of American Aid to Southeast Asia: The Griffin Mission of 1950* (Lexington, Mass.: Heath Lexington Books, 1971), pp. 3–4.

3. For typical, high-level assessments of the importance of Southeast Asia, see testimony

in Foreign Relations Committee, *Reviews of the World Situation,* pp. 156–63, 248–70, 279, 288–307; memo, Kennan to Acheson (conveying views of the JCS), 14 April 1950, *FR,* 1950, VI, pp. 780–85; "U.S. Economic Aid to Far Eastern Areas," NSC–61, 20 January 1950, NSC Files, Modern Military Branch, NA; Hayes, *Beginnings,* pp. 19–24; "Review of the World Situation," CIA 2–50, 15 February 1950, NSC Files, Truman Papers.

4. U.S., Congress, Senate, Committee on Foreign Relations, *Extension of European Recovery—1950, Hearings on S.3101, a bill to amend the Economic Cooperation Act of 1948,* as amended, 81st Cong., 2d sess., p. 359.

5. U.S., Congress, Senate, Committee on Foreign Relations, *Executive Sessions of the Senate Foreign Relations Committee,* Vol. 2, 81st Cong., 1st and 2d sess., 1948–49 ("Historical Series" of hearings held in executive session) (Washington, D.C.: GPO, 1976), p. 297.

6. Ibid., pp. 297–302.

7. For a legislative history of this act see U.S., Congress, Senate, Committee on Foreign Relations, *Legislative History of Committee on Foreign Relations, 81st Congress,* S. Doc. 247, 81st Cong., 2d sess., pp. 11, 14–16.

8. Hayes, *Beginnings; FR,* 1950, VI, pp. 4, 11, ftn. 5.

9. Letter, Webb to Griffin, 1 March 1950, U.S., Department of Defense, *United States-Vietnam Relations, 1945–1967, V.B.2, Justification of the War-Internal Commitments-The Truman Administration, 1945–1952, Book 1–1945–1949,* reprinted in sanitized form by U.S., Congress, House, Committee on Armed Services (Washington, D.C.: GPO, 1971), pp. 286–87.

10. Hayes, *Beginnings,* p. 8.

11. Letter, Johnson to Acheson, 1 February 1950, and memo, Bradley to Johnson, 20 January 1950, *FR,* 1950, VI, pp. 5–8.

12. Memo, Acheson to president, 9 January 1950, ibid., pp. 964–66.

13. Indicated in memo, Acheson to president, 9 March 1950, and memo, Ohly to Lemnitzer and Dickinson, 1 June 1950, ibid., pp. 41, 98.

14. Memo, Acheson to president, 9 March 1950, ibid., pp. 40–42.

15. Memo, Parelman to O'Sullivan, 10 January 1950, "Point IV for Indochina 1950–51" folder, Records of the Philippines and Southeast Asian Affairs Office, Lot 54D190, Records of the Department of State, RG 59, NA.

16. Letter, Truman to Acheson, 10 March 1950, *FR,* 1950, VI, p. 41, ftn. 2.

17. Memo, Burns to secretary of defense, 6 April 1950; and memo, Burns to Nolting, 7 April 1950, 091 French Indochina 1950, Records of the Joint Chiefs of Staff, RG 218, NA.

18. Memo, Acheson to president, 17 April 1950, *FR,* 1950, VI, pp. 785–86; memo, Lawton to president, 28 April 1950, "Mutual Defense—2" folder, White House Central File (Confidential), Truman Papers; letter, president to secretary of state, 1 May 1950, *FR,* 1950, VI, p. 791.

19. These amounts indicated in testimony in Foreign Relations Committee, *Executive Sessions, Vol. 2,* pp. 458–459, and International Relations Committee, 1943–50, *Policy in the Far East, Vol. 8, Pt. 2,* pp. 471–72, 492–93. In the print of the Senate hearings, the sum for covert operations is given once on the record as $650,000. In the House hearings, it is recorded twice as $6,500,000. In both committees, discussion of the money's use was placed off the record and thus not recorded by the stenographer or printed.

20. Truman's message is reprinted in International Relations Committee, 1943–50, *Policy in the Far East, Vol. 6,* pp. 183–86. The State and Defense Departments had originally wanted $100 million for the "general area" but the Bureau of the Budget cut the amount by $25 million, memo, Lawton to president, 17 May 1950, Truman Papers.

21. Memo, Acheson to president, 21 February 1950, *FR,* 1950, VI, pp. 716–17; memo of conversation, 3 February 1950, ibid., p. 719.

22. *New York Times,* 8 February 1950, p. 1.

23. Ibid., 22 February, 3 March, 15 March, and 16 May 1950, pp. 1, 10, 15, and 5. Memo of conversation by Acheson, 10 March 1950, *FR,* 1950, VI, pp. 752–53.

24. *New York Times,* 3 and 4 April 1950, pp. 17 and 22.

25. Ibid., 17 April 1950, p. 1.

26. Acheson's awareness of Bao Dai's unpopularity in Southeast Asia is indicated in memo, LBD to S/S, 9 March 1950, Acheson Papers.

27. Memo, Fosdick to Jessup, 4 November 1949, Raymond B. Fosdick Papers, Princeton University.

28. Memo, Jessup to Butterworth, 4 November 1949, 890.00/11–1849, RG 59, NA.

29. Memo, Butterworth to Fosdick, 17 November 1949; and memo, Reed to Butterworth, 15 November 1949, "Country File" folder, Lot 54D190, RG 59, NA.

30. Memo for the files, "Policy Toward Indochina," 16 November 1949, 890.00/11–1849, RG 59, NA. There is no direct evidence that Fosdick actually endorsed this paper. The assertion that he did is made by Jessup.

31. Telegram, Abbot (Jessup) to secretary, 29 January 1950, *FR,* 1950, VI, pp. 702–3.

32. Foreign Relations Committee, *Reviews of the World Situation,* p. 268.

33. Telegram, Stanton (Butterworth) to secretary (Merchant), 17 February 1950, *FR,* 1950, VI, pp. 738–39.

34. Memo, Ogburn to Butterworth, 21 March 1950, ibid., pp. 766–67. In letter, Gullion to Wallner, 17 May 1950, "Point IV for Indochina 1950–1951" folder, Lot 54D190, RG 59, NA, Gullion writes that he is "tempted to show them [the French in Saigon] some of the special pleading I have done for them in my wires."

35. Memo of conversation between Ogburn and Isaacs, 17 April 1950, "U.S. Policy Papers of Indochina" folder, Lot 54D190, RG 59, NA.

36. Acheson's view of the Chinese threat to the south is indicated in Secretary's Daily Meeting, 14 December 1950.

37. Foreign Relations Committee, *Reviews of the World Situation,* pp. 90, 159–60.

38. *New York Times,* 17 April 1950, p. 1.

39. Telegram, Bruce to secretary, 7 February 1950, *FR,* 1950, VI, pp. 722–23.

40. Memo of conversation, MacArthur and Chauvel, 20 February 1950, *FR,* 1950, III (Washington, D.C.: GPO, 1977), pp. 1360–62.

41. Telegram, Bruce to secretary, 22 February 1950, *FR,* 1950, IV, pp. 739–42.

42. Memo, "Military Assistance for Indochina," n.d., ibid., pp. 43–44.

43. State Department aide-memoire, 28 April 1950, ibid., pp. 789–90. The United States demonstrated its concern over developments in Vietnam in a graphic way when two destroyers from the 7th Fleet visited Saigon over the weekend of 18–19 March. The visit had the warm endorsement of the State Department and was met by Viet Minh-precipitated riots. *New York Times,* 20 and 21 March 1950, pp. 1.

44. See *FR,* 1950, IV, p. 735, first ftn. 1.

45. Daily Top Secret Staff Summary, 21 December 1949, RG 59, NA.

46. Telegram, secretary to acting secretary, 8 May 1950, *FR,* 1950, III, pp. 1010–12.

47. *New York Times,* 9 May 1950, p. 1. On 1 April, the *Times* carried a 31 March Associated Press dispatch on p. 4 stating that Truman had approved $30 million in principle for aid to Thailand and Indochina.

48. U.S., Congress, Senate, Committees on Foreign Relations and Armed Services, *Hearings on The Mutual Defense Assistance Program, 1950,* 81st Cong., 2d sess., p. 23.

49. International Relations Committee, *Policy in the Far East, Vol. 8, Pt. 2,* p. 489.

50. Foreign Relations Committee, *Executive Sessions, Vol. 2* pp. 455–58.

51. Ibid., pp. 523–25.

52. *FR,* 1950, VI, p. 831, ftn. 1.

53.   For a legislative history of the 1950 MAP bill, see Foreign Relations Committee, *Legislative History,* pp. 8–9.

54.   Telegram, Department of the Air Force to COMGENAMC, Wright-Patterson AFB, 6 June 1950, "Military Assistance-U.S. Vessels" folder, Lot 54D190, RG 59, NA; Edwin B. Hooper et al., *The United States Navy and the Vietnam Conflict, Vol. 1, The Setting of the State to 1959* (Washington, D.C.: Department of the Navy, 1976), p. 178.

Index